BRINGING DAVY HOME

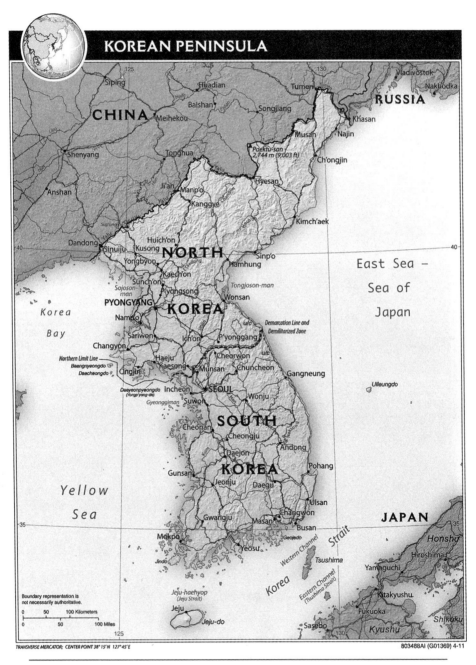

Central Intelligence Agency map (original), 1950. *Map courtesy of University of Texas Perry-Castañeda Library.*

BRINGING DAVY HOME

In the Shadow of War, a Soldier's Daughter Remembers

SHERRI STEWARD

Texas A&M University Press
College Station

Copyright © 2024 by Sherri Steward
All rights reserved

First edition

This paper meets the requirements of ANSI/NISO Z39.48-1992 (Permanence of Paper). Binding materials have been chosen for durability.

Library of Congress Cataloging-in-Publication Data

Names: Steward, Sherri., author.
Title: Bringing Davy home: in the shadow of war, a soldier's daughter remembers / Sherri Steward.
Other titles: Williams-Ford Texas A&M University military history series.
Description: First edition. | College Station: Texas A&M University Press, [2024] | Series: Williams-Ford Texas A&M University military history series | Includes bibliographical references and index.
Identifiers: LCCN 2023052496 (print) | LCCN 2023052497 (ebook) | ISBN 9781648432088 (hardcover) | ISBN 9781648432095 (ebook)
Subjects: LCSH: Steward, David Daniel, 1934–1950. | Child soldiers—Texas—Biography. | Korean War, 1950–1953—Psychological aspects. | Korean War, 1950–1953—Repatriation of war dead—United States. | Korean War, 1950–1953—Missing in action—Family relationships—United States. | Veterans—Mental health—United States. | LCGFT: Biographies.
Classification: LCC DS559.8.P7 S74 2024 (print) | LCC DS559.8.P7 (ebook) | DDC 951.904/242 [B]—dc23/eng/20231122
LC record available at https://lccn.loc.gov/2023052496
LC ebook record available at https://lccn.loc.gov/2023052497

For my two Davids:

David Daniel Steward . . .

the sixteen-year-old uncle I never knew but always loved,

and my son,

David Steward Sessions . . .

through whom the boy soldier lives

CONTENTS

Foreword by Larry C. Kinard... ix
Preface.. xi

      Prologue 1

PART I   The File

  1   The Blue House 7
  2   The Picture 15

PART II   Jumping Off

  3   Replacements 25
  4   Baptism 34
  5   Miracle at Remagen 43
  6   The Rock Quarry 53

PART III   Darkness

  7   The Homecoming 65
  8   Demons 72
  9   The Promised Land 82
  10   Boy Soldier 90

PART IV The Tempest

- 11 The Hermit Kingdom 101
- 12 Land of the Morning Calm 111
- 13 Stand or Die 124
- 14 A Million Miles from Home 135
- 15 Lost Battalion 142
- 16 Changjin 149

PART V Home

- 17 Grave 182 163
- 18 Finding Davy 173
- 19 Piney Wood Home 181

PART VI Forgotten

- 20 The Abyss 189
- 21 Forgotten Casualties 199
- 22 The Little Christmas Man 210

Acknowledgments 219
Notes 223
Bibliography 241
Index 255

A gallery of illustrations follows page 123.

FOREWORD

Larry C. Kinard

BRINGING DAVY HOME is an intimate look at war through the heart and soul of a soldier's daughter and niece. She tells the story of two brothers—her father, a combat veteran of World War II and Korea, and her sixteen-year-old uncle who served on the frontlines of Korea. The true story chronicles the brutal combat they endured and a mother's struggle to bring her fallen son home.

Like so many others who served during the Korean War, they received little acknowledgement for their sacrifice or the contributions they made in saving a country and its people. *Bringing Davy Home* poignantly portrays the story of most young Americans who went to war in Korea. Asked to serve in a "police action," many never fully understood why they were there. Today, we know why.

The decline of communism began with the Korean War. Often called the "Forgotten War," the Korean War is in reality the forgotten victory. The prosperous South Korean people now live in freedom and are in many ways the envy of the world—thanks to the thousands of young men who sacrificed there. Their everlasting gratitude to the soldiers who fought there provides strong evidence of victory.

I heartily recommend this book to all but especially to veterans and family members of those who served. Well researched and forthright, *Bringing Davy Home* accurately portrays the brutal fighting that young Americans endured in Korea. It provides us with new and vital insight into the heartache and anguish of those at home who must wait the return of our warriors.

As president of the National Korean War Veterans Association, my overarching hope was to help perpetuate the legacy of all those who served in the Korean War. Our efforts rescued a country and her people from the throes of communism. It is a legacy that deserves to be recognized and remembered. *Bringing Davy Home* informs us that those who died there did not die in vain.

Most Americans know little about the horrific and noble sacrifices of the Korean War. *Bringing Davy Home* reminds us all of those sacrifices—and the price of freedom. Read it carefully and you will understand why the legacy of those who fought and died there must forever be remembered.

Larry C. Kinard is a graduate of Texas A&M University with a bachelor's degree in mechanical engineering. He served during the Korean War as a first lieutenant in the Third Infantry Division. Kinard served as president of the National Korean War Veterans Association from 2013 to 2016, and as the national chairman for Tell America from 2004 to 2010. During his Tell America term, he helped to develop a national effort to educate school children about the "Forgotten War."

PREFACE

THIS IS THE STORY OF two small-town Texas boys—brothers and combat veterans, the likeness of millions of young Americans. Answering the urgent call to defend the freedom of people and nations they never knew, they willingly stepped forward and paid a bitter price. For months in a half-shelter grave, one lay nameless in the frozen Korean ground. The other, ravaged by two brutal wars, brought his teenage brother home to the piney woods of East Texas. Woven within is a heartbroken mother's undying resolve to bring one son home to American soil and the other home alive. For those who continue to await the return of precious fathers, brothers, sons, and uncles, this true saga has not ended.

Revealed in faded letters from army camps to frontline battlefields, this lost story is found. It cannot—and must not—be sugarcoated. This is an American journey of those who returned from war forever broken in body and mind. It is a journey of those who never returned at all—and of the forgotten casualties who loved them.

BRINGING DAVY HOME

PROLOGUE

We'll preserve for our children this, the last best hope of man on earth, or we'll sentence them to take the last step into a thousand years of darkness.

—President Ronald Reagan

BETWEEN THE YEARS of 1941 and 1945, more than 16 million young American men and women marched from their homes to fight in the Second World War. Some 400,000 of them would not return. After barely five years of peacetime, many would find themselves once again on the frontline of the "Forgotten War" in Korea "to defend a country they never knew and a people they never met."[1]

They kissed the cheeks of teary-eyed mothers and sweethearts, departing on massive ships in New York Harbor and from train stations deep in the piney woods of East Texas. They were the sons of presidents and of impoverished sharecroppers, but on the battlefields of Normandy, Iwo Jima, Remagen, and at a place called the Frozen Chosin, they were equals. Those who served in World War II were famously dubbed the "Greatest Generation." And for those of us who shared their lives, the moniker is befitting. But like the Korean War itself, the men and women who served there were simply forgotten as part of the Greatest Generation, though as many as 1.5 million served during both wars.

William Steward was one of those soldiers. To his children, grandchildren, friends, and neighbors, he was simply known as "Pop." And like so many daughters and sons of the World War II–Korea generation, I am filled at once with immense pride for having been a part of their lives and with a profound sense of emptiness as I witness their quiet passing.

I am today constantly reminded of how they came to be called the Greatest Generation and why there may never again exist such a selfless aggregation of Americans, or for that matter, human beings in our world. They are departing our world en masse—much as they did when they marched off to save the world from tyranny in World War II and Korea. They leave behind a legacy of freedom, dedication to country, and self-sacrifice rarely seen in our increasingly self-centered world. But the legacy is not lost, as their stories have been passed on to their children, sons and daughters like myself.

We treasure dog-eared photos of a father in combat, and we dutifully recite the names of his special band of brothers...from the Lightning Division at Remagen, or the 101st Airborne in Normandy, or the 1st Marine Division at Chosin. We return again and again to precious letters and the fading words of our heroes—our fathers, our uncles, our brothers, and our friends. We have memorized those words, written on cracked and yellowed Red Cross stationary, from somewhere near the Naktong River and from the front lines of Germany. We remember not only the sacrifices our fathers and mothers made for America and the world, but we cherish our role as part of that sacrifice. And in a miniscule way, we too have borne the sacrifice of our fathers' war.

Like so many others, my father struggled constantly to survive the agonizing torment of both a tragic Depression-era childhood and years of combat in two brutal, horrific wars. He, like many of his brothers in arms—at least the lucky ones—returned from World War II a survivor and hero, the demons of war momentarily silenced by the sound of parades, by love, and by a renewed hope for a better life. Six years later, William Steward returned from Korea and the horrors of the Forgotten War, broken in mind and spirit in a never-ending race against the hounds of war that would follow and haunt him until the end of his life.

The scars of war left an indelible imprint, not only upon my father but also on my two siblings and me, as well as our individual relationships with our father. But I was "Sherri-Bug," the towheaded baby girl of the family, so named for the way I flitted about like Sparky the Lightning Bug, mascot of the famed 78th Infantry Division. As he aged, the depth of his sacrifice was finally revealed and the bond between us strengthened. And like every devoted soldier's daughter, I went to inordinate lengths to accomplish the simple task of making him smile.

I have always believed that even as a child, my relationship with my father was steeped in a profound awareness of the demons that tormented him. I seem to have inherited from him the gift—or curse, depending upon one's individual perception—of a heart brutally exposed. My father and I were keenly aware of the triumphs, flaws, and fragility that made us who we were, and an unconditional love resulted from the unique understanding of two such kindred souls.

More at home with them than any, including my own cohort, I have lived a lifetime in the company of the World War II–Korea generation. I cherish these dear friends and heroes—a general who fought as a second lieutenant at Chosin Reservoir in Korea, an Easy Company Marine who barely survived Iwo Jima, a Navajo code talker, and a dear friend who landed with the first wave on Omaha Beach. Many of the most memorable moments of my life were spent in the company of these American heroes, hearing their stories and personal recollections of some of the most important episodes in our nation's history.

As I daily witness the passing of yet another member of their generation, I have come to realize that they were not only the guardians of my freedom but the foremost influence on my life. Searching for reason in a world I no longer recognize, I turn to them now more than ever. And as I witness the epidemic tumult of our times, I am filled with worry for those who must now live without them.

I have attempted to tell this story in its truest form. I sought authentication through hundreds of documents, such as United States Army records, ancestral records, scholarly journals, and original handwritten letters from the front lines of both Europe and Korea. My mother, Callie, and my dearest Aunt Judith were incredibly prescient in saving these precious historical documents, as well as extraordinarily benevolent in endowing them to me.

I included excerpts from frontline letters that are painful and disturbing to read. And while these are the words of my own father and Uncle David, they represent the thoughts and fears of countless others, so far away from home and family. These dark memories are not only essential pieces of American history but important reminders of what we ask of those who serve our nation. Above all, the words of these soldiers must leave us with unfaltering resolve to forever care for the brave men and women from whom we demand so much.

I have sought to authenticate details of events through numerous personal interviews of those who were actually present. Over the past decade, my dearest aunts, Judith, Helen, Donna, and Alma, were exceptional in sharing their memories of so long ago. I am grateful and fortunate that many years earlier, my son David, namesake of his great-uncle, possessed the foresight to record and preserve his grandfather's war memoirs, both digitally and in written record. This personal account of my father's combat days has been invaluable in unraveling the details of a story that began more than seventy-five years ago.

With regard to family history where no written documentation existed, I conducted multiple interviews from those who were present as well as family and friends. And while the many interviews with old-timers are cherished and extremely important to this author, I am fully aware that memories are often ebbing, especially when those events occurred more than seven decades ago.

As an adventurer, I have circumnavigated the globe many times. I have been fortunate to work in scientific and humanitarian endeavors, public education, and the corporate world. I have worked with some of the world's leading scientists, celebrities, and heads of state, yet I consider being a combat soldier's daughter and niece to be the greatest honor of my life. Witnessing the twilight of our World War II–Korea generation and the paling of my own life, I am compelled to tell this lost story. And as I delicately unfold another precious, yellowed news clipping or faded frontline letter, I am disquieted in knowing that I am possibly among the last to share it on a personal level.

This is a story of two small-town Texas brothers, both combat soldiers—the likeness of millions of others. They grew up during the Great Depression and the Dust Bowl. They endured World War II and Korea and suffered unspeakable family tragedy. Out of seven boys, my father was the only son to reach the age of thirty-six.

Long ago, I resolved to share this journey, a tale not only of William and David, but of thousands of American warriors and their families. It is a saga of how war changes those who endure it, as well as those who love and depend upon them. In a larger sense for those of us who still remember, this is a story we must teach our children—and as Americans, a lesson we must never forget.

Every measure of my being is the result of sharing my life with members of the World War II–Korea generation. The canvas of my own life bears the bright and radiant, as well as the darkened hues of a soldier's daughter. I have tried to tell this story without embellishment or partiality—yet I concede I have always seen the world through the eyes of a soldier.

PART I
THE FILE

1

THE BLUE HOUSE

It is so much safer not to feel, not to let the world touch me.

—Sylvia Plath, American poet

MY MODEST HOME in the tiny Texas town of Argyle, just north of Fort Worth, was built from the ground up during happier times. I painted it country blue and insisted that it be placed far back from the road, nestled deep in the woods among 200 mature oak trees.

Like Pop, I was creative, and decades of distance running provided me with a killer work ethic. I was constantly creating and building with my own hands. I built a koi pond, a bird aviary, and a meandering rock pathway leading to a beautiful flower garden. The Blue House became a gathering place for all the neighborhood kids. My son Dave would direct elaborately staged spaghetti western movies starring his classmates. The house was filled with love, especially during the many wonderful Thanksgiving and Christmas holidays. Pop preserved the memory of each holiday with an ancient video camera the size and weight of a sack of potatoes. "The Beast" accompanied him everywhere.

Each year, Dave would stage Grammy-worthy holiday performances. Inevitably, the star of the show was the one-and-only Pop, dressed as Michael Jackson or his favorite alter ego, "King William Rapper." Adorned in gold chains and sagging jeans, the aged World War II–Korean War hero—turned 1990s rapper—would traipse down the beautifully decorated staircase lip-synching and dancing to the latest hip-hop hits.

I hosted holiday feasts for my family and, invariably, for those who had no family. Beautiful Christmas lights twinkled, and everyone had presents under a tree decorated with treasured handmade dough ornaments from my son's grade school days. The Blue House seemed to be the happiest place on earth. Beloved even by the local wildlife, they flocked to the surrounding forest, where the sound of songbirds filled the morning air. The Blue House was a safe haven for three generations of foxes, dozens of bird species, and one soldier's daughter.

Since childhood, I had developed a propensity for driving myself beyond normal human expectations. "Perfectionism is the voice of the oppressor."[1] I couldn't just run the race—I had to win it. Whether it was making straight As, climbing the highest mountain, or being the "coolest mom," I always had something to prove.

My father separated from the military only a few days before my birth. But as children, my siblings and I were constantly changing schools, sometimes as many as four times in a single school year. As his demons would come and go, we wandered from place to place, constantly racing to escape them. Growing up with a father who left the army but not the battlefield was merciless. Each time we entered a new school, my brother, sister, and I struggled to fit in. We had to make friends fast—and get over losing them even faster.

I desperately wanted to escape the self-inflicted rigors I had heaped upon myself since childhood, a constant and never-ending addiction as I sought to validate my own self-worth. I pursued a quieter life and envisioned myself sitting on the front porch, drinking coffee and picking my guitar. I wanted solitude. I wanted to be away from the noise and traffic of the sprawling Dallas–Fort Worth metroplex. I wanted to be left alone, and the Blue House was everything I dreamed of—forsaking Pop's judicious warning, "Be careful what you wish for, it might come true."

Life had suddenly and unexpectedly come at me full throttle. It had careened off track, derailed by childhood trauma, failed relationships, financial woes, and crippling loneliness. My ill-fated wish had come to fruition, first with the devastating end of a long and painful relationship, followed by my son leaving home to study journalism at the University of Texas at Austin.

My only comfort was an elderly cocker spaniel named Miss Goma and Lovey, a fat and lovable cat of an even older vintage. Both had been with me almost as long as my son. They were dear to me, always offering their unconditional love without judgment, sustaining me through the darkest nights. But to add insult to misery, shortly after Dave left for college, my dear old friends died within weeks of each other. I was officially an empty nester, and brimming with profound emptiness, the Blue House lived up to its name in a sinister new way.

The Blue House was filled with photos and memories of better days—my son as a baby, as a teenager winning track meets, and the two of us perched triumphantly atop Yosemite's famed Half Dome on his eighth birthday. Like my father, I was plagued with constant insomnia. Unable to sleep, I would roam the Blue House alone, taking note of the sadness that engulfed me. I would stare for hours at iconic photos of past adventures: standing on the summit of Mount Kilimanjaro, holding a baby orangutan in Borneo, and arm in arm with my hero and friend, Dr. Jane Goodall.

I first learned of the world's most notable woman scientist on one of my frequent visits to a veterans' hospital waiting room. Surrounded by the famous chimpanzees of Gombe, she graced the cover of a 1965 *National Geographic* magazine. I later fulfilled my childhood dream of not only meeting her but also working with her in the United States and Africa. As a child, I often dreamed of my heroes: a beautiful woman who lived alone in a faraway land with the animals, a proud soldier boy, and my father—his signature army cap confidently perched on the side of his head. And as a woman, when love and life had failed me, night after night I returned to my dusty old dreams.

Every photo was a stinging reminder that once upon a time, I had been something special. Every photo represented a happier time that would never be again—accepting a prestigious teaching award, dancing with actor Jimmy Stewart, running alongside Olympians, blonde ponytail flying high. And as I fought to keep my head above water, my personal life seemed to drown in sadness. Ironically, my professional life flourished, and everything I touched turned to gold. I won highly coveted science and teaching awards, but like Pop, I couldn't seem to win the battle raging within me.

I would inevitably wind up at "the wall of heroes," the first piece of decorating I placed in my Blue House, right at the top of the stairs, for everyone—or no one—to see. Arm in arm with his band of brothers, there was Pop in Germany. And my teenaged Uncle David proudly wearing a new army uniform just before he was killed in action in Korea. In another favorite photo stood Pop on the front line in frozen Korea, a grenade strapped to his chest, and sporting the saddest eyes I have ever seen.

Each night I would read the framed Harry Truman–signed letter to my grandmother, presented to her upon the death of my Uncle David: "In grateful memory of PFC David D. Steward who died in the service of his country. He stands in the unbroken line of patriots who have dared to die so that freedom might live." As always, I would stop to gaze and touch the face of little sixteen-year-old David Daniel Steward. "Love, Tex," I would whisper aloud, as I had done for the entirety of my life.

The absolute solitude and silence of the Blue House began to swallow me. I recalled how Pop described being alone at night in a foxhole. I felt the same, alone with my ruminations and dread of what tomorrow would bring. I lost the energy to play my prized Jumbo Gibson guitar. I listened to sad music: Patsy Cline's "I Fall to Pieces," Itzhak Perlman playing the haunting theme from *Schindler's List*, and Townes Van Zandt's "Waiting Around to Die."

Each night I passed by the picture of the handsome, green-eyed soldier who captured my imagination from my earliest memories, and for whom I named my only child. Like so many others who died in Korea, no one really knew what happened to David. As my father aged, he could barely muster the word "Korea" and never dared to relive the horrors he endured there. I had always been persistent and inquisitive in learning about Uncle Davy, resulting in fractured bits and pieces of his death—grave 182, somewhere near the Naktong River, 1st Cavalry, and the breakout of the Pusan Perimeter. But like everything associated with the Korean War, the details of David Daniel Steward's death were a jumble of conflicting "facts."

As my father grew increasingly frail, I tried everything to broach the subject of his little brother. But each time, the bluest eyes I've ever seen invariably returned to the steely emptiness of the thousand-yard stare. The only person who possibly knew what happened to the boy soldier was my father. Back on the front line of Korea, only five years after the fierce combat he endured in World War II, my father served as special escort to his brother's remains from Tokyo, Japan, to the tiny southern town of Atlanta, Texas.

My father had recently undergone extremely risky surgery for an abdominal aneurysm, and I tried to prepare myself for losing the old soldier. On the night before his surgery, thinking I might never see him again, I sheepishly confessed to signing his name on a document requesting David's military death records. His response was filled with both relief and hope.

"Bug, I am so proud of you," he whispered. "Now you will finally know. It will be our special secret. You don't have to tell anyone about it if you don't want to, but I know you will never let David be forgotten."[2] His comments revealed a palpable sense of solace in knowing that, after decades, he was not alone in the burden of David's death.

Pop was one of the lucky ones. He managed to narrowly escape the fate of over 400,000 American men and women during World War II and nearly 37,000 in Korea. Against all odds, he was spared. He returned to his beloved piney wood home, raised a family and lived a simple life as he had planned. But nearly 172,000 warriors never returned to American soil after World War II.[3]

They were simply categorized as MIA (missing in action) or KIA (killed in action) and interred or memorialized in American cemeteries in places like Normandy, Henri Chapelle in Belgium, the Ardennes Forest, and throughout the Pacific and North Africa. At the beginning of 2023, nearly 7,500 Americans remained unaccounted for from the Korean War.[4]

Scattered like leaves throughout the Korean Peninsula, these fallen warriors are a painful reminder for family members that the Forgotten War has never ended. The Defense POW/MIA Accounting Agency continues to utilize forensic and DNA technology to identify remains of unaccounted for and unknown soldiers. Obtaining DNA samples from family members is key to identification and repatriation of remains. As immediate family members of Korean War servicemen age, a desperate effort to identify remains and return them to their families has recently ensued.

During Operation Glory in 1954, the remains of nearly 3,000 American servicemen in Korea were recovered. Many of these men were finally identified and returned to their families, but 866 remained "unknown soldiers" and were interred in the National Memorial Cemetery of the Pacific, known as the Punchbowl.[5]

By 1994, the North Koreans had returned 208 boxes of remains. Unfortunately, the remains were commingled, and the Department of Defense estimated the boxes contained more than 400 American servicemen previously listed as missing in action.[6] The total number of those still missing in Korea remains fluid as identification of remains continues.

Later in 2019, several soldiers were finally identified and brought home to families. Twenty-two-year-old Pvt. Frederick Eugene Coon was declared missing in action on July 29, 1950. His unidentified body was recovered and interred at the Punchbowl in Honolulu. As an unidentified soldier, he was interred in a grave marked "Unknown 830."

Private Coon's great-niece requested and was granted DNA testing on the soldier's remains, which were positively identified. Posthumously promoted, Corporal Coon was returned to his family in Missouri after nearly seven decades.[7] Sadly, so many heroes of the Forgotten War remain scattered in deep ravines and across the hillsides where they so gallantly made their last stand.

On Halloween night in 1950, a brutal North Korean Army major nicknamed "The Tiger" took command of more than 700 captured Americans, most from the green troops of the 24th Infantry Division. What followed was the infamous Tiger Death March, a savage 120-mile trek where POWs were stripped of boots, shirts, and jackets. In one of the most brutal winters on record, they were force-marched to an area near Chunggangjin, North Korea.

Weakened by the weather and deprived of food and water, many were unable to continue to march. Those who were wounded or could no longer walk were executed or left to die. Many were simply abandoned where they lay or hastily buried in shallow, unmarked graves along the death march route. Only 262 of the 700-plus Americans returned alive.[8]

The POWs were mostly American men, but among the multinational group were also twenty-three women, including Ann Marie Beatrix Edouard, a Carmelite nun from France, and Mother Mary Clare, an Anglican nun from County Wicklow, Ireland. Both were executed along the march in full view of other POWs. Any infraction or failure to keep pace resulted in merciless beatings or summary execution. The Tiger ordered the removal of all dog tags from the bodies of American soldiers.[9]

Among those who perished was a nineteen-year-old private first class, whose brother and sister-in-law later became my friends. The PFC from New Braunfels, Texas, survived the Tiger Death March but died at Hanjang-ni, North Korea, as a POW. Like so many other men who died in Korea, Anselmo Zamora's remains were never recovered. His brother, the last surviving immediate family member, exemplified the thousands of family members who would eternally feel the pain of wondering what happened, never knowing.

For each and every man lost—and especially for MIA and unaccounted for—a mother, daughter, son, or niece would forever feel the biting emptiness of the hole left in their lives. Regardless of age, a nine-year-old son or an eighty-eight-year-old mother, those left behind lack the solace of closure as they continue to conjure visions of their family member's ultimate fate.

Captivated since childhood by the image of the handsome young man we called Uncle Davy, I also felt an indescribable emptiness. He resembled my own son, reminding me of the grievous burden on his mother's soul. I wondered if I would ever find some sort of closure in knowing the details of little David Daniel's death. I desperately wanted him to be remembered and for my son to know of his namesake. But digging up such a sorrowful past left me intensely fearful of learning the truth. Would I find something so dreadful it might require a lifetime of silence—leaving me alone to burden the awful secret?

I wondered if members of my family were justified in the notion that I should simply let the secrets of David's death die with my father. "You should let it be," I was told on every occasion; indeed, not one family member encouraged me to find the truth. Aside from my father, perhaps no living soul actually knew the details of David's death in Korea. Would I be better off not knowing what happened? These are the fears and questions asked by thousands of family members each and every day of their lives.

Fridays were always the worst. My dear teaching friend of nearly three decades, Ruthann Parham, inevitably waved her friendly goodbye. With a worried voice she kindly implored, "Try to have a good weekend, Sherri." Weekend after weekend, theirs were the last human voices I heard until Monday morning. The forty-minute drive from my teaching job only intensified the dread of the silent misery in store for me.

I would stop at the mailbox before driving up the meandering dirt road to the Blue House. One Friday, as I steeled myself for yet another weekend of solitude, self-deprecation, and anguish, I made a determined effort to stop and drag myself out of my little blue truck to retrieve the mail. It was nearly dark, and I knew I would never have the strength or desire to walk the winding 120 yards back to the mailbox. Expecting to find a box full of bills, I pulled out a large manila envelope, stamped with huge red letters: "IDPF." It was thick and the postman had tightly rolled it in order to stuff it in the box. After a quick glance, I was sure it was someone asking for money. I threw the file on the front seat of my truck and then on the kitchen counter.

Exhausted, I dropped my bag full of ungraded student papers and collapsed into my old chair. Wait a minute—IDPF? Oh, my God!" I screamed, having completely forgotten that I had completed the forms for an Individual Deceased Personnel File for David Daniel Steward more than a year ago. With a burst of energy I hadn't felt in weeks, I ran to the kitchen and grabbed the thick file again. My hands began to shake as I read the words: "Department of the Army, U.S. Total Army Personnel Command."

I held the package to my chest and paced the floor. Should I open it now—on dreaded Friday? Would the contents of the file unleash upon me the witches' brew I knew so well? Perhaps I should wait until Monday. But the answers for which I had waited a lifetime were in the envelope and I knew it.

How did a sixteen-year-old Texas boy find his way to the front line of one of the most brutal wars in history? Exactly where and how did David Daniel Steward die in the Korean War? Did he die mercifully—or did he share the grim fate of so many who were captured? Was he actually with the beleaguered 24th Infantry Division as my research led me to believe? Or did he die with his 1st Cavalry buddies as his family proudly proclaimed on his tombstone? What was it about David's death in Korea that my father so fiercely guarded, dodging my queries with vagaries? "Oh, I think he died at Inchon." What compelled him to remain silent for nearly five decades?

As darkness enveloped the Blue House, I turned on the lamp next to the empty chair where I had so often held my furry companions. With trembling hands and tears streaming down my face, I poured myself a full glass of courage and placed the Individual Deceased Personnel File on my lap. After witnessing almost fifty years of silent anguish on my father's face, I began the long and arduous journey to unlock the secrets of the boy soldier's death.

2

THE PICTURE

There are moments such as these when time stands still.

—Dorothea Lange, Depression-era photojournalist

WE MOVED A LOT. By the ninth grade, I had attended eighteen schools in four states. After my father's discharge from the U.S. Army Hospital in Camp Chaffee, Arkansas, we were no longer an army family. But we moved as if we were. Like Winston Churchill, who famously referred to his chronic depression as the "black dog," William Steward was constantly on the run, with the black hound nipping at his heels.

As a small child and later as an adult, I felt an inexplicable bond between Pop and me. By most standards, he was not the best parent—but as if by some divine power, I recognized his demons. I was also mysteriously and intensely drawn to the memory of my teenaged Uncle David, whom I never knew.

As an adult, I devoured scientific research on posttraumatic stress disorder (PTSD) in combat veterans, developing a keen interest in the effects of war upon their children. I found myself in a new and curious position after the 9/11 terrorist attack on the World Trade Center and subsequent wars in Afghanistan and Iraq—as an educator, I became an unwitting observer of these children. In many of them, I witnessed a disturbing resemblance to my own childhood. It brought me home again—to the home I never had.

My older brother and sister did not reap the benefits of being the baby, nor did they share my propensity for childhood illnesses, which likely garnered some special attention from my father. I was born after he returned from the misery of the Korean War, when perhaps finally he could reconcile that he had survived not one but two ghastly wars. My brother was born just before the start of the Korean War and my sister while Pop was on the front lines of Korea.

Being born during the tumult of war undoubtedly had significant disadvantages for my siblings. They were older, and like many children of combat veterans whose tangled minds are burdened with the psychological effects of war, they bore the full brunt of it. We all came to know my father's demons. We lived with them. And like nomads roaming from place to place during our childhood, we ran to escape them—just as he did.

It was fear of the unknown that I remember most. Where would I be next month? How long do I have with my new best friend? What about Midnight, my newly adopted kitten—what would happen to her when we leave? Would we have a plan, perhaps waiting until the end of the school year—or would we simply leave without notice in the middle of the night or on a school morning as we often did? I was a highly organized child, and by the age of eight I developed my own personal exit strategy.

More often than not there was little warning. Many of our possessions, such as furniture, toys, clothes, and pets, would have to be left behind. Developing a system I continue to use after nearly six decades, each of my personal treasures was prioritized. I knew exactly which friend would be the recipient of prized belongings that might be left behind. Everything I really loved—my stuffed animals, my drawing book, and my picture album with its secret pocket and photo of Uncle Davy—was *Semper Paratus*, always ready. Sure, there would be heartbreak, but I learned quickly. Be ready to roll, Bug.

Most of our travels were along old Route 66 from Santa Monica to Riverside to Needles, California, just across the line from Arizona. From Kingman to Williams to Petrified National Monument, we stayed just ahead of the black dog chasing my father. Petrified Forest, which became a national park in 1962, was a welcome relief for three small children cooped up in the backseat of a '49 Chevy. Some 60 years later, I vividly remember the nearly 1,700-mile excursion as a grueling 30-hour journey that never involved an overnight stay—stopping only for gas, and when we were lucky, a couple of breaks with an actual flush toilet.

Set amidst the vast nothingness between Albuquerque and Santa Rosa, the infamous Clines Corners travel stop was my favorite destination. A combination gas station, souvenir shop, and cafe, Clines Corners was the brainchild of Roy Cline. Cline dreamed of creating a respite for weary travelers along Route 66. After the Santa Rosa cutoff was approved in 1937, Roy's dream came true when he moved and convinced mapmakers to put Clines Corners on the map. It quickly became the only game in town for weary Route 66 travelers—and three disheveled children escaping the demons of war.

My father would fill the tank with twenty-four-cents-a-gallon gas, buy a handful of nickel candy bars and peanut patties, and drink a few cups of boiling hot coffee. Momentarily released from our backseat prison and the humdrum of the blacktop, we marveled at the strange souvenirs in the famous Route 66 curio shop. Fortune-telling machines, animal skulls, Native American charms, Gila monster ashtrays made of petrified wood—Clines Corners had it all. Back on the road again from Tucumcari to the state line of Texas, we resigned ourselves for what lay ahead—eleven more hours and just shy of 600 miles to the East Texas town of Atlanta.

Rolling across the desert hour after hour, we played rock-paper-scissors, sang "Ninety-Nine Bottles of Beer on the Wall," and anxiously waited for sunset and the skyline of "Big D." Finally it was there—Pegasus, the famous Flying Red Horse atop Dallas's first skyscraper, the Magnolia Hotel, built in 1934. With noses pressed against the curved rear window of the old Chevy, three wide-eyed children gazed in awe as the giant winged horse faded into a tiny red speck on the Texas horizon. Bedraggled and tired, we waited for our father's inevitable and familiar words, "You kids need to go to sleep. 'The sun is riz, the sun is set, and here we is in Texas yet.'"

From the tall pine forests of East Texas to San Something, California, the hand-tinted 1950 photo perennially appeared on our wall as if by magic. In its unassuming eight-by-ten metal frame, the picture mystified me. From my earliest childhood recollections, I was profoundly captivated by the image of the handsome, smiling, green-eyed teenager in the photo. And racing through the house at breakneck speed, I would respectfully come to a screeching halt at the picture, where I would dutifully touch the frame and whisper, "Love, Tex," in deference to my uncle's signature at the bottom of the photo.

I had questions, lots of them. But I learned early in life to keep my queries to a minimum when it came to the subject of my Uncle Davy. On one occasion, running at full tilt with hands overhead to break my fall, I slammed into the wall, knocking the picture to the floor just as my father rounded the corner. He let out a bloodcurdling scream. With veins popping on his forehead, he shouted, "Now look what you've done, you broke it, you broke Davy's picture."

Being Bug, I was rarely the recipient of such malice from my father, and as a result I immediately began wailing sobs of apology for my crime. Biting his lip and kneeling on one knee, he grabbed my hand and looked square into my eyes.

"I'm sorry, Bug," he said. "But you know how much Uncle Davy meant to me, and I hope he will always mean something to you too. Please be careful with his picture, because that's all we have left to remember him by."

I would never forget the palpable sorrow in my father's eyes as he struggled to conceal the years of burden he alone had quietly borne. From that day forward I became the self-appointed guardian angel of my Uncle Davy, and six decades later I still pause in passing the beautifully framed photo on my wall to whisper "Love, Tex."

• • •

At 11:00 a.m. on January 29, 1934, David Daniel Steward, like most of the Steward children, was born in the East Texas town of Atlanta in Cass County, twenty miles south of Texarkana.[1] He was the sixth child born to William Henry and Delta Ray, both bone-tired of the struggles their family had endured during the past few years of the Great Depression. There was no doctor present for the birth, only the equally tired and hungry neighbor women who hoped this one would come without complications, so they could continue tending their nearly barren gardens.

As was the case with most poor farm children during the Great Depression, there would be no celebration to welcome the tiny newcomer. His grand entrance into a troubled world was acknowledged only by a handwritten record by country doctor Joe D. Nichols later that day and officially filed on February 5, 1934.[2] Thirteen months earlier, on March 4, 1933, Franklin Delano Roosevelt was inaugurated as the thirty-second president of a nation deeply immersed in the throes of staggering poverty and hunger. Unemployment had reached 25 percent, and in his inaugural address, Roosevelt attempted to calm an anxious, weary nation with his famous words, "The only thing we have to fear is fear itself."

In the early years, the Great Depression became the great equalizer, unleashing misery and suffering on all who endured it. Politicians initiated campaigns to bolster optimism and convince a beleaguered public that recovery was just around the corner. Beloved by his countrymen, Henry Ford joined the effort to restore calm as he announced at the end of 1929, "Things are better today than they were yesterday."[3] Attempts to buoy the confidence of farmers and laborers failed miserably as they began to feel even more of poverty's sting than they were perennially accustomed to.

Inhabited by those forced off the farm, hobo jungles began to appear on the outskirts of cities such as Fort Worth, Houston, and San Antonio. Often called "Hoovervilles," they were temporary places of refuge for rootless riders of the rails. More than two million men rode the rails in search of a better existence across a jobless nation. Walter Ballard was one such displaced farm boy. Famously photographed by Dorothea Lange in Hardeman County, Texas, in

1937, Walter shared his experiences on the rails, "You're not a goin' anywhere, you don't care, you just ride . . . You're going to eat, that was more than you was doing at home."[4]

As a result of budget constraints, veterans' services were almost nonexistent. World War I veterans like David's father suffered enormously. Although he was gassed at Meuse-Argonne in France and suffered from significant respiratory problems, like other seriously wounded veterans he received no benefits.[5] Veterans and their families joined the ranks of the Great Depression's destitute masses. As David grew older, life became an intolerable ordeal for his father. To feed seven hungry mouths, he worked the sawmill ten hours a day, seven days a week. He earned eight dollars and fifty cents per week in a dangerous job where production was often pushed to the limit, but he was grateful to have any job. The entire country was in the throes of both economic and environmental devastation.

David Daniel Steward was a child of the Dirty Thirties. He was born at home during the first of three waves of crippling drought that would leave American families even more desperate for food—for themselves and what little livestock they had left. Food and agricultural prices fluctuated wildly. In order to stabilize prices, the federal government ordered the slaughter of six million pigs, almost none of which reached the mouths of hungry children. The meat was simply wasted. Children like David, born in the South during the 1930s, got a double dose of misery as they made their unfortunate arrivals amid both the Great Depression and the devastating Dust Bowl.

The year of David Steward's birth has officially been recorded as the worst drought to occur in a thousand years. Temperatures soared, and 1934 proved to be one of the driest and most destructive years in American history.[6] It simply stopped raining in 1934. Weeks after Davy's birth, as if to foretell what lay in store for him, a "black blizzard" rolled through the Southwest, blowing 350 million tons of precious, life-giving topsoil as far as New York City.[7] The city of Boston lit streetlights at midday as visibility was often reduced to three feet. The Great Dust Bowl was in full swing, adding to the misery of the deepest and longest-lasting economic devastation of the industrialized world. The result became one of the worst manmade ecological disasters in human history. In one of the largest mass migrations in American history, over two million people left the Plains states.

Hundreds of thousands of families fled their barren farms with nothing more than their possessions tied to worn-out jalopies and high hopes of a better life in places like California. From Oklahoma, Missouri, Arkansas, and Texas, they were referred to as "Okies," a derogatory invective for the downtrodden souls who left the misery of their farms to feed their hungry families. Many would find only more hardship and shame in California's promised land.

Across Texas as far as the East Texas piney woods, once thriving gardens became deserts. Milk cows and goats vanished with the last rain—as with the children, there was nothing left to feed them. To help feed livestock, government programs began providing farm families with hominy and corn deemed inedible for humans. Their livestock long gone, the Steward children were happy to eat it.

The early years of the Depression were especially difficult for children, who suffered from malnutrition and diseases such as valley fever, a fungal lung infection, and rickets, a crippling bone disease caused by lack of nutrition. One of America's most iconic folk singers penned songs about the poor and their lives during the 1930s. Referring to the devastation of the Great Depression and the deadly pneumonia of the Dust Bowl, Woody Guthrie sang "I Ain't Got No Home" and "Dust Pneumonia Blues."

Malnourished children with weakened immune systems were much more susceptible to infectious disease, which claimed the lives of thousands. During the 1930s and into the 1940s, childhood pneumonia and influenza remained among the six leading causes of death in America. By early 1940, pneumonia remained the leading infectious cause of death in the nation.[8]

For David Daniel, the heartache was only beginning. On August 3, 1940, six-year-old David became a proud big brother. He adored and doted over his blonde-haired baby brother, Kenneth Carl Steward. But in the spring of 1941, Kenneth developed bilateral bronchial pneumonia. Just nine days later, not yet a year old, little Kenneth was laid to rest in the old Beech Creek Cemetery in Atlanta, Texas. An ancient, somber photo immortalized the unbroken grief of the Steward family as they gathered around the tiny graveside. Frozen in time, the doleful face of young David lay bare his heartache—and forecast the sorrow yet to come for him.

Amid an unremitting cloud of despair, the Steward family trudged through their daily struggles after baby Kenneth's death. They were weary of the hardships they had suffered. School photographs of the six remaining Steward children accurately displayed the deprivation and burden on their somber faces. Seventeen-year-old William was restless. He constantly talked of joining the military. But his father had witnessed the true horror of combat in the trenches of the Great War, and the old soldier tried everything to discourage his eldest son from becoming a soldier.

The Great Depression hit the tiny East Texas town of Atlanta hard. Established in 1871 with the building of the Texas and Pacific Railway, Atlanta relied heavily on harvesting the rich diversity of the pine forests as an important part of the economy. By 1885, lumbering and sawmills became the chief industry in Atlanta. As the economy boomed from the timber industry, the population of the newly incorporated town swelled to nearly 2,000, and by 1929, there were over 105 businesses. But as the Great Depression ravaged the nation, many businesses in the once-prosperous town were forced to close their doors. Until the opening of the nearby Rodessa oilfield in 1936, the long hours and dangerous work at the sawmill remained one of the few sources of income for laborers.

Like children everywhere, David found ways to escape the misery and hunger of the Depression. He entered Bloomburg Grade School, which sat on the border of Atlanta, and he immediately found a best friend in David Murphy. Murphy, who was the same age as David, described his friendship with the young Steward kid.

> We were best buddies in grade school. We had the same name, and we were both kinda shy. We pretty much kept to ourselves in school. Bloomburg School sat on about five acres of woods and we had long recesses. They would ring the bell for recess, and it might be one or two hours before they called us back. We linked together, talking and sharing our thoughts, watching the big boys play ball. We would play marbles, washers, or a game called 'Land.' You used your pocket knife to mark off your circle—and whoever got the most territory won the game.[9]

Murphy possessed a keen memory of growing up in Atlanta during the Great Depression. He recalled the details of the hardships that both families endured:

> Life was hard, and everybody who had land farmed it. Most everyone canned food and hunted just to put food on the table. I remember that David liked to hunt squirrels, and like others, [his family] ate them. There was no money to buy things, so naturally cash was a problem. There were no jobs for the men, and there was no way to earn money. When we had it, David and I took our lunch to school in a fruit jar, or maybe we had a biscuit left over from breakfast. Kids just didn't have any of the things that they have today. As kids, we had to invent our own entertainment.

But the one good thing about the Depression is that we were all in the same boat, and that made it a little more acceptable.[10]

When asked if he remembered anything special about his childhood friend, Murphy responded without hesitation. "The first thing that comes to mind when I think of David was that he was the embodiment of young men growing up during the Depression and World War II. He was the image of all of those young men."[11]

It was during this time of drought, depression, and hunger that David's father planted the seeds of a better life to come, and he prayed they would come to fruition in time. Like many of the Okies before him, he dreamed of moving his family to an area that would ultimately become one of the nation's breadbaskets—Imperial Valley, California. But his dream of moving the family to the booming agricultural area of Southern California would have to wait.

He was one of the lucky ones. As a trimmer at the Atlanta sawmill, he earned almost $500 per year, the second-highest salary at the mill.[12] For the time being, the old doughboy would endure ten-hour days and the unabating struggle to feed and clothe his family in Texas.

PART II

JUMPING OFF

3

REPLACEMENTS

But they who love the greater love / Lay down their life . . .

—Wilfred Owen, World War I soldier-poet,
killed in action November 4, 1918

WILLIAM STEWARD ENTERED THE WORLD during the calm between two fierce storms. Born after his father returned from the horrors of World War I and just five years before the beginning of the Great Depression, William was the second born of Delta Ray and William Henry Steward. His older brother, Robert, had lived only a few days, making William the eldest and chieftain of the younger Steward children.

In the year of William's birth, Johnny Weissmuller became America's Olympic hero after winning three gold medals in swimming at the 1924 Paris Olympics. As boys, deep in the piney woods of East Texas, William and his brothers spent hours pretending to be Weissmuller's famed Tarzan the Ape Man character.

British prime minister Stanley Baldwin resigned and was reelected by a landslide that same year. Benito Mussolini, the Italian dictator and World War II Axis leader, made formidable gains in power over the Italian people. And just eighteen days after William was born, Adolf Hitler was tried for high treason in Munich. Turning the tables on German leaders who surrendered in 1918, Hitler proclaimed during his trial, "There is no such thing as high treason against the traitors of 1918."[1] Seventeen years later, William Steward and Adolf Hitler shared a destiny that would change the world.

At only five feet five inches and 130 pounds, William was the smallest of the Steward boys, but he was the fastest boy in school and brimming with pluck. His tattered farm overalls and small frame often made him a favorite target for bullies and ruffians. But despite his slight stature, William didn't shrink from a fight, and in Cass County he earned legendary status for his mettle. At the old Bloomburg School, where older and younger students were often grouped together, four of the school's older and most notorious bullies surrounded him and pummeled him into oblivion. He was forced to miss several days of school due to the severity of his shellacking, but it served only to buy time for his plan of retribution.

The bullying taught William valuable lessons in the tactics of survival and battle—and years later on the battlefields, those lessons helped him stay alive. He quickly learned that intellect, lickety-split thinking, and grit were far more valuable than brawn. While he healed, he laid his clandestine battle plans to find and sequester each of the boys alone. Armed with a rope and a lead pipe, William taught each of the bullies a lesson he learned from his mother. And as he finished his schooling, he recited Leviticus: "And if a man cause a blemish in his neighbor . . . breach for breach, eye for eye, tooth for tooth."

After William's severe thrashing, the impoverished Steward kids resolved to take actions into their own hands. The four boys, William, Earl, Mickey, David, and the fiercest Steward kid of all—tiny, fiery-haired sister Helen—proclaimed, "If you pick on one of us, you'll have to fight all of us."[2] The Steward youngsters were intelligent, scrappy, and like all poor children of the time, they either learned to fight or suffered the consequences.

Beautiful and diminutive, Helen was fiercely protected by her brothers. But after her vicious right hook broke the jaw of and coldcocked a male tormentor twice her size, her brothers—and potential bullies—allowed her a much wider berth.

Much of the rural South continued to suffer the lingering effects of the Great Depression into the early 1940s. Like most Texas boys, William tired of farm chores. He watched his father rise before dawn to tend to the farm before leaving for his usual ten-hour job at the sawmill. No matter how hard his father worked, there was never enough money to feed and clothe his family of eight. William grew tired of poverty, being bullied in school, and the misery he endured at home. He dreamed of seeing the world, but more than anything he wanted to be a hero like his father. He couldn't wait to trade his blue-and-white striped government relief overalls for the uniform of the United States Army.

After baby Kenneth's death from pneumonia in 1941, William solidified his plans to join the army. Rumors of a new war raging throughout the world deeply troubled Americans, but most remained optimistic for a peaceful resolution.

In Yugoslavia, the resistance fought fiercely against German aggressors, prompting an infuriated Hitler to heap revenge upon its desperate citizens.

Germany's fearsome air force, the Luftwaffe, pummeled English cities, and German troops marched into the ancient city of Athens, placing citizens under martial law. In desperation, Greek Prime Minister Alexandros Koryzis committed suicide by gunshot. Two weeks later, Greece surrendered to the Germans. William's father witnessed a terrifying and uncanny resemblance to the black clouds of war he had seen brewing just before World War I—and he agonized over his son's constant talk of becoming a soldier.

Like millions of Texas boys, William "Billy" Steward was the son of a soldier, and he couldn't wait to be like his father. Younger brother David listened with intent, hanging on to every word of William's talk of soldiering. Playing soldier in the piney woods, David soon traded his coonskin Davy Crockett hat for an old army hat. He desperately wanted Billy to become a soldier and to teach him everything he knew.

Their hero and father, William Henry Steward, was a decorated "doughboy" of the 3rd "Rock of the Marne" Division during World War I.[3] He was born in East Bernstadt, a coal town in Laurel County, Kentucky.[4] Life was hard for miners and employees of the company, and there was little opportunity for them to own their own homes and farms. Coal miners were often paid in coal scrip, a substitute for legal tender, which could only be used at a specific locality like a company store. The mining companies rented out houses and provided employees with credit at the company store. In remote areas of Kentucky, coal miners were often indebted to the company and doomed to work in the mines for the remainder of their short lives.[5]

William Henry's father, John Jackson Steward, briefly worked in the mines but later rented a house on acreage, where he farmed. The fruits of his labor were then sold at the company store, to which he seemed perpetually indebted.[6] Determined to save his son from a life in the mines, John Steward moved his entire family to (New) Boston, Texas, twenty-two miles from Texarkana. Like many children of the time, his son dropped out of grade school to help his father on the new family farm.[7] In Texas, William Henry Steward would escape the blackness of the mines—but at the age of twenty-one, he would not be spared from the darkness of the trenches.

He enlisted on December 4, 1917, in Texarkana, Texas.[8] After basic training, William Henry shipped to France with Company K, of the 30th Infantry Regiment on April 23, 1918.[9] Eyewitness to the carnage of the Great War, the old infantryman became one of more than 320,000 American casualties. He recognized war for what it was—inglorious, "obscene as cancer, bitter as the cud."[10] And he prayed his sons would never endure the horrors of war that still tortured his soul.

William Henry's 30th Infantry Regiment received the French Croix de Guerre with palm for valor on the battlefield in the Champagne-Marne campaign.[11] At five feet six inches, the fiery-haired Scotch-Irishman saw horrific combat in some of the worst battles of the First World War. Steward fought in battles of the Château-Thierry sector of France,[12] Aisne, Champagne-Marne, the Aisne-Marne offensive, Saint-Mihiel, and Meuse-Argonne.[13]

Adding to the wretchedness of the bloody trench warfare was the first large-scale use of weaponized toxic chemicals—and there was no greater cause of terror than frantic calls from fellow soldiers, "Gas! Gas, boys!" On April 22, 1915—ironically, the date we now celebrate as Earth Day—the German army delivered the first mass use of poison gas on the western front. Releasing 168 long tons of chlorine gas over a four-mile radius near the Belgian city of Ypres, the surprise attack accomplished the German goal of breaking the deadlock in the trenches. A gaping hole was punched through the lines of the French, Canadian, and British divisions. And a new and terrifying form of warfare was unleashed upon mankind.

Caught in the path of the yellow wall of gas, every living creature was in some form wounded or killed. Men, horses, dogs, domestic livestock, and insects suffered a painful, withering, hellish death. As the attack at Ypres came to an end, casualties were estimated at more than 6,000 and a new kind of war neurosis emerged—gas fright. Remembering the horror of the scene, a survivor recounted the German gas attack near Ypres.

> We saw figures running wildly in confusion over the fields. Greenish-gray clouds swept down upon them, turning yellow as they traveled over the country blasting everything they touched and shriveling up the vegetation.... Then there staggered into our midst French soldiers, blinded, coughing, chests heaving, faces an ugly purple color, lips speechless with agony, and behind them in the gas-soaked trenches, we learned that they had left hundreds of dead and dying comrades. It was the most fiendish, wicked thing I have ever seen.[14]

By the end of World War I, gas attacks accounted for a staggering 1.3 million casualties and more than 90,000 deaths.[15] In the hours of darkness between October 4 and October 5, 1918, William Henry Steward was gassed in the second phase of Meuse-Argonne.[16] Like many thousands of American soldiers who were gassed, he survived but suffered respiratory and neurological problems for the remainder of his life.

In the Meuse-Argonne alone, one of the deadliest campaigns in American history, the Allies expended more ammunition in three hours preceding the attack than that used by both sides in the entire four years of the American Civil War.[17] American losses were staggering. In less than six weeks, 26,277 American Expeditionary Forces soldiers were killed and 95,786 were wounded.[18]

In addition to being gassed, William Henry was wounded in the lower part of his right hand on August 3, 1918. For the majority of his life, he carried a well-calcified fragment of a rifle butt deeply imbedded in his hand. His grandchildren often queried him about the large lump on the palm of his hand, to which he quietly replied, "Something from the war."[19] The painful lump abscessed after more than forty years and was surgically removed before he died in 1961.[20]

William and David's father rarely spoke of the Great War. The elderly soldier's only mention of the "war to end all wars" was of the dying horses he was forced to shoot on the battlefields of the Château-Thierry sector.[21] And after recounting the only battle story he dared to utter, the aging farm boy who loved horses would unfailingly leave the room, tears streaming down his red and contorted face. There was little doubt among family and friends that William Henry Steward was a casualty of the First World War, still suffering from the effects of gas and what was then termed "shell-shock disorder." Although many dismissed William's father as a shell-shocked old soldier, his son could not wait to become a hero like his father and namesake.

The younger William was one of 750,000 Texans, including more than 12,000 women, to heed the call of a desperate nation at the onset of World War II. While Americans gathered around their radios to hear President Roosevelt's famous "Day of Infamy" speech, only one in six Texans had a radio. At the time of the Japanese bombing of Pearl Harbor on December 7, 1941, the Lone Star State was largely rural with most citizens living on small farms and ranches. Texas's two largest cities, Houston and Dallas, had a combined population of less than one million. New York City had a higher population than the entire state of Texas. Only 20 percent of Texans owned an automobile, and less than half had received a high school diploma. Nevertheless, Texas became critically important to the war effort during World War II.[22]

The oil boom shifted the population from rural agriculture to urban manufacturing. The war effort reverberated from the smallest Texas town to the fast-growing cities. Texas was a staging ground for some of the Second World War's most important heroes: the Pacific Fleet Commander, Adm.

Chester Nimitz; the Supreme Allied Commander, Gen. Dwight Eisenhower; and the army's most decorated soldier, Audie Murphy. More than 1.5 million men received military training in Texas, including Gen. Douglas MacArthur, whose family had moved to San Antonio in 1893. William Steward—like many Texas boys—dreamed of becoming such a hero.

On September 29, 1941, at the age of seventeen, William hitched a ride to the Army Induction Station in Dallas and finally became a soldier like his father before him. While war appeared imminent in America, it was simply deemed an emergency prior to the surprise attack on Pearl Harbor. Even before that pivotal moment, William decided not to wait for the official declaration of war he knew was coming. Nazi Germany had already invaded Poland; Austrian Jews were being deported to Polish ghettos. In England, the Luftwaffe battered Liverpool, London, Plymouth and Bristol. The Auschwitz concentration camp was expanded and Rudolf Höss, chosen by Hitler himself, was appointed commandant.

Like so many other proud Americans, William couldn't wait to get in the fight. Because he was a volunteer rather than a draftee, William knew he could request a specific duty. He hoped for China duty. "I wanted to see all the faraway places since I had never been any place but Cass County, Texas," he remembered. "Besides, an enlisted man made twenty-one dollars a month—and if I got China duty, I could live like a king!"[23]

After enlisting, William was sent to Fort Francis E. Warren, Wyoming, for basic training. Years later he recalled, "It was one of the coldest places I'd ever been." He trained with fierce commitment, and earned and maintained Expert Marksmanship Badges in rifle, grenade, machine gun, and bayonet. But sixty-nine days after becoming a soldier, William's life—and the world—changed forever. After Pearl Harbor, America was officially at war.

By the time the Japanese struck Pearl Harbor, William had completed most of his basic training. With China duty now out of the question, his unit prepared for combat missions on a new front in North Africa. The Axis powers of Germany and Italy sought to control the Suez Canal and disrupt supplies of Middle Eastern oil to the Allies; and if accomplished, the strategy may well have resulted in an early defeat for the Allies.

Fighting in North Africa had been costly for all sides. In February 1941, Erwin Rommel, the brilliant German general known as the Desert Fox, arrived to take command of what would ultimately become the famed Deutsches Afrika Korps. By 1942, led by pistol-packing Maj. Gen. George S. Patton, American troops landed in Casablanca, Morocco. By the end of the North African campaign, the Germans and Italians suffered more than 620,000 casualties, and the British lost 220,000 men.[24] Americans suffered almost 20,000 casualties, but William Steward, who was still stateside, was not one of them.

The Axis powers weren't the only enemies bedeviling the U.S. Army. Infection by hemolytic streptococci had been a common cause of bacterial pneumonia, which had been sufficiently virulent to greatly complicate the influenza pandemic of 1918. Additionally, during the prewar expansion of 1941, outbreaks of scarlet fever and rheumatic fever were recorded simultaneously within several U.S. Army training camps. Between December 1941 and April 1942, bacteriologic studies were performed at Fort Warren, where William was completing his basic training. The U.S. Military Commission on Hemolytic Streptococcal Infections concluded that army medical officers "did not recognize" the relationship of streptococcal disease and scarlet fever, nor did they make any connection with rheumatic fever.[25]

Just before shipping out to North Africa, William came down with a severe case of bacterial pneumonia and was instead shipped to the army hospital. Pneumonia remained the leading infectious cause of death in the United States, and even the army took the deadly disease seriously, especially at Fort Warren. In a strange twist of fate, the deadly disease that months earlier claimed the life of his baby brother likely saved William's life.

Still recuperating from bilateral pneumonia and weighing only 126 pounds, William was given the coveted job of driving a jeep for high-ranking officers. Later, he was assigned to guard B-17 bombers in the Nevada desert near Las Vegas. In 1943, Lady Luck spared him a second time. He received orders to ship out with his unit to the Pacific, where some of World War II's most brutal battles were raging. But just one day before he was to set sail, William was diagnosed with a serious case of measles and again had a lengthy hospital stay.

"I thought I was going to miss the whole damn war and I was pretty upset about it," he said decades later. "Looking back, I can't believe how naive I was, but that's the way we were. We wanted to be in the fight, we wanted to do our part. And none of us had a clue what we were in for."[26]

William finally recovered from his long string of infectious illnesses. He grew strong and packed lean muscle onto his small frame, and his weakened immune system improved. William received his orders for Europe and his dream of "seeing faraway places" was about to come true. He was one step closer to becoming a combat soldier—and like so many others, he felt ready for anything the Germans could throw at him.

After special combat training at Camp Howze, Texas, William finally entered combat on the Normandy coast of France as a replacement. During

World War II, once a soldier was sent to a combat division, he was generally replaced only if he was wounded or killed in action. The World War II replacement system continues to be an issue for debate even today. In the European theater of operations (ETO), the U.S. Army Ground Forces Replacement System was at best flawed. At worst, many military experts believed it was not only broken but a serious detriment to unit cohesiveness that resulted in the unnecessary loss of lives.[27]

The German army deployed nearly 300 divisions; the Japanese deployed around 100.[28] The U.S. replacement system was based upon the bold and calculated 90-Division Gamble, proposed by the army chief of staff, Gen. George C. Marshall. The War Department determined that ninety divisions would be the absolute maximum number of divisions to be scheduled for mobilization. The plan judiciously attempted to balance manpower calculations for battle with the needs of the vast American war industry, deemed the "arsenal of democracy."[29] But toward the end of 1944, as battles raged in the Hürtgen Forest and the Battle of the Bulge, the manpower shortage became a critical problem.

Military planners conceded that original estimates of manpower required for the ETO had been vastly underestimated. But part of the problem was the way in which planners prepared their estimates. Obviously, riflemen would have higher casualty rates than supply clerks, but the army calculated percentages of replacements purely from their tables of organization. If a unit had 5 percent supply clerks, they would receive 5 percent replacements. This created a surplus of noncombat-trained support troops, such as cooks, clerks, and transport truck drivers. As manpower shortages became more critical, these men were sometimes given combat training in as little as three weeks, converted to infantrymen, and sent to the front. While the infantry accounted for only 6 percent of all U.S. Army service, by the end of 1944, infantrymen accounted for 83 percent of all casualties.[30]

The psychological pitfalls of the replacement system in the ETO cannot be overstated. Early on in World War II, units would complete basic training and then be sent to their divisions as an integrated unit. By the time they arrived overseas and on the front line, they had sometimes been together for several years. This created cohesive fighting units, such as the 101st Airborne, portrayed in Stephen E. Ambrose's *Band of Brothers*. Army replacements had no such unit training, they participated in little or no unit field maneuvers, and were often sent to the front lines knowing absolutely no one in their assigned units.

Due to high casualty rates among replacements, battle-hardened veterans simply avoided them—they neither trusted their judgment in battle nor wished to see them get killed. Unlike the few who received some unit training at the division level or those who began the war as cohesive fighting units, esprit de corps among these replacements was almost nonexistent. From a replacement training center in the United States to the front lines of Europe, a replacement would be herded into a dizzying array of brief stops:[31]

> **Replacement Depot:** Up to one week, nicknamed "Repple Depple," usually in a U.S. port.
>
> **Reception Depot:** On the continent of battle for one or two days; usually a large tent city where replacements got a first glimpse of the sights and sounds of war.
>
> **Stockage Depot:** A few hours; replacements received ammunition and weapons.
>
> **Forward Depot/Forward Battalion:** Introduced to commanders for unit history.
>
> **Replacement Company and Platoon:** Sent to the front lines as individuals, after being separated from the men with whom they trained and met on their journey from America.[32]

Replacements were alone and scared, and many died before members of their platoon even knew their names.[33] By the end of 1944, both Eisenhower and Gen. Omar Bradley admitted the replacement system was flawed. Bradley observed, "Casualties among replacements greatly exceeded those of battlewise veterans on the line."[34]

Historian and author Max Hastings detailed the serious flaws within the U.S. infantry replacement system, noting, "It created deep unhappiness among many men, and contributed to the Army's alarming total of almost a million battle fatigue cases in World War II."[35]

One young infantry soldier described the fear and loneliness of being a replacement: "Being a replacement is just like being an orphan. You are away from anybody you know and feel lost and lonesome."[36] Recalling the psychological burden of being a replacement, another infantry soldier wrote, "We were just numbers. We didn't know anybody and I've never felt so alone, miserable and helpless in my entire life. We had been herded around like cattle at roundup time."[37]

William Steward was about to receive his baptism of fire—as a replacement.

4

BAPTISM

It takes a hero to be one of those men who goes into battle.

—Gen. Norman Schwarzkopf, leader of coalition forces during the Gulf War

THE FINAL MONTHS OF 1944 were a watershed for the Allies, but the cost was horrific. In Operation Overlord, which began with D-Day on June 6 and ended on August 30, the Allies suffered more than 209,000 casualties, including more than 125,000 U.S. ground forces casualties. On D-Day alone, more than 10,000 Allied forces were killed, missing in action, or wounded; 6,603 of those were American casualties.[1]

Beginning on September 19, 1944, the battle of Hürtgen Forest was the longest single battle in United States history. The U.S. First Army suffered more than 33,000 casualties on what author Edward Miller called "a dark and bloody ground."[2] A staff sergeant observed the brutality and bitter losses of the Hürtgen Forest: "We lost between one-quarter and one-third of our troops each day—so there was a constant turnover of company personnel. If a rifleman lasted three days he was a veteran."[3]

The savage fighting and staggering casualties from September to December 1944 shifted farther south from the Hürtgen Forest on December 16 as the Germans launched a new and blistering offensive. In an astounding tactical feat, three German field armies secretly managed to assemble in the Ardennes as fighting continued in the Hürtgen. As a result of the surprise Ardennes offensive, Allied forces were summoned to contain the Germans at the epic Battle of the Bulge.

In what is widely considered one of the bloodiest battles of World War II, U.S. forces were faced with crushing artillery fire, subzero temperatures, blizzards that grounded air support, lack of cold-weather preparedness, and lack of food and supplies. The battle was fought from December 16, 1944, to the end of January 1945. During the Battle of the Bulge, Americans sustained almost 90,000 total casualties (killed, wounded, missing, captured). More than 47,000 were wounded, over 23,000 were missing in action, and 19,246 were killed in action. Most of the casualties were "dogface," or infantrymen, famously immortalized by World War II cartoonist Bill Mauldin.[4]

By the end of 1944, American casualties escalated dramatically, resulting in a critical need for replacements on the front lines of the European theater of operations (ETO). William Steward spent the fall of 1944 in intense preparation for combat. After months of enduring basic and desert warfare training, disease, and guarding B-17s, he departed first from Boston and on to the Port of New York. In a fifty-seven-ship convoy loaded with replacements, William sailed at top speed across the Atlantic.

> We were so excited to finally get out of port and to finally be assigned to a fighting unit. We were ready to do our part and we were tired of waiting around. We pulled out of port on a huge ship with 5,000 dogface onboard. It hadn't occurred to any of us that the reason we were replacements was because the poor dogface before us had gotten himself killed or badly wounded. But once I got on that ship and out to sea, I had a bad feeling. I began to wonder if I would ever see home again.[5]

William landed at Le Havre in the Normandy region of France at the Fifteenth Replacement Depot, a reception depot for arriving troops. The allies liberated Paris in August 1944, but Le Havre remained under German occupation until September. Adolf Hitler declared the important port city a *Festung*, or fortress—and demanded it be held to the last man.

German commanders ordered the evacuation of all French citizens, but few of them left their homes. In early September, Allied forces demanded a surrender that Nazi command flatly rejected. In a desperate effort to prevent the vital Channel port of Le Havre from being lost by the Allies, the city was subjected to massive bombings as wave after wave of Allied bombs were dropped. In one day alone, British bombers dropped 1,820 explosive bombs and 30,000 firebombs.

Amid the smoke and rubble in Le Havre's city center, only the ghostly silhouette of the World War I memorial remained standing. Le Havre became a martyr city and after a twelve-day siege, the people of Le Havre finally emerged free of Nazi tyranny. For over 80,000 homeless French citizens, the liberation brought little joy. With more than 5,000 civilians killed, almost every family lost a loved one.

When finally the city was freed of German occupation, Gen. Charles de Gaulle pronounced to the battle-weary citizens, "To Le Havre injured for the sake of France, but alive! And which will be great!"[6] Among the troops climbing down from nets stretched across the huge troop ship was a wide-eyed young Texan from Atlanta, Texas. William saw a city and a people ravaged by war.

> I got my first glimpse of what war looked like in Le Havre. The city was in ruins, there was no law and order, buildings were reduced to rubble, there were wrecked military vehicles everywhere, and little children were begging for food and scrounging through the rubble for food and clothing. There were about 150 of us together and we were all replacements. We knew we were going straight to an infantry unit on the front line. I had gone all the way through combat training with my best buddy, Tony. Tony was kinda funny; he was a poor infantry soldier, he had trouble rolling his pack and with infantry weapons. I wondered if we would be placed together.[7]

The replacements were later placed on narrow gauge trains, called "Forty and Eights." "They were big enough for forty men or eight horses," William recalled. By morning William and other replacements arrived amid heavy snows in Verviers, Belgium.

> While we were there . . . a train pulled in from the east; it was carrying wounded American soldiers and we got another shocking sight. We saw the wounded being taken off the cars. They were moaning and groaning, some had bandages on their heads, some on their arms, and some of them were shot all to pieces. This was the first time I realized what war was really like. And I realized all of a sudden that I was in a place I did not want to be.[8]

The replacements were issued ammunition and told to drop the huge packs they were carrying. They were to carry only essentials: poncho, overcoat, blanket, and a clean pair of socks, which they packed next to their bodies for warmth. Remembering the wave of loneliness that swept over the anxious replacements, William recalled parting from his only buddy, Tony.

By late afternoon it was snowing very heavy, and Tony and I were wondering if we were gonna be sent to the same outfit. But we weren't. Tony's name was called first for the 3rd Division and my name was called for the 78th Infantry Division—we were broken up. The lieutenant that was in charge of my bunch—I asked him if I could say goodbye to Tony and he said 'Yes.' I dashed over . . . and I told Tony I would be in the 78th Division and the lieutenant said if he wanted to write me, he could . . . to APO 78th, NY, NY, and I'd get it. Well, it was a pretty emotional thing because Tony told me . . . that he didn't believe he would make it back. Well, unfortunately Tony was right . . . after I'd been in combat I got a letter from Tony's lieutenant—and a sniper got Tony.[9]

William and his group of 78th Infantry replacements were placed on trucks for the drive to the German-Belgian border. They were then marched through a foot of snow to the regimental command post. William vividly recalled the ordeal at the command post: "They gave us three K-rations and told us to only eat one. We could hear rumbling off to the east and see flashes of light from the big guns that were firing. And I knew we were very close to the front line.[10]

William and fifteen other replacements were assigned to the 309th Infantry Regiment of the famed 78th Infantry Division. Units of the 78th had endured some of the most vicious fighting of the war in the subfreezing temperatures of the Hürtgen Forest. The division took and held the Siegfried Line against violent German attacks throughout the bitter winter of 1944—and they needed replacements badly.

Except for the flashes of light from the big guns, it was pitch dark. It was freezing cold and snowing heavily. The commander of the battle-weary 309th Infantry Regiment was Col. John G. Ondrick, privately known as "Uncle John" by the GIs he led. Insisting upon personally greeting each group of replacements, Colonel Ondrick stepped from an old barn set up as the 309th Command Post. William was instantly impressed with Uncle John.

He was tall, weighed about 180 pounds, his boots and battle jacket were clean, and he had on a steel helmet with a silver eagle right in the front. By this time the rumblings to the east were heavier and the flashes of light greater. It looked and sounded like a real bad East Texas thunderstorm. Needless to say, we were a very scared bunch of young men. He stepped up to each man. He asked me where I was from, and I told him Texas. He said, "Good, I like Southern men, they make good fighters."[11]

Colonel Ondrick then asked William, "Are you any good with that rifle?" William proudly replied, "Yes, sir! I qualified expert!" Just before moving on to the next replacement, Uncle John told William, "Good. That's what we need on the front." William deeply admired Colonel Ondrick, who spoke personally to each replacement. He forever remembered Uncle John's words as he addressed the group of cold, hungry, and now fearful replacements.

> Colonel Ondrick said our codename was "Diehard." This was kind of a shock to me because I thought it was a pretty bad name for an outfit that was gonna take casualties, as all combat units do. He said he had the best damn regiment in the U.S. Army . . . his unit did not retreat, we hit the enemy hard, and we hit them often. He told us we would work and fight eighteen hours of every twenty-four, and sometimes more.[12]

William was assigned to K Company, along with four other replacements that would later become his dear friends. Artillery fire was intense, so they were taken to an old farmhouse, the home of an elderly man and woman. The deadly German eighty-eight-millimeter antitank artillery guns were now sending rounds at shorter intervals and closer to the farmhouse. The infamous flak gun was one of the most feared and devastating weapons of the war, producing a screaming sound that instilled terror in the heart of every infantryman. William recalled moving toward the front line in frighteningly vivid terms.

> About every thirty seconds, we are hitting the ground. Here's a bunch of green replacements, scared out of our gourds and every time a shell hit, we hit the ground whether it was close or missed us by a good ways. By now the rounds were falling pretty close; they were German eighty-eights and they screamed when they came in. The sergeant told [the elderly couple] to go to the basement to be safer. There was a little white dog tied in the backyard and he was terrified. I decided to go out in the backyard and free the little dog. [Cpl. Elmer] Nance came to the door and yelled at me, "Get back in here." It was a good thing I did—a round came crashing in and killed the little dog, it tore him half in two.[13]

The new replacements for K Company moved out at daybreak to find company headquarters and receive their platoon assignments. As they continued up a dirt wagon road, they received sporadic harassing fire and were told to lie flat in a grassy field until they were called upon for their assignments.

William was assigned to the 2nd Rifle Platoon, along with three other replacements who would join the group later. He was luckier than most replacements—at least he knew the names of three men he had met in Le Havre at the reception depot. But just as William stepped out of the half-standing cottage where K Company headquartered, two eighty-eight rounds came roaring in and hit the grassy field. Lying in the grassy field, Pfc. "Wilky" Wilkerson became a Purple Heart recipient before being assigned to his platoon.

By the time William got to the old house to report to his 2nd Platoon, he was shaking with anxiety. Things did not improve—he counted only five men. Along with the platoon leader and staff sergeant whom he had met back at headquarters, there were a total of only seven men. Knowing that a full-strength rifle platoon consists of thirty-nine men, William nervously asked, "Where's the rest of our platoon?"

"You're lookin' at 'em," replied a weary and grizzled man lying on the floor.

"Welcome to the 2nd Platoon," cracked another dogface with a wry grin. William described meeting the men who would later become his lifelong band of brothers.

> They were the filthiest, sorriest looking bunch I'd ever seen. Now Hob [Norman Hobson] was over there on the floor of this old farmhouse we were in, cleaning his gun. I'll never forget that. All you could see were his eyes, looking out from under that helmet. He was cutting those eyes over at me, singing this little song to the tune of "The Wabash Cannonball." He was just trying to get my goat. He knew I was scared to death.
>
> *I heard that eighty-eight a comin' with a mighty screamin' start.*
> *Before I got to my foxhole, I'd won the Purple Heart.*
> *It's a dirty, mean contraption, known quite well by all.*
> *It's a modern combination known as Hitler's cannonball.*[14]

Most men were given nicknames; Pfc. Clifton Fortune from Texas was "Cliff," and Hobson from California was "Hob." Before William arrived on the battlefront, Cliff and Hob had been through bitter combat together and were good friends. William later remembered the man who became his best friend. "Cliff was an exceptional person," William said. "He had a wife and a new baby girl he'd seen once while on a pass. He talked mostly of getting back to Cross Plains, Texas, to his farm and his family."

Being small-town Texas farm boys, Cliff and William hit if off instantly. William quietly asked Hob and Cliff if the platoon was "jinxed." Hobson could see the jittery replacements were scared to death and quietly explained that the 2nd Platoon drew a lot of tough missions because of their leader, Lt. John McCrea—one of the best and brightest combat leaders in the 309th Regiment. Hob looked at Cliff and with a wide grin said, "I think we'll call him 'Dodie.'"

As darkness closed in on the 2nd Platoon, the lieutenant and Sgt. Bart Assarian arrived. Assarian was a tough, battlewise combat soldier. He was husky with coal-black hair and eyes and a fast-growing black beard. Known as "Blacky," Assarian was interim platoon sergeant in the absence of Sgt. Dale Patton, who had been wounded and evacuated to the field hospital.

The replacements had not yet learned an important infantry lesson—don't volunteer for anything! The lieutenant asked if anyone was good with a BAR, or Browning automatic rifle, often used as a light machine gun in the infantry. Corporal Nance, the replacement who earlier saved William as he tried to free the white dog, stepped up to proudly report, "I'm an expert, sir!" Nance was loud and brash. William had a sneaking suspicion he wouldn't be as brave with Germans shooting at him on the front line.

Sergeant Assarian turned to William, "And I understand you're expert with an M-1, Steward; you're up with Hobson. You'll be a scout, and you'll be on point."

Throughout the night the artillery became fierce in a back-and-forth duel.

"The Germans were shooting at our artillery behind us, and our guys were shooting at them," William said of his first night on the front line before battle. "We were right in the middle. The whole horizon was flashing like lightning and the ground shook from the big guns. It was frightening."[15] Just before daybreak, Lieutenant McCrea shouted a command that William would hear for many months, "Hook 'em up boys, we're jumping off. Hob and Steward, take the point."

Years later, William recounted his feelings on entering battle for the first time.

> It seemed like every hour brought something else to me that I wasn't sure I really wanted. I didn't have knowledge about anything else, just my platoon. The 2nd Platoon was my world; they were my family. We were three-quarters of a mile from live German soldiers who wanted to kill me. I was scared and anyone who wasn't was a damn fool. . . . I made my mind up to do the best I could because I was there—and there was nothing I could do about it.

> The 1st Platoon was ahead of us and just around the bend, I saw my first dead man. He was laying on his back. He'd been killed by the artillery in the night. His eyes and mouth were open and he was clutching his throat and . . . I thought he had a look of fear. Well, I was trying to grapple with this thing when a 1st Platoon man stepped out of rank, reached over and took the man's wristwatch off and put it on his own. I was really shocked. I really couldn't believe an American soldier would do such a thing. But after you've seen so much of this . . . they did it to us, we did it to them.[16]

After reaching a hilly area, the rifle platoons were ordered to allow several Sherman tanks to pass through their ranks. Taking the opportunity as a smoke break, the green replacements lit their cigarettes and watched the Shermans roll by. Sergeant Assarian's words quickly ended their relaxing break: "You dumb shits can have a smoke break in a few hours—if any of you are still alive." His words terrified William, who began to check and recheck his battle gear. He recalled the fear, smoke, the sight and smell of becoming a combat veteran.

> Sherman tanks began to move ahead of the 1st and 2nd Platoons. They immediately started firing on the hill in front of us. The Germans answered with mortar and small-arms fire and an intense firefight ensued. The lieutenant was screaming, "Move up and take the ridge." It was very frightening. It was my first taste of live combat and to me it was the Alamo, Bull Run . . . all rolled into one. You see the enemy and you keep firing until he doesn't move anymore. You can only hear the lieutenant and platoon sergeant giving orders—and you just obey them.[17]

Corporal Nance, the replacement who bragged about what he would do in combat and his expertise with the BAR, did all of that and more. William described the scene as two German soldiers tried to move a machine gun around their left flank.

> Nance raised up on his knees with German riflemen shooting at him, and he cut down on them with that BAR—they didn't have a chance. He stopped the machine gun from getting to our left flank. That's what Nance was like. There he was—the first time he'd been in combat and he saved our bacon that morning. . . . I think he was the gutsiest man I've ever seen.[18]

K Company had taken the ridge and several prisoners. The 2nd Platoon had several wounded, but none devastating and none killed in action. The sergeant told everyone to dig in. After digging his foxhole with Hob, William's hands were still shaking. He could barely hold his canteen. As Hob helped the shaken replacement, he said, "Well, Dodie, what do you think of your 'baptism of fire?'"[19]

5

MIRACLE AT REMAGEN

They weren't warriors. They were American boys who by mere chance of fate wound up with guns in their hands, sneaking up a death-laden street in a strange and shattered city in a faraway country in a driving rain.

—Ernie Pyle, World War II journalist,
killed in action April 18, 1945

IT DIDN'T TAKE LONG for William Steward to know he was in a tough outfit. Arriving in the European theater of operations in October 1944, some of the men of the 78th "Lightning" Division had already been in the fierce combat of Germany's Hürtgen Forest for months. William's 309th Infantry Regiment had been fighting from city to city in Simmerath, Witzerath, and Bickerath against large numbers of German troops. In the middle of one of the most brutal winters on record, the 309th repelled ferocious German counterattacks in Kesternich, against overwhelming numbers of German soldiers. Dangerous house-to-house fighting made the situation grim as casualties began to mount. The 309th Regiment held the line at Kesternich "in the face of the fiercest German drive since D-Day."[1] William learned early on that it would be difficult to survive in this unit.

After capturing several towns and villages, continuous firefights, and house-to-house combat, William's unit received Field Order Number 3 on February 3, 1945. The 309th would attack the town of Schmidt and attempt to secure the high ground overlooking the important Schwammenauel Dam. The dam held twenty-two billion gallons of water and remained under German control. American commanders feared the Germans would blow up the dam and destroy not only the towns along the Roer River but also American troops and equipment. The dam had to be intact in order to make the all-important river crossings.

Gen. Dwight Eisenhower, the Supreme Allied Commander, personally deemed seizure of the Roer River dams to be of critical importance, even delaying attack plans in the Eifel mountain range pending capture of the dams.[2] Capture of the Schwammenauel Dam was of paramount importance in advancing to the Rhine River and ultimately piercing the heart of the Third Reich. The Lightning Division was to seize the dam at all costs—and no one thought it would be easy. The 78th boys had been there before during the brutal December fighting of Hürtgen Forest. Lt. Col. Andy Lipscomb of the 311th Regiment described the obstacles facing his soldiers. "We were fighting the elements," Lipscomb said. "The men were tired when they moved up the hill.... They were so very numb and tired that they couldn't hit the ground when the artillery and mortar fire fell beside them.... Every house contained the enemy."[3]

The lessons learned were bitter for the Lightning Division. And as the brutal winter began to thaw, the streets of Schmidt were filled with muddied shell holes, dead animals, and dead American soldiers.

On February 7, the Lightning Division commander, Gen. Edwin Parker, committed all three regiments to taking the dam. Later that evening, he ordered William's 309th Infantry Regiment to take the all-important dam across the Roer River. In preparation, William's 3rd Battalion was to complete the dangerous mission to capture the town of Kommerscheidt, an important step in seizure of the dam. The men of his battalion were exhausted from the elements, constant shelling, lack of sleep, and fatigue. After capturing the town, the regiment was to push through another regiment to capture the dam.

On February 8, 1945, William spent his twenty-first birthday in the final phase of capturing the Schwammenauel Dam. Of the house-to-house fighting amid constant and intense shelling, one commander later wrote, "I can remember the shelling was so heavy that I couldn't make the company commanders hear me except by shouting in their ears individually."[4]

On the ninth of February, elements of William's 309th Infantry Regiment came to a clearing in a fir forest blanketed with fresh snow. At 188 feet high and 1,000 feet across, the Schwammenauel Dam lay just below them. The fight for the important dam had been costly, with one platoon sustaining 75 percent casualties. From this moment on, William was no longer a replacement. He was a battlewise combat veteran of the 309th Infantry Regiment. In a special commendation sent to Lightning Division's headquarters, the commanding general of V Corps summarized the importance of the 309th Regiment's determined efforts.

> Had it not been for the determined assault of members of the 309th Infantry Regiment in the face of direct artillery and small-arms fire, which resulted in the capture of Dam No 3, further complicated winter operations against the enemy on the northern front would have been impossible. Although the 78th Infantry Division is relatively new in combat, you have given ample proof that in future operations you will add new honors to those you have already achieved.[5]

The 78th Lightning Division captured the Schwammenauel Dam and finally crossed the Roer River—and the historic race to the Rhine River was on. After crossing the Roer, William's 309th fought every step of the way to reach the bone-chilling waters of the great Rhine. His "Diehard" regiment slogged nearly fifteen miles, capturing twelve towns and taking more than 500 German prisoners.

From the important enemy stronghold at Vlatten to Eppernich and Wallesheim, every town was filled with snipers and enemy soldiers. Many were battered soldiers from the Volkssturm, a ragtag national militia established in the final months of the war, but others were die-hard remnants of the German army. In Vlatten, the infamous German 5th and 8th Parachute Regiments made a last-stand effort with deadly machine-gun crossfire. William's K Company took the lead in crossing a fiercely defended stream between Vlatten and Wallesheim, encountering intense small-arms and machine-gun fire. By dark, the exhausted K Company boys had taken the town of Eppernich.[6]

William's 309th Infantry Regiment received daily orders to proceed with their blistering pace, attacking southeast in order to maintain constant contact with the 9th Armored Division. In the area near Lovenich, they ran headlong into elements of the German 9th Panzer Division and 3rd Parachute Division. After fierce firefights, William's K Company was ordered to remain in position through the night. The men were fatigued, but no one slept.

At daybreak, the weary American dogface soldiers received new orders, none of which involved rest or sleep. They were to push through the 311th Regiment to "seize and secure a bridge over the Ahr River."[7] The weather and constant shelling added to the misery of infantry soldiers. William described his regiment's historic journey to the Rhine.

We slugged across the Roer River. The shelling was constant, day and night, and I began to wonder where in the world they got all the artillery rounds they fired on us. It would snow on us. Then it would melt, then it would rain on us. Our clothes got wet. We'd move into one firefight, then another, then we'd move on to another offensive. We survived on two to three hours sleep, sometimes we ate one meal a day, sometimes two—and they were always K-rations. The K-rations gave me very bad heartburn; everyone had it. They had it so rich, just to keep you alive. We all had bad heartburn. I weighed about 135 pounds . . . and I was carrying nearly ninety . . . but we made it to the Rhine River and there it was—the bridge at Remagen.[8]

The 78th Division had accomplished its mission of reaching the great Rhine River. To prevent the Allies from crossing the river and piercing the heartland of the Third Reich, Adolf Hitler personally ordered the demolition of all bridges on the Rhine. After the U.S. First Army captured the city of Cologne, the 3rd Armored Division raced to cross the river. But just before their arrival on March 6, German engineers blew the Hohenzollern Bridge. Only one bridge remained intact over the Rhine River.

As it flows by the small village of Remagen, the Rhine is nearly a thousand feet wide, swift, and extremely cold, hovering around forty-five degrees Fahrenheit until summer. The Rhine has been a formidable natural barrier to invading forces for centuries. Two thousand years before William Steward reached the Remagen Bridge, Julius Caesar crossed the Rhine at Andernach, less than twelve miles south of Remagen. Using local lumber, his massive 40,000-man army built a bridge over the swift river in only ten days. The last breaching of the Rhine came when Napoleon's army crossed in 1805. American military leaders believed the last natural barrier to Germany's heartland would be anything but a cakewalk.

German Gen. Gustav von Zangen believed the Americans would cross precisely at Remagen. "The Americans would have to be stupid not to take advantage of this hole and push tanks toward the Rhine. I think they will use this valley—like water flowing downhill."[9]

General Zangen pleaded with German Field Marshal Walter Model to secure the Ludendorff Bridge with troops of two German army corps. But Model refused, saying, "Only a fool would try to cross the Rhine where the cliffs rose steeply on the opposite bank."[10] Model's miscalculation would later be seen as a lethal blow to the Third Reich.

The famed Ludendorff Bridge (called the Remagen Bridge by Americans) was built during World War I and named for German Gen. Erich Ludendorff. It was built to carry two railway lines, transporting troops and equipment to the western front during World War I. The total length of the bridge spanned 1,300 feet, and at its highest point the Ludendorff soared over ninety feet above the Rhine.

The Ludendorff Bridge connected the town of Remagen on the west bank of the Rhine and the village of Erpel on the east. Erpeler Ley, the basaltic mountain on the east side of the Rhine, rises to over 500 feet and is cut with a 1,299-foot pedestrian and railway tunnel. The steep cliffs of Erpeler Ley provided a strategic defensive advantage for the Germans, giving defenders a direct overlook of the bridge and wide river below. The geographical surroundings made crossing the Rhine at Remagen an almost impossible task.

Crossing the Ludendorff at Remagen would allow the establishment of an important bridgehead for the transport of Allied troops and equipment into the heart of Germany—and it became an intensely psychological advantage for Americans. The Ludendorff was the last standing major bridge on the Rhine, and crossing it symbolized the last stand for Hitler's empire.

Hitler took a personal interest in the bridge at Remagen. He ordered it blown, with an explicit command that the eastern bank of the Rhine be defended to the last man. The Führer's do-or-die defense of the Rhine River involved the entire Wehrmacht, the unified forces of Nazi Germany, which included the army, Luftwaffe, and Special Forces Command of the navy. The plan called for immediate destruction of the bridge after German land forces retreated across it. The strategic importance of the Ludendorff Bridge could not be overstated—and both sides knew it. Of the Ludendorff Bridge, General Eisenhower and his chief of staff said, "It is worth its weight in gold."[11]

The Ludendorff Bridge was designed to hold demolition charges in sixty structural locations, each capable of holding over eight pounds of explosives. Connected by electrical cables were zinc-lined boxes capable of holding a payload of explosives. The explosive charges could be safely detonated in unison from the Erpeler Ley tunnel. A system was also developed to manually ignite the charges should the cables fail.

In 1944, American bombers detonated charges on the Mulheim Bridge in Cologne and blew the bridge. As a result, Hitler personally demanded that demolition charges on all German bridges be set only when the enemy advanced within a specific distance to the bridge. He also ordered that bridges could be defensively destroyed only with written orders of commanding officers. The Führer's orders undoubtedly provided another fatal blow to his do-or-die defense of the eastern bank of the Rhine.

Elements of the 78th Division were alerted for movement to the bridgehead. In an effort to ensure a unified and expedient attack on the Ludendorff, it was decided that units of the 78th Infantry Division would attach to the 9th Armored Division. In the race to the Rhine, the 9th Armored Division seized the opportunity to capture the Ludendorff. The division reached the banks of the Rhine on March 7 and seized the town of Remagen. Gen. William M. Hoge, commanding general of Combat Command B/9th Armored, immediately received an unsettling message. Captured enemy soldiers revealed German plans to blow the bridge at 4:00 p.m. In his historic reply, General Hoge was emphatic, "You've got forty-five minutes to take the bridge."[12]

German machine-gun fire from the tall stone towers, small-arms fire, and sniper fire rained down on the Americans. Just as they approached the bridge, German defenders set off explosive charges on the bridge. The explosion blasted a thirty-foot gap in the supporting truss on the south end of the battered Ludendorff Bridge. But when the smoke cleared, the bridge was still standing.

Artillery fire was called in to create a cover of smoke for Company A, led by 22-year-old Lt. Karl Timmermann. Under withering machine-gun fire, Sgt. Alexander A. Drabik from Ohio became the first American to cross the Rhine River on the Ludendorff Bridge. But before he reached the German-held side, he witnessed an amazing act of heroism. Lt. John W. Mitchell, an engineer from Pittsburgh, braved fierce machine-gun fire to cut demolition wires and keep the bridge intact. Sergeant Drabik recalled the scene and the incredible bravery of Lieutenant Mitchell.

> While we were running across the bridge—and, man, it may have been only 250 yards but it seemed like 250 miles to us—I spotted this lieutenant, standing out there completely exposed to the machine-gun fire that was pretty heavy by this time. He was cutting wires and kicking the German demolition charges off the bridge with his feet! Boy, that took plenty of guts. He's the one who saved the bridge and made the whole thing possible.[13]

By 4:00 p.m., Americans had finally seized the Ludendorff Bridge. Elements of the 78th, still under command of the 9th Armored, were instructed to cross the bridge and attack. On March 8, units of William's 309th Infantry Regiment began crossing the Ludendorff into the night and throughout the next morning. Their orders were clear: "When you get across, turn right and attack."[14]

On March 8, Hitler was informed that Americans had captured the intact Ludendorff Bridge. The Führer was furious. Hitler immediately ordered the bridge destroyed at all costs. Over the next nine days, the Germans used every weapon in their arsenal to destroy the Ludendorff. From March 8 to March 16, German pilots flew over 400 sorties in attempts to destroy the bridge. Along with constant, fierce artillery fire, the Germans utilized armored vehicles, infantry, howitzers, floating mines, superheavy mortars, and even demolition frogmen.

The Luftwaffe, the aerial warfare branch of the Wehrmacht, was deployed in full force as 367 different aircraft attacked the bridge over the next week. The German High Command dispatched the Arado 234 turbojet bombers and Messerschmitt Me 262 jet fighter-bombers, used for the first time in an attack of a tactical target. The fighter bombers could fly at 410 miles per hour, so fast that American antiaircraft batteries had difficulty locating them.[15]

Propeller aircraft were used even more frequently in the attempt to destroy the bridge. Me 109s and the famed Stuka dive-bombers were a constant threat to infantrymen crossing the bridge, especially from March 8 to March 10. The infamous Stuka dive-bomber made a screaming sound, often referred to as "the siren of death." In addition to their bomb payload, they carried two wing-mounted MG-17 machine guns for strafing troops on the bridge. Although the Luftwaffe was phasing out the Stuka, it was nevertheless a deadly and terrifying weapon threatening those crossing the bridge at Remagen.

On March 8 and 9, Germans were successful in hitting the bridge more than twenty-four times, on one occasion blowing a fifteen-foot hole in the decking. In response, Americans assembled the largest concentration of antiaircraft weapons during the war, leading to the "greatest antiaircraft artillery battles in American history."[16]

At 4:44 p.m. on March 8, eight Stuka dive-bombers and a 109 fighter harassed troops and attempted to hit the bridge in daring, low-lying attacks straight up the Rhine. Thirty minutes later, eight more Stukas arrived but were shot down.[17]

On the morning of March 9, William crossed the bridge at Remagen. The German welcome party quickly dispatched seventeen aircraft to attack the bridge, which was now loaded with American troops and military vehicles attempting to cross. William's 2nd Rifle Platoon led K Company as they crossed the Rhine on the Ludendorff Bridge. William recalled crossing the bridge in the early morning light of March 9.

The river was swift and ice cold. If you fell and the fall didn't kill you, and you didn't drown from the weight of your pack, you would probably freeze to death or be picked off by snipers before you got out. I wanted to get off that bridge as quick as possible.... Hob and I took the point and we were about two-thirds of the way across the bridge when a Stuka D came roaring down the river ... he threw the first bomb but it missed. I thought a second hit the superstructure, you could feel the old bridge shake. Everyone was shooting at him, riflemen and everybody. He was skimming the water to keep out of the way of American antiaircraft fire, but they couldn't get to him because of the cliffs on the Rhine ... then two of our P-38s came after him.

He made a second run and the two P-38s were on him. This time he came back with strafing fire—and believe me, I was clinging to that old bridge. The last time I saw him he was dodging, flying off with those two P-38s on his tail. Let's face it, I've seen men do some brave things in my lifetime, but I've never seen one any braver that that German pilot.[18]

To the dismay of his military leaders and as a last-ditch effort to destroy the bridge, Hitler ordered the use of V-2 ballistic missiles, the first use of such weapons on a tactical target. The world's first long-range guided ballistic missile, the V-2 was fueled by liquid rocket propellant. Just days after D-Day, the V-2 became the first manmade object to travel into space.

Hitler ordered use of the V-2 "vengeance weapon" to serve as devastating retribution for the bombing of German cities. By the end of the war, the Wehrmacht had launched over 3,000 V-2 missiles against Allied targets, including the cities of London and Antwerp.

Although technologically ahead of their time, V-2 missiles were inaccurate and as a result, posed a grave threat to both German troops and civilians. On March 17, eleven V-2 rockets were fired from Holland at the Ludendorff Bridge. None reached its target, but one landed in Remagen, killing numerous civilians and three American soldiers while wounding thirty.

Civilians and soldiers later recounted the blast "felt like an earthquake."[19] Joseph Goebbels, the German minister of propaganda, wrote in his diary of the American capture of the bridge at Remagen.

It is quite devastating that the Americans should have succeeded in capturing the Rhine bridge at Remagen intact and forming a bridgehead.... The Remagen bridgehead causes the Führer much anxiety, ... Nevertheless, it must be assumed that the failure to blow the Remagen Bridge may well be due to sabotage, or at least serious negligence. The Führer has ordered an inquiry and will impose a death sentence on anyone found guilty.[20]

The Führer was indeed enraged at the failure to destroy the Ludendorff Bridge. He personally ordered the court-martial and execution of all officers responsible for failing to demolish the bridge. Four German officers were court-martialed, convicted, and executed only days later by the Führer's personal Flying Court, which acted as judge, jury, and executioner. Prior to their execution by gunshot, each of the four officers was allowed to write a last letter to their family. Hastily buried in shallow graves, the officer's letters were burned, and their families were denied military pensions.

At 3:00 p.m. on March 17, 1945, after enduring months of bombing, demolition attempts, and hundreds of artillery hits, the weakened and battered Ludendorff Bridge finally collapsed into the Rhine. As engineers attempted to repair the bridge, its massive structure crashed into the icy waters of the Rhine, killing twenty-eight American engineers and wounding ninety-three. Only the four huge stone pillars remained; they still survive today.

American news was filled with the capture of the Ludendorff Bridge, as journalists began to call it the "Miracle at Remagen." On March 8, the Associated Press reported the capture of the Remagen Bridge:

> The swift, sensational crossing was the biggest military triumph since the Normandy landings . . . a battle feat without parallel since Napoleon's conquering legions crossed the Rhine early in the last century.[21]

General Eisenhower summarized the incredible capture of the Ludendorff Bridge:

> We were across the Rhine, on a permanent bridge; the traditional defensive barrier to the heart of Germany was pierced. The final defeat of the enemy . . . was suddenly now, in our minds, just around the corner.[22]

From March 7 to 17, six American divisions and 25,000 American troops crossed the Rhine at Remagen. The U.S. military believed the war was shortened—and many American lives were likely saved—by the gallant efforts at Remagen.

In the aftermath of capturing the all-important bridge at Remagen, Americans prayed for respite from the bitter fighting. But Hitler had a new plan for the thousands of American soldiers who crossed the bridge. In his diary, Joseph Goebbels echoed the Führer's sentiment.

> The Führer considers the bridgehead a definite thorn in the flesh of the Americans. He has now ringed the bridgehead with heavy weapons whose job it is to inflict the greatest possible casualties to American forces concentrated in the bridgehead. It may well be, therefore, that the bridgehead will not be all joy for the Americans.[23]

The Rhineland battle was costly for both the enemy and Americans. More than 60,000 Germans were killed or wounded, and nearly 250,000 were captured. Americans suffered 6,570 killed in action and thousands more wounded.[24] With the establishment of the vital bridgehead, William and the boys of Diehard hoped the Germans would capitulate, bringing the war to an abrupt end. They were wrong.

6

THE ROCK QUARRY

We few, we happy few, we band of brothers;
For he to-day that sheds his blood with me
shall be my brother.

—William Shakespeare, *Henry V*, Act IV

DIEHARD AND THE LIGHTNING DIVISION were about to be confronted with the Third Reich's last stand. Hitler planned a last-ditch defense for the German heartland. In addition to the Wehrmacht, the People's Militia, or Volkssturm, was formed. It consisted of undersupplied and hurriedly trained units of conscripted boys and men between the ages of sixteen and sixty, though many were much younger or older. William remembered the Volkssturm for the remainder of his life.

"Once we crossed that Rhine, we began to see a lot of old men and young boys," he said. "I'll never forget some of those faces. We just hoped and prayed they would give up. But they didn't. They fought hard. It's hard for me to think about that now. It was really so sad. But you know, we just did what we had to do."[1]

Fighting was fierce as Hitler ordered the Wehrmacht to defend Germany's western front to the last man. Moving east of the Rhine, the 78th Division began the dangerous job of capturing one village after another. Dragging on, day after miserable day, the fighting continued. In his dispatch to the *New York Times*, war correspondent Ernie Pyle described the plight of the American infantrymen. "Forget about the glorified picture of fighting you have seen in the movies," Pyle wrote. "The picture you want to get into your mind is that of plugging, filthy, hungry, utterly weary young men struggling half-dazed and punch-drunk, and still somehow getting up and beating the Germans."[2]

William's 309th K Company began their campaign of village-hopping. Dangerous house-to-house fighting ensued as many villagers refused to surrender. After a bullet tore through the left side of the runner and messenger's face, William received an assignment for which there were few volunteers. The track star from Texas became the new K Company runner. William described the perils of village-hopping.

> Sometimes when we moved on a village, we could see white flags hanging out of windows . . . telling us the villagers wanted to surrender. Most of the villagers actually wanted to surrender, but not this one. We all knew they were ready to put up a fight. All of a sudden, an enemy machine gun opened up on us from the left flank. We scrambled for cover. The first few men moved forward and took cover behind some bushes. There were nine of us and I was one of them. The rest of the platoon scrambled back behind a small rise. This left the platoon split into two groups. That also left the nine of us exposed and in big trouble.
>
> I suddenly felt something slam into the left side of my helmet, ripping it off my head. I was holding my 536 radio to my left ear. I had no idea what happened, but was sure it had ripped open my left ear. . . . I could see my helmet a few feet from me with a nasty looking scar down the left side. My radio was a mass of wires and tubes. I saw the dirt kick up just inches from my face and then I heard the sound of a rifle firing. Then everything suddenly became quiet. A German officer walked out waving a white flag. Dumb old me, I thought they wanted to surrender.[3]

"Come out with your hands up!" the German ordered in perfect English. "We have you covered from your left flank with machine gun and another from the front. There are twenty-five rifles pointed at all of you at this moment. Come out with your hands up."[4]

• • •

William remembered his greatest fear: "If there was anything that frightened me more than a sniper, it was the thought of surrendering to an enemy who excelled in making prisoners talk."

Given the alternative, William was ready to carry out his next order: run for smoke!

"If you make it," said the sergeant, "Get the platoon sergeant's radio. Call for mortar to drop smoke between our positions and the Krauts. Good luck—we're all counting on you."

As the German officer saw no response to his surrender demands, he turned to walk back toward the village. And William ran the fastest race of his life.

> I could hear that machine gun chatter and I saw something in the little trail in front of me. It was the body of a replacement who joined our platoon less than twenty-four hours before. As I attempted to jump over his body, I went sprawling ... and the two extra clips from my Tommy [Thompson submachine gun] went flying. Finally, I got back to my feet to join the rest of the men.[5]

As Sergeant Assarian called for covering smoke, he screamed to William, "You get back up there and tell them to sit tight, I'm calling for smoke."

William was confused by the order. "Go back up there, Sarge?" he replied in amazement. "You gotta be out of your mind! I nearly got killed getting down here!"

Red-faced and screaming, the sergeant repeated his command. "You're the runner, aren't you? Then do your job!"

Preparing himself for the run, a disheartened William told his sergeant, "That machine gun will cut me to pieces, Sarge."

In a stroke of luck, William made it back to safety absent of enemy machine-gun fire. Of the German machine gunner, William said, "I guess he thought if I was dumb enough to go back, he would just let me go."

Under the cover of smoke screen, Lieutenant McCrea led the men of 2nd Platoon under the German guns and over a small rise to safety. Decades later, an edgy William recalled the day he received the Bronze Star.

> I reported the position of our dead replacement. Other than a skinned elbow and hands, I had no wounds, only two bullet holes in my field jacket. I never saw my scarred helmet again. That evening as we dug in, Lieutenant McCrea told me he was recommending me for the Silver Star for saving members of the 2nd Rifle Platoon. Well, I got the Bronze Star instead, and I was happy. All my buddies lived. I was just happy to be alive. Anyway, I was scared to death, but like Sarge said, I was just doing my job.[6]

After crossing the Rhine and attempting to break out of the bridgehead, William's battle-weary 309th Infantry Regiment received a new, urgent order. They were to seize control of a ridge overlooking the Reichsautobahn. The autobahns were the pride of the Third Reich.

Although the Führer had little to do with construction, the Reichsautobahn was often referred to as "Hitler's roads." The Americans knew that controlling the autobahn would cut the vital transportation of the Wehrmacht. It was one of the last great barriers facing the Americans.

The 309th was ordered to take the ridge overlooking the autobahn and hold it. Whoever controlled the ridge, controlled the autobahn.

"We moved out and we moved into an area we called the Rock Quarry," William remembered of the ordeal. "Our orders were to take and hold the ridge at all cost. We had no sleep and almost no rations for three nights."

The Rock Quarry remained vivid in William's memory for the entirety of his life, becoming the source of nightmares for years to come. Noted in the 309th official history, the stone quarry was formed by Hill 335 and near Hill 330. It proved to be the site of the "most stubborn opposition" in the mission to take control of the autobahn.[7] William recounted the battle at the old Rock Quarry.

> By this time I had been in combat long enough I was thinking for myself. I didn't have to ask what to do. I dug in behind a bush. We usually dug in two to a hole but our platoon was whittled down to the point where it was one man to a hole. Hob dug in next to me—I knew we were gonna get hit. Sure enough, at daybreak we got hit. We stopped them. We stopped them the next morning. . . . The next evening we were down to seventeen men in the platoon. We knew we would get hit the next morning.
>
> They poured artillery on us 'til way past midnight. I just knew they were gonna blow us all to kingdom come. Daybreak came and it was overcast. There was no sun to catch us in the eyes. They didn't come and I thought they were whipped. I was relieved. Hob said, "Stay in your hole and keep your head down." Well, I had one ration left and no sleep.
>
> I Company was to our right and all of a sudden, there was small-arms fire to our right. I heard the radio of our platoon sergeant, "Get ready." We were in a half-moon shape set up on the ridge. The lieutenant screamed, "Fix bayonets." My hands were shaking so bad I could hardly fix my bayonet. We later learned I Company was in hand-to-hand combat. Well, an armored car started up the hill—it had a seventy-five-

millimeter cannon and it was spraying the hillside with machine-gun fire. Behind it was fifteen to twenty infantry soldiers. Whitey and Kline went running to the right with our bazooka and BAR to take out the armored car.

There was so much smoke you could only see the silhouettes of German soldiers. I aimed at the silhouette and pumped as many bullets into it as I could, reloaded, and if he was still coming I pumped some more. It was chaotic—the lieutenant was screaming and you can't hear anything for all the firing and everyone was scared. We turned them back and they ran back... and firing ceased a bit. Then mortar fire came, and they came at us with a light tank and about twenty-five infantry soldiers. I had no way of knowing how many of our men had been hit... the only chance you have is to stay in your position and keep firing, which I did.

I heard the bazooka go off, then a second time, knocking off one of the tracks of the light tank. The machine gunner came up in the turret and fired at us. Kline's BAR began to rattle and I didn't hear the machine gun again. I thought there should have been another round on the bazooka because just a track was gone and the tank hadn't been disabled. I didn't hear our bazooka fire anymore—there was a good reason for that, Whitey was dead. We really cut down on 'em. The attack was over. We could not have stopped another attack.

Moving up to our rear were GIs from another platoon in the 310th to take over our position. They said, "Get your gear and go to the rear, a GI cook truck will fix you something to eat." Hob and I left together; neither of us had a scratch. We were wore plum out—tired, hungry, and filthy, but we didn't have a scratch. The cooks were good to us. They made coffee for us, but my hands were still shaking so bad I could hardly hold it. We sat on an ammo box waiting for chow.

The lieutenant came up and he was hit in the arm, but not bad. Then Cliff came up and he was hit on the hand, but OK. Our platoon sergeant had a thigh wound. It was me, Cliff, Hob, Sergeant Assarian, and Lieutenant McCrea. I can't remember seeing anyone else coming up. I asked the lieutenant, "Where is the rest of our platoon?" and he said, "You're probably looking at 'em." It was really more than I could take. I'm not embarrassed to say, I just put my face in my hands and cried.

They brought Nance down, he was hit in the thigh and as usual he was yelling, "I'm gonna be back and I'm going to kill a thousand Krauts." They brought Little Joe down, he had a piece of shrapnel in his throat and there was blood all over his field jacket. Wellington was dead. Our medic, Doc Richardson, was dead. Two of the young replacements who joined us only a couple of days earlier were dead—I didn't even know their names. Kline was hit bad in the groin. We had six dead and many wounded . . . and evacuated. I Company suffered hand-to-hand at the Rock Quarry with heavy casualties. My platoon was almost annihilated there.[8]

The boys of the 309th finally had the bridge at Remagen and the Rock Quarry behind them. The autobahn was seized by March 14, but they had no rest as they fought their way to the Sieg River. William's K Company dug in near the river. His platoon once again drew a tough assignment. They would be given the duty of furnishing three outposts. Positioned between the American main body and the enemy, an outpost served as a sort of early warning system to prevent a surprise attack on the main body of troops. No one wanted that assignment due to vulnerability and proximity to the enemy. William described the unusual events near the Sieg River.

This is where the English-speaking German women set up speakers and played music for us at night. It was a propaganda thing and we got a big kick out of it. They played American tunes, like the Andrew Sisters, and after each song they would give us the propaganda. We liked it—until they started dedicating some of the tunes to the outposts, our company, and our platoons. It got a little serious then.[9]

Each night a reconnaissance patrol was sent out to spy on the enemy. William remembered, "This is where we lost Johnson and several others." Johnson, a rifleman from Fort Worth, Texas, was wounded and taken prisoner along with several other K Company soldiers while on patrol. William's 2nd Rifle Platoon was dug in for five days near the Sieg River. On April 6, the 78th Division crossed the Sieg and pushed forward into a dangerous area known as the Ruhr Pocket, heavily defended by 370,000 German defenders, Panzer divisions, SS, the Volkssturm, and everything else the Germans could muster to stop the advancing Americans.

At daybreak on April 7, moving toward villages, the 2nd Platoon took heavy artillery, small-arms, and mortar fire. At 9:00 a.m., they moved into a wooded area where William and his Texas buddy, Clifton Fortune, took the right flank. William recalled the scene that would haunt him for the remainder of his life.

There was a lot of fog and when I stepped in those woods, for some reason it made the hair on the back of my neck stand up. It just didn't seem right. We were in the forest about ten or fifteen minutes when I heard a shot fire out near me. I thought at first I might have been hit, but I wasn't... but my buddy Cliff wasn't so lucky... a sniper got him. I heard him and tried to get to him, but I couldn't. Every time I moved, [the sniper] started firing at me and I figured I was next. I got down behind an old log and he couldn't get me. In a few minutes some of my platoon came in and killed the sniper. But my buddy, poor Cliff, was dead. He had a twenty-year-old wife and a baby girl he'd only seen once. I promised myself I wouldn't get close to anybody else in combat. I didn't want to get close and have to lose them. Things were never the same for me.[10]

Two days later, William received the Purple Heart for wounds received during a firefight in the Ruhr Pocket. After everything he had seen, he considered himself lucky to be alive as his wounds were not severe enough to leave the front. As the fighting raged during World War II, soldiers were often "patched up" and sent back to the front lines as "walking wounded."

Describing the situation behind lines with medics, William said, "There was no goofing around in the field hospital because you knew your friends needed you. Like everyone else, I went right back up to the front."

For nearly seven years, William carried a keepsake of the Ruhr Pocket—a piece of shrapnel deeply embedded in his right shoulder.

The Ruhr Pocket was planned as a coordinated squeeze—the 78th Infantry Division pushing northward and other First and Ninth Army units pressing in from the east and north.[11] Included within the pocket were Germany's largest industrial cities. The Ruhr cities had become the war machine of Germany, supplying machine tools, oil, iron, chemicals, coal, and necessities for the Third Reich's war. As the last remaining hope for Nazi Germany, the pocket was fiercely defended for thirteen days.

The First and Ninth Armies linked up on April 14, 1945, splitting the Ruhr Pocket in two. When the pocket was finally reduced, William's Lightning Division and other units liberated thousands of slave laborers and captured over 300,000 German soldiers. Knowing American soldiers treated their captives well, tens of thousands of German soldiers, Hitlerjugend (Hitler Youth), and Volkssturm were eager to surrender. William and other American soldiers shared their K-rations and cigarettes with the battered Volkssturm soldiers, many barely walking with untreated wounds.

Of the German infantry and Volkssturm, William tearfully remembered, "They were just foot soldiers like me, some of them just young boys or old men. They didn't want to be there any more than I did."[12]

The large industrial city of Wuppertal surrendered to the Lightning Division on April 15, 1945. With a prewar population of over 400,000, Wuppertal was critical to the Third Reich's war machine. For the boys of Diehard, Wuppertal was the first of many war-ravaged German industrial cities. For the first time, they saw the emaciated bodies of those they helped liberate—thousands of Jewish citizens, French, Czechs, Dutch, and Poles, enslaved by the Nazi war machine for more than four years.

More than 100,000 German soldiers died fighting in the Ruhr Pocket, many of them much younger or older than typical fighting age.[13] Americans sustained over 10,000 casualties in the Ruhr Pocket. William and his best buddy Cliff were just two of them. Cliff was buried in a temporary grave in Ittenbach, Germany before being reinterred at a U.S. cemetery in Holland. He finally went home to Cross Plains, Texas in 1949, where he was laid to rest with full military honors in his family cemetery. On May 7, 1945, Germany surrendered unconditionally, and the war in Europe was over. But William's dream of being home by Christmas was not to be.

The 309th was supplied with new replacements and renewed to full combat strength, preparing once again for war with the invasion of Japan looming. But after the Americans dropped atomic bombs on Hiroshima and Nagasaki, the surrender of Imperial Japan was announced on August 15, just three weeks before William and his 309th Regiment were to depart Europe for the invasion of Japan. The official surrender was formally signed on September 2, 1945, aboard the USS *Missouri*. As a result, elements of the 78th Division received a new mission. The 309th and 310th Regiments were ordered to Berlin as the occupational force for Germany's capital city.

With a beautiful and peaceful snow silently falling on his field jacket, the last Texan in the 2nd Rifle Platoon grabbed the hand of his dear friend Hob and jumped aboard a truck in the huge convoy headed for Berlin. On November 22, 1945, William and his brothers in arms entered the once great city and witnessed the total devastation of war.

• • •

William resolved to live through the occupation of Germany, the suffering of children, and the devastating horror the Second World War heaped upon his soul. His mind was a jumble of joy, grateful relief, sorrow, and guilt. He was lucky. He would return to his family, while his friends—Cliff, Doc Richardson, Whitey, and Shea—lay beneath white crosses so far from home.

To escape the demons of war, William dreamed of home, of reuniting with his mother, father, brothers, and sister. And for the first time since climbing down the ship ropes and setting foot on French soil, he began to believe he would actually live to see his home and family. He could almost smell his mother's fried potatoes and biscuits as he prepared his mind for coming home.

Half a century later, scientific researchers investigated the homecoming experiences of warriors returning from war. Studies reveal that homecoming experiences of combat veterans are of critical importance in predicting combat-induced psychological impairment. Within the first six months of returning from combat, those who exhibit marked feelings of isolation, shame, negative personal interactions, and unregulated emotions are more likely to be symptomatic of psychological trauma.[14]

Since ancient times, warriors have returned from the epic psychological trauma of war only to be hurriedly reintegrated into family and normal life. Recent studies of negative homecoming experiences of Vietnam veterans have provided us with better understanding of reassimilation from the battlefield to the home front.

In a study of 247 inpatient combat veterans with PTSD, Johnson et al. found that homecoming stress was the most significant predictor of current PTSD symptomatology—often "superseding combat exposure, childhood, and civilian traumas."[15] In other words, what happens after soldiers return from the battlefield is clinically significant. It is generally accepted that positive homecoming experiences serve to mediate the intensity of trauma. Unfortunately, negative homecoming experiences of traumatized warriors have been linked to an increase in intensity and development of the traumatic experience.

For veterans returning from the horrors of World War II and Korea, there was almost no understanding of combat-related psychological trauma. These men were simply alone in dealing with the demons of war. The symptoms and behavioral changes associated with combat trauma have remained the same for centuries—difficulty sleeping, nightmares, flashbacks, extreme startle responses, feelings of guilt and shame, irritability, agitation, depression, anger, and aggression.[16]

More than fifty years before clinical research affirmed the significance of reassimilation to the home front, twenty-two-year-old William Steward became a case study. He was about to experience the worst psychological trauma of his life—upon his homecoming.

PART III

DARKNESS

7

THE HOMECOMING

I've been immersed in it too long. My spirit is wobbly and my mind is confused. The hurt has become too great.

—Ernie Pyle, World War II journalist,
killed in action April 18, 1945

THE PINEY WOODS OF EAST TEXAS were blanketed in an eerie silence that morning, broken only by the sound of desperate footsteps and labored breathing. Racing through the pines, fleeing his invisible enemy, William Steward's frenzied mind was a jumble of chaos and confusion.

There's a sniper in that tree ... no, no! No dogwoods near the Rhine. Am I in Germany? I am, I am ... I saw the sniper, he killed him. He killed the boy. I know he is dead, I saw him. Oh God, I heard him.

Frantically running deeper into the woods, he began to wonder if this was real at all. The curious sound of every step was muffled in thick layers of pine needles; the sickening sound of cracking limbs added to the confusion of a tangled mind on the edge of reality. The faster he ran, the more it all seemed like a surreal dream, performed in exaggerated slow motion. Suddenly, the peculiar sound was punctuated by the loud crack of a broken limb hitting his face, sending William ducking for cover on the forest floor.

The damn Kraut got Fortune. Oh, God. Cliff is dead. I've got to get out of here! No, no, no ... none of this is right. Fortune is already dead, I heard him take his last breath at the Sieg. There were no dogwoods. Where are the Krauts?

Chapter 7

Finally back in his beloved piney woods, under a spring dogwood in full bloom, the dazed soldier dropped to his knees in resolute despair.

I am home. I did make it home. Dear God, I am not in Germany. There are no Germans in these woods, because I am home. I'm the one who killed the boy.

It was March 13, 1946, and life seemed on the verge of normalcy again. William and his brother Earl had been granted a second chance at life, returning from a horrific war that took so many lives. The cruelty of the Great Depression had subsided, the Great Dust Bowl had ended, and a good-looking soldier with a chest full of medals could easily find work and a beautiful girl who needed a real-life hero.

Now that World War II was over, William was imbued with hope. Most memories of the war were unbearable, but no longer having to anguish about surviving each day, he saw promise in his future. He had some pocket money, owned a couple of new suits for the first time in his life, and was a bona fide war hero.

William's brother, Earl Wayne, served in the navy. Like his older brother, he was lucky to be alive. While at sea on a minesweeper during the height of the war in the Pacific, his ship sustained damage from a near-miss kamikaze attack. Earl was severely wounded. Along with many of his crew, he was thrown into shark-infested waters near Iwo Jima. Many of those who went into the water died of their wounds or shark attacks within the first few hours. Some of the sailors, including Earl, remained in the water much longer before they were rescued. Earl received the Purple Heart for his wounds—and like brother William, he continued to struggle with recurrent war memories.

Their brother Aubrey Carol, nicknamed "Mickey," had grown into a robust young man and was now helping his father at the sawmill. When William joined the army, his youngest brother, David Daniel, was just seven years old. But when William returned nearly five years later, little David had grown into a strapping country boy who could navigate his way through the dense East Texas forests, bringing home stringers of fish for the family.

The older boys were beside themselves with joy. Against all odds, they had returned to their family and the old home place in their beloved piney woods. Of the more than 16 million men who marched off to war with the Steward boys, more than 400,000 would never again see home. The Steward boys were blessed with luck and they knew it.

They would celebrate the homecoming with a hunting and fishing trip in the woods behind the old Kennedy farm settlement. Grandfather and Grandmother Ollie Wood would join them for an old-fashioned feast in the Steward house later that evening. Mother, who was expecting baby Judith within the month, would make her famous buttermilk biscuits and "Sis" would bake her delicious sweet potato pie. The elation that swept over William was ephemeral, interrupted mostly at night in the dark, frightening corners of his mind.

William continued to suffer from nightmares and sleeplessness. Each night, he quietly struggled to comprehend why he had been spared while his buddies had not. He thought continually of his dear friend Clifton Fortune and wondered how his wife and baby daughter were getting by without him. What about poor Bernard Shea's family? In the midst of a firefight, Shea's last words had been to William: "Keep your head down, Tex." Now Shea rested in Henri Chapelle American Cemetery in Belgium along with more than 7,900 American casualties of World War II. Agonizing over his friend's misfortune, William was deeply troubled that even in death, Shea was never reunited with his family.

For brothers William and Earl—and for thousands of combat veterans returning from the Second World War—a type of dysfunctional guilt referred to as "survivor's guilt" was prevalent but not fully understood. Studies of World War II, Korean War, and Vietnam combat veterans have shown that their suicide rates far exceeded those of civilians of comparable age. In a large study of Vietnam veterans, "Combat-related guilt was found to be the most significant explanatory factor."[1]

William constantly thought of his buddies who landed with him on the coast of France and slogged through the never-ending rain and mud. His mind returned again and again to the freezing temperatures, the screaming sound of German eighty-eights, and the ghostly silhouettes of attacking Germans at the Rock Quarry. The relentless memories of the bitter winter of 1944–45 and the sight of frozen bodies were etched in his mind for the remainder of his life. It was exactly as the famous war correspondent Ernie Pyle had described. Pyle, the beloved voice of every infantry soldier, depicted William's nightly thoughts: "The unnatural sight of cold dead men scattered over hillsides and in the ditches."[2]

In spite of several fitful nights, William used the quiet time to lay his plans for the promise of a wonderful day with his family. Surely it was just the excitement of being home that had caused his restlessness. And for the first time in years, he was free of army rules and regulations, free of the misery of combat, and free of the perennial fear of death.

A long stringer of fish would be easy pickings for supper, so he stacked three fishing rods and reels near the doorway alongside a brand-new tackle box, paid for compliments of the U.S. Army. He could hardly wait to see his old stomping grounds, which harbored plenty of wildlife. In those days, East Texas bayous, creeks, and rivers teemed with huge bass, catfish, and white perch. By the time he was fourteen, William had become a skilled outdoorsman, an excellent shot, and he knew precisely when and where the fish were biting. On many occasions before he joined the army, the old pines and the creeks flowing through them had supplied dinner for his hungry family.

He had a curious feeling of uneasiness as he arranged and rearranged the rifles on the weathered oak dining table, rechecking the chambers at least a dozen times to make sure they were empty. Baby brother Howard Neil had already attempted to pick up an unloaded rifle and was scolded to tears by his hero big brother. Like all rural southern families, hunting and fishing were not only an integral part of the Steward boys' upbringing, but during the darker days of the Great Depression, those skills were life-sustaining for the family. Unlike his older brothers, William was an expert combat rifleman. He was well aware of the consequences of carelessness when using a weapon. Everything had to be just right.

William had last held a long gun just before he departed Germany; rifles were just one of the many reminders of the hellish combat days he was so happy to leave behind. He guessed the lack of sleep contributed to his newfound edginess, but he was determined to shake it off and enjoy the beautiful pines and the family he had so longed for. Decades later, in her eighties, William's sister Helen remembered her brother's homecoming.

> He always had the shakes; that was something I'd never seen in Bill before. I remember he had a hard time baiting a hook when we were fishing because he had the shakes so bad. And boy, you couldn't drop anything—you know, make a loud noise or yell out, even if you were just kidding around. At first we got a kick out of it and we'd just do it for fun, but it would make him mad so we stopped doing it. He was just real jumpy all the time.[3]

There was a joyful mood in the Steward home on this serene spring day. The dogwoods were in full bloom, the boys were back home, and Mother and Helen sang hymns as they prepared biscuits and gravy for breakfast. William was exuberant, happy to be alive and reunited with Mother, Dad, and his siblings. His sister teased him and reminded him how pretty her best friend

Callie had grown to be. Maybe tomorrow he would look up the lovely girl he had left behind in what seemed like an eternity. So often, as he lay in a snow-covered foxhole, cold and alone and halfway across the world, he had dreamed of this homecoming day. And on this glorious spring morning, he could scarcely contain himself as he realized his prayers of coming home had at last been answered.

Young Howard Neil worshipped his three older brothers, especially William. After all, William was a war hero, just as he dreamed of becoming. Howard Neil was born the seventh child of the Steward children, and his mother was tired. Sister Helen, only fourteen at the time, became his surrogate mother when their mother worked in the garden and attended her church functions.

Aside from his sister, there were few children for Howard to play with. David was three years older, but he often worked in the neighbors' fields before and after school to earn extra money. His brother William was in the army almost half of Howard's eight years of life. Earl was in the navy, and Mickey was working with his father at the sawmill. And while life had improved, the Steward family still suffered from the lingering poverty of the Great Depression.

Howard Neil was the hapless recipient of all that was secondhand. He wore the older boys' worn-out clothes, played with worn-out toys, and still wore the dreaded Depression-era relief overalls, which were the subject of much scorn from more affluent children. Howard was small like his brother William, and like so many impoverished country kids, he was often bullied and taunted by others in school.

Howard's rough-and-tumble sister Helen schooled him on numerous techniques for self-defense—or in her case, something more akin to blitzkrieg. She tried to teach him to throw the stinging right hook for which she was a Cass County legend. But Howard did not share his older siblings' penchant for fisticuffs. Despite his station in life, little Howard Neil wore a perpetual beaming smile on his tender face.

Howard had his fill of household and farm chores, which were inevitably delegated to him. It just didn't seem fair to him—all the boys would go hunting and fishing, but Howard Neil was told he wasn't old enough for the hunting trip. When Howard began to cry, William once again reminded him that hunting was a dangerous sport: "You have to know what you are doing anytime you are using a firearm, Babe—and I've already seen too many young men die."[4]

What followed would remain unspeakable. Indeed, many family members would never speak of it again. For decades, others dared not query the details of the homecoming. All those present were scarred for life, some more indelibly than others. There would be no therapeutic solution for those who witnessed the accident, as the consensus among all was to bury the tragedy into the deepest recesses of their minds.

Among the old-timers who were queried about the incident nearly seventy years later, the story seemed to elicit such heartbreaking sorrow that it seemed cruel to merely broach the subject. After the death of Aubrey Carol (Mickey) in 1965, there were no living witnesses to the actual accident—except William Steward, who remained unable to utter the name Howard Neil for the entirety of his life. Other family members, including William's sister Helen, were present but did not witness the actual accident.

Most family members and residents of the small town were reticent to speak of young Howard's death. Years later, however, Mickey recalled the horrific details of the deadly mishap to his wife. Saddened by the news of young Howard's death, schoolmates struggled to understand what had happened to their smiling young friend. David Murphy, best friend of Howard's older brother, David Daniel, revealed the sentiments of teachers and students.

> The whole school was so sad about it, and everyone quickly heard of the tragedy. I had a little brother, Kenneth, who was in the same grade as Howard Neil. Naturally he was very sad to find out that his friend had been accidentally shot. No one really knew the details, but everyone was very sad about it.[5]

The details of what happened on that misty March morning varied slightly from storyteller to storyteller. But two significant details remained universally consistent—what happened at the old Steward farm on March 13, 1946, was one of the most tragic accidents in the history of the tiny East Texas town of Atlanta. And not one soul believed that William Steward would survive the ordeal.

"The baby was trying to play soldier."[6]

"There was a struggle for the gun, he said it had a hair trigger."[7]

"The scene was horrible, everyone was screaming."[8]

"Billy was on his knees crying so hard."[9]

"Billy went crazy after the accident; he ran like a wild animal straight into the woods, screaming all the way."[10]

"Years later he told Dad he was sure he was back in Germany with his buddy who got killed, but when he finally realized he was home, he just fell to his knees and asked God to please take him."[11]

"When he finally come out of the woods that night, he had a big gash on his head, he was white as a sheet."[12]

"Everyone knew it wasn't just the end of Howard Neil . . . it was the end of Billy, too."[13]

With a sobbing brother and mother kneeling beside him, Howard Neil, William Steward's beloved baby brother, lay dying in the red Texas clay. As their panic-stricken father ran for help, a frantic William ran deep into the forest. Aubrey Carol and their mother waited for the inevitable sound of a second gunshot from the piney woods. By the time Howard's tiny body was loaded into the neighbor's old Ford, it was already too late.

Only two written records of the tragedy remained: Dr. Joe D. Nichols's death certificate, which read, "Accidental gunshot wound to the chest with .22 rifle," and a dog-eared, tear-stained photograph bearing my father's handwriting on the back: "I am so sorry my little darling."[14]

Howard Neil Steward was pronounced dead on arrival at 11:00 a.m. in Cass County, Texas. He was eight years, five months, and four days old.

Having survived some of the fiercest combat of World War II, one of the most brutal wars in history, and after only fifty-one days of peace, William Steward was once again at war.[15] But this was a new kind of war—one he could never win. And one he would fight until the end of his days.

8
DEMONS

I remember the experience as I do a nightmare. A demon seemed to have entered my body.

—Audie Murphy, World War II hero

WILLIAM STEWARD'S WAR did not end in 1945. After the tragic death of eight-year-old Howard Neil, William once again found himself on the battlefield. But unlike the battles he fought in Belgium, France, and Germany where so many of his friends were lost, William's war continued to rage in the battlefields of his mind. Before her death, his sister Helen recalled the months following his separation from the U.S. Army.

"I saw him sitting by the creek, and I decided to sneak up on him," Helen said. "I thought he was fishing, but as I got closer I saw that he had his head in his hands and he was sobbing like a baby. I said, 'Billy, what in the world is wrong?' And he just said, 'Please, please, please, Sis—just go away.'"

Helen recalled, "I caught him crying a lot. But he never wanted any of us to see him crying."[1] He would simply disappear into the woods for no good reason. He no longer had an interest in his favorite things. He didn't want to hunt or fish anymore, telling Helen, "Even when you throw 'em back in the water, Sis, it hurts them real bad." Rough-and-tumble William had become very sensitive, but his sister remembered that he would "fly off the handle at the smallest things."[2]

On one occasion, his brother David became the recipient of the hellfire that raged within William. Accidentally, David had mortally wounded a mockingbird with his pellet gun. And as the hapless creature flailed on the ground, Helen witnessed a frightening rage in William that she had never seen before. He grabbed the pellet gun from his younger brother and "bashed it into a thousand pieces on an old oak tree," she recalled. As David began to cry,

William grabbed his terrified brother by the collar and screamed, "What did that little thing ever do to you?"[3]

The evolution of war psychology remained in its infancy, and since there was little understanding of combat-induced neurosis, an official diagnosis of combat fatigue was virtually meaningless. Unfortunately, for the thousands of broken warriors returning from the horrors of World War II, and according to many military experts, no such condition would officially exist for nearly forty years.

For as long as humans have committed warfare against each other, there have been psychiatric casualties of war. Referenced in the annals of antiquity, combat psychiatric casualties have not been limited to modern warfare. At the battle of Marathon in 490 BCE, the Greek historian Herodotus described a soldier who was wounded in no part of his body, yet was permanently blinded upon witnessing the battle death of a fellow soldier.

Herodotus later wrote of one of military's most famous last stands at the battle of Thermopylae Pass in 480 BCE. During seven days of savage fighting, a Greek force of 7,000 soldiers held off nearly 150,000 invading Persians. During the slaughter, the commander of the Spartans, King Leonidas, clearly recognized that some of his warriors were no longer battle-worthy after days of intense fighting. "They had no heart for the fight and were unwilling to take their share of the danger."[4]

During the Civil War, "homesickness," or "nostalgia" became a deadly problem, reaching the highest levels of command in both the Confederate and Union armies. A Union surgeon, who treated the malady now known as post-traumatic stress disorder (PTSD), claimed that it "killed as many in our army as did the bullets of the enemy."[5] Officers reported, "Many good soldiers were possessed of a homesickness . . . that amounted almost to a mania."[6]

American novelist and Civil War nurse Louisa May Alcott described the psychological trauma she witnessed in a young Union soldier: "His mind had suffered more than his body. . . . He lay cheering his comrades on, hurrying them back, then counting them as they fell around him, often clutching my arm, to drag me from the vicinity of a bursting shell, or covering up his head to screen himself from a shower of shot."[7]

During the Civil War, surgeons described the symptoms of homesickness and nostalgia—a morbid yearning for home, trembling, vacant stares, hallucinations, delirium, and even heart pain and palpitations. Unaware of the significant connection between combat stress and heart damage, surgeons reported that heart-related symptoms among soldiers were likely due to nervous excitement and anticipation of danger. Recently, researchers have found that serious disease, including heart disease, is inextricably linked to PTSD. In a recent study of 8,248 combat veterans, those with a diagnosis of PTSD were 47 percent more likely to develop heart failure.[8]

One of the more intriguing cases of American battle fatigue occurred in 1876 at the Battle of Little Bighorn, where the Sioux Nation decimated Gen. George Armstrong Custer's U.S. 7th Cavalry. Maj. Marcus Reno, General Custer's second in command, saw intense combat action in the Civil War; indeed, Reno's leg was broken when his horse was shot out from under him during battle. Later decorated for meritorious conduct, Reno survived horrendous combat in Gettysburg and again at Cold Harbor. Many researchers now believe that Major Reno had not fully recovered from the psychological trauma of the Civil War prior to the battle at Little Bighorn.

Amid the carnage of Little Bighorn, Major Reno's Indian scout, Yellow Knife, was struck in the face with a bullet, spraying Reno with flying fragments of tissue and brain matter. Reno reportedly began to "foam at the mouth." Crying loudly and uncontrollably, he later recounted voices in his head. So paralyzed with fear were some of Reno's men, like the warriors at Thermopylae, they could not fight. The Sioux refused to kill them, believing that to kill such cowards would bring only shame upon themselves.[9]

Swiss military physicians were perhaps the first to identify a clear and concise set of psychological behaviors resulting in what is now known as PTSD. They called it "nostalgia" in reference to soldiers' constant ruminations about home. Other symptoms were extreme anxiety, insomnia, lethargy, and weakness, and physiological symptoms such as cardiac palpitations, fever, and dry or foaming mouth.

Military physicians from every country recognized and had a name for the psychological trauma of war. In France, physicians referred to it as *maladie du pays* (country disease) or nostalgia; Spanish soldiers were said to be broken (*estar roto*), and in Germany, *heimweh* was the debilitating condition of the homesick soldier.

By World War I, a new name for an old condition had emerged—the doughboys were said to have neurasthenia, or "shell shock" disorder. But once again, military experts missed their mark. Shell shock was thought to be partly a function of physiological brain trauma due to modern weaponry such as advanced artillery, but primarily a function of emotional and individual weakness rather than psychological brain trauma. Soldiers of World War I, whom we now recognize to have been victims of severe PTSD, were even executed as cowards. In World War II, the Germans court-martialed and shot more than 10,000 "cowards," many of whom were combat soldiers suffering from severe PTSD.[10]

British poet Wilfred Owen was perhaps the world's most famous victim of shell shock disorder. Much of the poetry pertaining to the soul-crushing misery of World War I is credited to Owen. As a second lieutenant, twenty-three-year-old Owen was severely wounded with a concussion from mortar fire that killed his fellow officers. Unconscious and lying among his dead comrades, he languished several days before he was discovered and sent for treatment.

After being diagnosed with neurasthenia, or shell shock, Owen was sent to Craiglockhart Military Hospital in Edinburgh. Craiglockhart was established to accommodate the enormous number of psychological casualties of World War I's bloody trench warfare. Owen's poetic portrayals of fellow shell-shocked warriors exposed an imagery which could be derived only from one who had himself witnessed "the carnage incomparable."

In "Mental Cases," one of his darkest poems, Owen hauntingly depicted the broken and tormented souls at Craiglockhart.

> Who are these? Why sit they here in twilight?
> . . . what slow panic,
> gouged these chasms round their fretted sockets? . . .
> —These are men whose minds the Dead have ravished . . .
> Treading blood from lungs that had loved laughter.[11]

Owen returned to the battlefields in the summer of 1918 and was awarded the Military Cross "for conspicuous gallantry and devotion to duty." Twenty-five-year-old Wilfred Owen was killed in action during the crossing of the Sambre-Oise Canal, exactly one week before the end of the war. His mother received the telegram of her son's death on Armistice Day.

Of the 16.1 million Americans who served in World War II, only about 6 percent were involved in sustained combat. Of those who saw actual combat, a staggering 37 percent were discharged due to "combat exhaustion" (later referred to as combat fatigue).

After the battle of Hürtgen Forest, one medic remembered his joy at surviving but also his persistent depression: "This was my personal Valley of the Shadow. I left with an incredible relief and with a sadness I had never so far known."[12]

One of those who saw sustained and horrific combat was iconic American writer J. D. Salinger. Salinger landed at Utah Beach on D-Day, suffered through two of the bloodiest battles in history—Hürtgen Forest and the Battle of the Bulge—and then participated in the liberation of Dachau concentration camp. Carrying manuscript pages of his novel *The Catcher in the Rye* with him from Utah Beach to Dachau, Salinger was changed by the war—and he deeply embedded his own persona and wartime experiences in his beloved character Holden Caulfield.

When the war in Europe ended on May 8, 1945, Salinger sat on his bed clutching his .45-caliber pistol. After coming perilously close to ending his life, he checked himself into a hospital in Nuremberg for treatment of severe depression and battle fatigue, which he fought for the duration of his life. Decades later, unable to forget the horrors of Dachau, he told his daughter, "You could live a lifetime and never really get the smell of burning flesh out of your nose."[13]

In 1943, two incidents created a firestorm of controversy regarding the legitimacy of combat-induced neurological trauma. During the Allied Italian campaign, one of World War II's greatest generals, Gen. George S. Patton, stopped to visit troops at the 15th Evacuation Field Hospital. The general, whose flamboyant and tough-as-nails persona was both feared and respected, was known to be a brilliant military tactician. When "Old Blood and Guts" queried an eighteen-year-old private about his injuries, the 26th Infantry rifleman confided in the general: "I guess I can't take it."[14]

In full view of medical personnel, Patton infamously pulled the soldier to his feet, slapped him across the face with his glove, and called him a coward. The general then chased the soldier from the tent and gave him a swift kick to the rear. Patton promptly released a memo to Seventh Army headquarters regarding hospitalized soldiers who were "nervously incapable of combat."

> Such men are cowards and bring discredit on the army and disgrace to their comrades, whom they heartlessly leave to endure the dangers of battle while they, themselves, use the hospital as a means of escape. You will take measures to see that such cases are not sent to the hospital but dealt with in their units. Those who are not willing to fight will be tried by court-martial for cowardice in the face of the enemy.[15]

A few days later, the general stopped at another field hospital, approached a twenty-one-year-old artilleryman from South Carolina, and inquired as to his condition. The soldier replied, "It's my nerves, I can't stand the shelling anymore."[16] Patton, who saw no physical wounds on the patient, struck the soldier on his face. Surrounded by seriously wounded soldiers, a deeply agitated Patton screamed at the soldier, "Hell, you're just a goddamned coward...

you're going back to the front lines. I ought to shoot you myself, you goddamned whimpering coward."[17]

The Commander of Allied Forces in Sicily, Dwight Eisenhower, vigorously rebuked Patton's behavior. While Eisenhower's August 1943 letter of reprimand was private, it was no less forceful.

> I clearly understand that firm and drastic measures are at times necessary in order to secure the desired objectives. But this does not excuse brutality, abuse of the sick, nor exhibition of uncontrollable temper in front of subordinates.... I feel that the personal services you have rendered the United States and the Allied cause during the past weeks are of incalculable value; but nevertheless if there is a very considerable element of truth in the allegations accompanying this letter, I must so seriously question your good judgment and your self-discipline as to raise serious doubts in my mind as to your future usefulness.[18]

General Patton was ultimately relieved of his command of the Seventh Army; however, due to his prodigious acclaim as one of the world's most brilliant military strategists, the incident served to further polarize those on both sides of the combat neurosis issue. But many physicians were beginning to realize that these soldiers were not simply suffering from concussive shock of artillery, they were not simply homesick, and they were not cowards or weak in character.

In a 1946 report on combat exhaustion, psychiatrists reported that "Psychiatric casualties are as inevitable as gunshot and shrapnel wounds."[19] Of the soldiers still alive after sixty days of sustained and intense combat, such as Normandy and the Hürtgen Forest, over 90 percent became psychiatric casualties. On Okinawa alone there were more than 26,000 documented cases of combat fatigue. The bloody fighting in the Pacific produced the highest number of battle fatigue cases—and 40 percent of all evacuations in 1943 were deemed "mental cases."[20]

It was not until later that the army understood the relationship between brief periods of rest from intense combat and the overall health of its fighting men. In the 1946 combat exhaustion study, researchers reported, "Each moment of combat imposes a strain so great that men will break down in direct relation to the intensity and duration of their exposure."[21]

As evidence, British riflemen in Europe were given four days of rest for every two weeks on the front line and appeared to avoid combat exhaustion for longer periods. But American troops remained on the front lines in sustained combat for as long as three months without a single break. The mental toll on these men was enormous and long-lasting.[22]

The seeds of change were slowly planted, as World War II became not only the most widespread conflict in human history but also the deadliest. The notion that battlefield symptoms were following soldiers back to the home front became obvious; nevertheless, attitudes at the highest levels of military medicine continued to disavow the existence of psychological war trauma as either real or even of any importance. Incredibly, it would not be until 1980—after another generation of scarred veterans returned home from Vietnam—that the American Psychiatric Association recognized and added PTSD to the third edition of the *Diagnostic and Statistical Manual of Mental Disorders* (DSM-III). As a result, teams of researchers, physicians, and military organizations rushed to determine etiology and treatment for warriors returning from later wars.

Increased awareness of PTSD among the general public and the medical community has undoubtedly led to better treatment. While many factors led to a change in attitudes regarding PTSD, two factors remain highly significant: advancements in neuroscience and post–Vietnam War popular culture. Scholarly understanding of the PTSD brain has increased dramatically since the Vietnam era. But American popular culture pushed PTSD into the national consciousness.

When combat veterans returned from the brutal Vietnam War to an often heedless American populace, it became glaringly evident that many veterans were deeply affected by war trauma. Popular war movies brought their suffering to the public forefront. Michael Cimino's epic *The Deer Hunter* was released in late 1978, winning five Academy Awards. A few months later, Francis Ford Coppola's *Apocalypse Now* hit theaters, adapting Joseph Conrad's classic novella *Heart of Darkness* into a nightmarish examination of abnormal psychology in wartime.

Beginning with the 1980 addition of PTSD to the DSM-III, policymakers have been tasked with keeping the pendulum from swinging too far—between essentially minimizing the existence of PTSD, as in the past, to potentially overdiagnosing the condition.

Veterans Administration disability claims and tax-free compensation for PTSD have skyrocketed over the past two decades. In its 2019–20 Report to Congress, the Veterans Benefits Administration stated that PTSD was the fourth-most claimed VA disability.[23]

To receive PTSD compensation in the past, a veteran's trauma had to be service-connected, and supporting records were necessary. But the VA significantly changed the rules in later years: a supporting record of trauma was no longer required, and veterans were no longer required to have been exposed to violence or to have witnessed it. Simply expressing a "credible fear of being attacked" was enough to qualify. Additionally, the VA included non-war-related trauma, such as accidents, that may occur while off-duty.[24] Many combat veterans fear that the system will become overburdened, resulting in fewer benefits for those who need them the most.

In 2020, the Department of Veterans Affairs, Office of Inspector General (OIG) released a review of the PTSD claims processing system. The review found that "PTSD Claims Processing Training and Guidance need improvement." The OIG recommended immediate action for improving the system, which will undoubtedly benefit those who suffer from combat-related PTSD.[25]

Recent studies reveal that after more than forty years, over a quarter-million Vietnam veterans have full-blown PTSD and as many as 31 percent have partial PTSD. For many aging Vietnam veterans, the symptoms appear to be worsening with time.[26] To further complicate PTSD studies among combat veterans, researchers found that major depressive disorder (MDD) and PTSD are unequivocally linked. Almost half of those diagnosed with PTSD have also been given a diagnosis of major depressive disorder.[27]

The comorbidity between major depressive disorder and PTSD is chilling; researchers have shown that major depressive disorder increases the risk of suicide.[28] One study found the rate of suicide for World War II veterans was four times higher than their civilian peers. By 2015, the Veterans Administration also released data showing higher suicide rates among World War II veterans as compared to their civilian peers.[29] In September 2017, the Veterans Administration released a dismal statistic. After examining over fifty-five million veteran records, with adjustments for age and sex differentials, the risk for suicide was 22 percent higher among veterans compared to U.S. non-veteran adults. Of the veteran suicides reported each day, nearly three-fourths were not under Veterans Administration care.[30] While veteran suicides appear to have decreased since 2017, the Veterans Administration reported that the U.S. veteran suicide rate in 2019 was "substantially higher than the rate among non-veterans."[31]

New studies involving the neurological mechanisms of PTSD have shown that brain tissue and physiology may actually be altered in combat veterans with PTSD. In a study of Vietnam combat veterans with and without PTSD, positron emission tomography (PET) scans revealed that cerebral blood flow was correlated to traumatic reminders of combat stress.[32] In addition, trauma and stress are known to result in alterations of the brain's chemical systems, which can cause long-term changes in the brain.[33] And although the mechanism by which PTSD affects the brain is highly complex, a generalized public understanding is relatively uncomplicated.

Brain imaging studies have allowed us to determine two important areas of the brain that are altered in those with PTSD. Research has shown that volume is significantly reduced in the hippocampus of the PTSD brain.[34] This area of the brain is important because it regulates both past and present memory. The hippocampus aids the higher thinking portion of the brain in regulating the amygdala, an almond-shaped structure which is responsible for emotional response, including "fight or flight."

A simplified example exists in the perception of immediate danger—you see a man with a gun. But seeing a man with a gun does not always mean you are in danger; perhaps you are walking the aisles of a gun show. The hippocampus and the areas of the brain involved with higher thinking will alert you that everything is OK, and the experience is placed in the context of nondanger. Quite simply put, these higher thinking areas serve as a check and balance on the amygdala and its response to trauma or danger.

In the PTSD brain, simply seeing a man with a gun may cause the amygdala to run amok. It remains unchecked by the memory and higher thinking areas of the brain. In the PTSD brain, researchers have found that in addition to a marked decrease in the volume of the hippocampus, there is also significant overactivity of the amygdala.[35] This provides us with some understanding of why certain sights, noises, and even smells can trigger an episode of PTSD.

Insomnia, nightmares, flashbacks, feelings of guilt and shame, irritability, depression, inability to regulate emotions, William Steward had them all. And by all accounts, he was a textbook case of PTSD—if only the malady had existed.

After Howard Neil's death, William wandered about aimlessly, constantly moving from one odd job to another. Decades later, his sister recalled her brother's wildly swinging emotions after the death of his youngest brother. "We didn't know if he would hug us and cry, or if he would fly off the handle for no reason at all," Helen said. "It was so sad because we all knew how bad he needed someone to help him. But us kids—and everyone else—just tried to stay away from him.[36]

Helen characterized his behavior saying that "he became a loner," avoiding contact with friends and family. She remembered a disturbing conversation with her brother about the existence of God. "I don't know how someone like me could have survived all this," William told her. "It just makes me believe once and for all that Mother is wrong; there is no God. If he was real and as good as they say, he wouldn't let innocent people die, little children and good people . . . then let a worthless someone like me live."[37]

More than sixty years later, his sister-in-law vividly recounted her memories of William. She was one of the only surviving family members privy to the horrible details of the tragic spring day on which little Howard Neil was accidentally killed. Donna was the beloved wife of Aubrey Carroll (Mickey), William's brother, who with his mother held the child in their arms on that fateful day. "Those were dark days for Billy," she remembered. "He just seemed to be a lost soul. Everyone knew the boys who came home from that war were never going to be the same again. We all knew those boys had seen things that no human being should ever see. But at first, he seemed to have been able to handle it. After the war and Howard Neil's death, he just went crazy."[38]

9

THE PROMISED LAND

I'm going simply because there's a war on and I'm part of it, and I've known all the time I was going back. I'm going simply because I've got to—and I hate it.

—Ernie Pyle, World War II journalist,
killed in action April 18, 1945

LIKE SO MANY BROKEN WARRIORS, William Steward was haunted by erratic demons. His severe symptoms were transitory, punctuated by fleeting periods of normalcy. Before the war he had been a gifted musician, and with his mustering-out pay he bought two new guitars, one for himself and one for his brother David. But William would find no solace, even in his love of music. As he battled to understand the web of confusion, guilt, and darkness that seized him, he desperately searched for a glimmer of light. The eternal light that would burn for William had been there all along—in his sister's best friend. Her name was Callie.

Callie lived just down the hill from the Steward farm with her sister and mother. William's sister Helen and Callie had been best friends since the age of six. He had seen Callie on many occasions, but never paid much attention to his sister's little friend. Helen honed her matchmaking skills on William and Callie for years, but William made it plain that he just wasn't interested. "Sis, she's just a kid," he would always say.

Callie's mother, Vera Kennedy, was deeply religious. And she insisted on keeping "those Steward rascals" far from her two daughters. The three older boys, William, Earl, and Mickey, were infamous for fisticuffs and carousing after the war, and William had begun to drink even more after the death of his little brother, Howard Neil. After a Saturday night at the notorious Louisiana-Texas State Line honkytonk, the boys would pass Mrs. Kennedy's house rejoicing loudly to the old gospel tune "Bringing in the Sheaves." Years later, Callie recalled her disgusted mother's warning, "I pity the poor girl who ends up with one of them boys."

Helen and Callie were inseparable friends for their entire lives. In the fall of 1946, they attended the Oak Grove Revival, a large church event. As they listened to the preacher's fiery tale of sin and damnation, the sky blackened with the full fury of an East Texas thunderstorm. As the thunder, lightning, and torrential rain swallowed the little country church, the three Steward boys ducked into the church for cover. Drenched and obviously in a celebratory mood, they sat on the back row next to Helen and Callie under the disdainful eye of Callie's fuming mother. The girls could not contain themselves, and Helen told Callie, "We'd better get out of this old church—with those three in here, it's sure to fall in on us." Later that evening, William asked his sister about the good-looking girl she was sitting with. "Oh, Billy, that's just Callie," Helen said. "She's only sixteen—she's just a kid!"

William was a twenty-two-year-old combat veteran who had seen the worst of the world. Callie was a sweet, ivory-skinned sixteen-year-old who had never been out of Cass County, Texas. He made an effort to follow her as she walked home from school. "He was always holding my hand," she remembered.

Callie sought to help William through the tragedy of Howard Neil's death. Being deeply religious, she asked him to be "saved," and she was certain that with God's mercy and goodness he would become a new man. They talked for hours about the war and the German orphans he saw, and his dream of becoming a successful singer and songwriter. Callie told him she would pray for him every night and she was sure the Lord would help him escape the sorrow of his past.

Over the next few weeks, William seemed to be more at ease after his walks with Callie, his demons temporarily silenced. He began to play his guitar and write songs about his newfound love. But Mrs. Kennedy was determined to keep her daughter from going astray with the likes of William—and on several occasions she made her case face to face while holding her double-barreled shotgun.

Although he had fallen in love with Callie, William knew it would never work. He knew Mrs. Kennedy was a wonderful person, but she would try everything to keep them apart and he didn't really blame her. He was a worldly sinner hardened by war, and her daughter was an innocent and God-fearing lamb of God. He told himself it didn't matter anyway, he and his father planned to leave Texas to look for work and a new home in Southern California. Even if he stayed, her mother would simply not allow it under any circumstance. And if he waited until Callie's eighteenth birthday, he was sure another Cass County boy or soldier would win her over in his absence.

A heartbroken William resolved to leave behind his pain and sorrow to start a new life in California. But he would not forget the pretty young angel who kept his demons at bay. He would always remember seeing teary-eyed Callie for the last time, hearing her sweet words of encouragement as he turned and walked away: "For He will command His angels . . . To guard you in all your ways . . . and on their hands they will bear you up . . ."[1]

After receiving news of high-paying jobs with excellent benefits, William and his father left for the nation's breadbasket. Almost entirely below sea level and a subregion of the Sonoran Desert, the Imperial Valley is extremely dry but boasts some of the richest soil on Earth. The valley is bordered by the Salton Sea, the Colorado River, and to the south, the international border between Mexico and the United States. The county seat of El Centro is known for extreme temperatures, ranging from below twenty degrees Fahrenheit to over 120 degrees in the summer.

Formed in 1911, the Imperial Irrigation District was created to supply the fertile valley soils with water from the Colorado River. At eighty-two miles long, the All-American Canal was completed in 1942, supplying water to one of the nation's most important agricultural areas, the Imperial Valley. After the war and the canal's completion, jobs were plentiful in the world's greenhouse, especially for skilled workers who understood farming and irrigation. And like the thousands of Okies who came before him, William's father did not hesitate to move his family to the promised land of Southern California.

He landed an excellent, on-the-spot job with the Imperial County Irrigation District. He was elated with the benefits and starting pay. William helped his father find a new family home close to work in the desert town of El Centro, the antithesis of their East Texas piney wood home. In January 1947, they returned to Texas with good news. They found a wonderful new home, a wonderful job, and a better way of life. And while William was happy for his father and family, William's nightmares and depression returned with a biting vengeance.

Since returning from the front, and especially after the tragedy of Howard Neil's death, William was mercurial, restless, and suffered with headaches and pain. Since being wounded at the Ruhr Pocket, he experienced trouble with his right shoulder but never understood the source of the pain. After medics removed several pieces of shrapnel from his arm, he had insisted on getting back to his 2nd Rifle Platoon buddies, knowing they desperately needed him. For several years William would bear a constant reminder of the Ruhr—a forgotten piece of shrapnel deeply embedded in his right shoulder. He was given medicine for pain and continued to use it, but he developed severe ulcers, which plagued him for many years. He continued to suffer from night sweats and vivid nightmares, long stretches of sleeplessness, and other symptoms of battle fatigue. Years later William vividly remembered the move to California.

> I felt like I was on the world's biggest roller coaster going a hundred miles an hour. One minute I would be on top of the world having a good time, looking forward to starting a new life, then the next thing I knew I would hit rock bottom. I couldn't forget about your mom [Callie], and no matter how hard I tried, she was the only thing that made me feel better. It seemed like everything happened so fast. I finally got out of the Army and things just went crazy. So many nights I laid in a foxhole thinking about making it home, fishing in the creeks—and now we were leaving everything I ever knew, Granddad and Grandmother, and moving to the desert. One minute I couldn't wait to get away from Texas, then the next thing I knew, the thought of leaving would literally make me sick. I really didn't know what was wrong with me.[2]

The Steward family would never be the same after the homecoming tragedy that ended little Howard Neil's life. By the end of 1946, William's mother had lost three children. They survived World War I, the death of their firstborn son Robert, the Dirty Thirties, and the Great Dust Bowl. They survived the hunger and poverty of the Great Depression, the pneumonia death of eight-month-old baby Kenneth, World War II, and finally, the tragic death of their precious eight-year-old Howard Neil. Like so many impoverished southerners, William's father had long dreamed of moving his family to a better life in the promised land of California.

There was every reason to leave the sadness and misery their family had so long endured. As William's mother put it, God had compelled them to "leave this sorrowful old place behind." Surely they would "find peace and the glory of God" in the Golden State. They sold most of their possessions, tied the remainder to an old Ford, and tearfully waved goodbye to the children's brokenhearted grandparents.

William was still reeling from the ghastly ordeal of his brother's tragic death and the horror of his combat days. Both experiences were now profoundly entangled in his fragile and tormented mind. He vowed never again to see the wretched sight of eight-year-old Howard Neil's death. And as he pulled away from the only home he had ever known, he whispered to his father, "I will never have to see this place again." In the middle seat of the old Ford, as close to William as possible, sat his younger brother and greatest admirer, David.[3]

• • •

Bouncing from job to job in the desert town of El Centro, William drove a cab, played rhythm guitar and sang in a band, and worked at several other odd jobs. He missed the piney woods, the creeks and bayous where he fished, and he missed his grandfather. His shoulder ached constantly, especially after driving a stick shift or holding his guitar all night. But he loved writing and playing his songs, and he made more money than ever playing in Southern California honky-tonks.

He was a good-looking war hero who never had to buy a drink, and alcohol was simply a part of the music business. The bigger the crowd, the more they drank, the more money he made—and the more often his demons returned. Through a stroke of luck, William met a man looking for talent for radio station KIOX in Bay City, Texas. The station's house band needed a singer-songwriter, and William fit the bill perfectly.

The radio station job was just the break William needed. A more respectable job in the music industry would provide him the opportunity to save some money and get his life back on track. Since returning from war, only one thought quieted the tumult within his mind. William laid plans to return to Texas and the two people he most loved, his grandfather and, of course, Callie.

William left the California desert town of El Centro for his grandfather's farm. His grandfather, James Theodore Wood, was a successful farmer and entrepreneur, a proper man who wore a tie and fedora each and every day of his life. He was known as an honest man of his word, a wonderful role model, and pillar of his church and community. It was William's grandfather who years earlier, by the glow of coal-oil lantern, wakened him on the morning he left for overseas: "Son, it's time to go. Your country needs you."

More than anyone, he was the person William most respected and to whom he turned for advice. William knew his grandfather would lead him in the right direction regarding Callie, who would soon turn eighteen. Always a gentleman, William's beloved grandfather advised him to inform Mrs. Kennedy of his love for her daughter and that he would wait for her. If she still wished to marry him, he would ask Mrs. Kennedy for her daughter's hand—and no matter what, he would abide by her wishes. He vowed to return after her eighteenth birthday and promised her mother he would clean himself up and make a wonderful son-in-law. He told Callie he loved her and intended to marry her if she would have him when he returned.

William honed his musical talents at the Bay City radio station and began to play at larger venues like the Louisiana Hayride, a radio and television broadcast second in the world of country music only to the Grand Ole Opry. The Louisiana Hayride launched the careers of some of music's greatest performers and showcased up-and-coming new talent. Performers on the Hayride included Hank Williams, Elvis Presley, Johnny Cash, George Jones, Kitty Wells—and local World War II hero William Steward.

William made good money, but like so many other budding entertainers, drinking and constant parties surrounded him. His plan had been to leave the honky-tonks of Southern California, to clean himself up, save money, and marry the love of his life. But his nightmares were back, and he was once again depressed and mercurial. He lost weight, failed to show up for performances, and feared a return to the hellish year of his homecoming from the war in Europe.

The notion of losing Callie and his dream of becoming a singer and songwriter was more than he could take. He constantly tried to think of a way out of the black hole, but in fact there was only one thing he really knew—being a soldier in the U.S. Army.

In July, William returned to the desert. On July 29, 1948, he walked into the Fort MacArthur Army Recruiting Station in San Pedro, California. He emphatically told the recruiter he had his fill of combat—but he was sure he could be of value to his country in training new recruits. He had served his country for four years, two months, and two days. Somehow, he had survived the war to end all wars, and it was now peacetime.

"Don't worry, you'll never have to return to war," laughed the recruiter. "You'll be training troops on the beaches of sunny California, son."[4]

It would be a three-year peacetime reenlistment contract, and the army could provide just the stability he needed to marry Callie and begin a family. William Steward was once again a soldier.

Like his brother, David was not impressed with desert life. There were no creeks teeming with fish, there was no hunting, and the young people seemed different. Summer and weekend nights in Texas had been filled with musical picking parties, guitars, banjos, fiddles, and mandolins. David was a natural musician, learning to play anything with strings, but his favorite was the guitar.

Back home in Texas, neighbors and kinfolk would join in playing and singing gospel music. They played the songs of Bob Wills, Ernest Tubb, and an up-and-coming troubadour named Hank Williams. By the time he entered high school, David had become an accomplished musician. He missed playing his guitar on the front porch of his grandfather's old home place. The students in California laughed at his southern drawl, at the music he loved, and at the way he dressed. They called him "Tex," a name he proudly accepted—as it was one of only two things he found tolerable about Central Union High School in El Centro.

Central Union High School had an elite Cadet Corps for male students aspiring to serve in the military—and it was a dream come true for David. His father and brother were his two greatest heroes, and he had dreamed of becoming a soldier his entire life. The Cadet Corps not only provided early military training, it would also help him enter the Junior ROTC. By the age of twelve, David had his fill of heartache, losing two younger brothers, baby Kenneth and Howard Neil. William had never been the same since the war and the tragic death of little brother Howard. In some ways, David felt he had also lost his big brother and hero, William.

Finally, David's dreams seemed to be coming true. The hardships and sadness he suffered in Texas seemed to disappear with his newfound excitement of becoming a soldier. He could hardly wait until his seventeenth birthday, the age at which he could officially enlist with his parent's signature. Biding his time, David was fully aware that the circumstances called for restraint and patience.

Becoming a corps member was not an easy task. The Cadet Corps required all cadets to maintain the highest character, to be in good academic standing, and to contribute to both families and community. They were required to demonstrate and provide proof of unyielding work ethic and stability. David laid plans and vowed to fulfill his dream of becoming an elite member of the Cadet Corps, his sole reason for attending school in El Centro. He needed an after-school job—and a birth certificate.

Like so many rural children born at home in the 1930s, David's only official record of birth was filed on February 5, seven days after his birth on January 29, 1934. It was signed by the Cass County registrar and Dr. Joe D. Nichols in Atlanta, Texas.[5] David's birth record existed in only one other place, the Cass County Family Census Blank, an ancient, enormous black book containing handwritten records of children's birthdates and ages for the purpose of entering public school.[6] While his brother William made plans to win the hearts of Callie and her mother, David continued his plan of achieving excellence in the Cadet Corps and achieving his ultimate goal of becoming a soldier. He wrote to the Cass County courthouse and requested the birth certificate required for a new job.

In February 1949, following his Grandfather Wood's advice, William followed through on his promise to ask for Callie's hand in marriage. Things were different now. He had a pocketful of money and wore a new army dress uniform, proudly pinned with his Bronze Star, Purple Heart, and treasured Combat Infantryman Badge. Mrs. Kennedy hoped her daughter would find a man dedicated to preaching the gospel. But as promised, a dapper William had both honored his word and served his country well, and she reluctantly submitted.

On February 5, 1949, Vera Kennedy accompanied her daughter and William to Texarkana, Arkansas, where they began their six decades of marriage. After a tearful goodbye to her mother and sister, Callie left the piney woods for the first time in her life. She was officially an army wife, accompanying her soldier-husband back to California for the first in a long string of army bases.

The move to the promised land began just as William and his brother David had dreamed. William began his new life with Callie as the recruiter promised, "On the beaches of sunny California." On December 4, 1949, William and Callie joyously returned to their Fort Ord Quonset hut with Michael, their new baby boy. Meanwhile, David received his birth certificate from Texas, landed an after-school job, and was accepted into Central Union High School's elite Cadet Corps. The days of poverty, depression, death, and war were finally over for two small-town Texas brothers.

Decades later, both William and sister Helen described a foreboding sense of apprehension in forsaking Texas. Although they missed the old homeplace, the mysterious feeling of dread dissipated with the excitement of a fresh start. But as they bathed in the perennial sun of their new Southern California lives, a fierce and violent storm was brewing in the ancient land of Chosun—Korea.

For brothers William and David Steward, the move to the promised land was full of empty promises. And as if the black blizzards and despair of his 1934 birth forecast the future for young David Daniel Steward, the promised land move would seal his fate.

10

BOY SOLDIER

My friend, you would not tell with such high zest / To children ardent for some desperate glory, / The old Lie: Dulce et decorum est / pro patria mori. [It is sweet and fitting to die for one's country.]

—Wilfred Owen, World War I soldier-poet, killed in action November 4, 1918

Dearest Mom and Dad,

Please don't worry, Mom. . . . I'm sending a $25 bond each month. . . . You and Dad keep half and save me half. Put a bond every other month away for me, okay?

Boy! Isn't this a swell plan? I can soon buy me a good guitar. . . . I have a chance to get on the music squad and go to music school. If I do, I'll be coming home about every two weeks. Isn't that swell? Boy, Oh Boy! . . . I also took shots and vaccinations today.

All my love,

David[1]

Underage soldiers have served their countries in combat since ancient times. The Spartans of Greece began military training at age seven. It is estimated that almost 20 percent of all soldiers in the American Civil War were under the age of eighteen, and almost 100,000 Union soldiers were younger than fifteen.[2] Nearly fifty boy soldiers under the age of eighteen have received the Medal of Honor for valor on the battlefield—and eleven of them were not yet sixteen.[3] They commonly shared romanticized illusions of war, but their glory was quickly supplanted by the horror of combat and the total devastation of war.

John Cook was only fifteen when he received the Medal of Honor for his actions at the Battle of Antietam. Elisha Stockwell, another fifteen-year-old, recounted his memories from the Battle of Shiloh. "As we lay there and the shells were flying over us, my thoughts went back to home, and I thought what a foolish boy I was to run away and get into such a mess as I was in."[4]

While there is no true record, estimates for underage American soldiers in both World War II and Korea are more than 250,000. World War II alone accounted for an estimated 200,000 underage soldiers, and 50,000 more were sent home when their underage status was discovered.[5]

Like David Steward, sixteen-year-old Audie Murphy dreamed of being a soldier. America's most decorated combat soldier, Murphy falsified his birthdate after Pearl Harbor to enlist in the army. At only five feet, five inches tall and 112 pounds, baby-faced Murphy was turned down for being underweight and underage. After his sister provided a notarized document that falsified his birthday by one year, Murphy became a soldier and served in some of World War II's most fierce fighting.

By the age of twenty-one, the fearless Texan was World War II's most decorated soldier, receiving every U.S. Army military combat award for valor. In the Colmar Pocket of France at the age of nineteen, Murphy held off an entire company of Germans and six supporting Panzer tanks for more than an hour. For his bravery in saving his entire company from being overrun by the Germans, Murphy received the Medal of Honor. After the war, the beloved Texas soldier became an enormous success as a Hollywood movie star, but untreated for the debilitating posttraumatic stress disorder he suffered, Murphy paid a terrible price.

> War ... takes something from you and it leaves something behind in its stead. It burned me out in some ways so that now I feel like an old man. . . . It made me grow up too fast. You live so much on nervous excitement that when it is over you fall apart.[6]

There is no official military record of underage servicemen. Since the legal age of enlistment is seventeen with parental consent, those who enlisted fraudulently simply did not exist. Calvin Graham became the embodiment of underage military service at the age of twelve. A decorated seaman, Graham is thought to be the youngest who served during World War II.[7]

In the vicious fighting at Guadalcanal, Graham was severely wounded when his ship was hit, yet he continued to pull his shipmates to safety. For his bravery, he was awarded the Bronze Star for valor and the Purple Heart. When his true age was discovered, he was booted from the navy—minus an honorable discharge—stripped of his medals, and denied benefits.[8] Forty years later, his disability benefits were finally restored but not his Purple Heart. At the age of sixty-two, Calvin Graham died at home in Fort Worth, Texas, and more than a year after his death, his widow was presented with his Purple Heart by the Secretary of the Navy.[9]

Perhaps the best-known group of underage soldiers was the Hitlerjugend. During the Second World War, the Hitler Youth was composed of males aged fourteen to eighteen. By 1936, the Hitlerjugend had grown to over five million youths—and by 1940, the organization had over eight million registered members. Mandatory membership in the Hitler Youth was enforced for all Aryan boys. Parents who objected were investigated and interrogated, and as a consequence, the majority of Germany's teenage boys became members.[10]

The 12th SS Hitlerjugend Panzer Division of more than 10,000 boys served in Normandy, suffering over 60 percent casualties. As the Third Reich became more desperate in the waning months of the war, the German national militia conscripted boys over the age of twelve to fight. Near the end of the Second World War, American soldiers captured German boys as young as eight years old.

Underage soldiers often lived in constant fear of exposure. After serving their country with honor, some were subjected to loss of benefits, such as Veterans Administration health care. For underage soldiers killed in action, even the death benefit provided to their families was subject to scrutiny. Falsifying military enlistment documents and birth certificates could have serious consequences for both the soldier and his family. For the many underage soldiers who proudly served their country during some of the most brutal fighting in World War II and Korea, a code of silence was the only option.

On January 30, 1950, the day after David Steward's sixteenth birthday, thoughts of war were nonexistent for most Americans. Less than five years earlier, World War II had been the most destructive war in human history, but Americans were on the winning side. Thoughts of the horrible combat endured by his father and brothers never entered David's mind. After all, he could serve his country during peacetime. American troops were stationed around the globe. And if he was lucky, he might get to see Germany, Japan, or even Hawaii, as the recruiting posters promised.

No one would ever need to know the circumstances of his incorrect birth document. Was it a simple clerical error—as a cracked and yellowed news clipping suggested—or was it deliberately falsified?[11] While local newspapers reported that sixteen-year-old David enlisted just one day after his sixteenth birthday on January 30, 1950, army records revealed his enlistment date as February 2, 1950. One certainty remained—within three days of his sixteenth birthday, David "Tex" Steward became a proud soldier boy.[12]

One Christmas Eve, my teary-eyed Aunt Judith greeted me with a stack of yellowed letters, more than fifty years after my teenage uncle penned them. The cherished letters were a Christmas gift, written by my Uncle Davy and gently placed in my hands by the little sister he loved so dearly. The faded envelopes, tied together with a tiny, pink ribbon, had obviously remained untouched for decades. The letters were written from California army camps, Okinawa, and the front line of Korea. Tearfully relinquishing the treasured letters she had so long protected, Judith Steward proclaimed the sobering responsibility that was now mine. "I know you will never let our little David be forgotten. David has meant so much to you—I think you must have been sent to Earth as his guardian angel. You are the one person who should have these, Bug."[13]

"Kiss little Judy for me, Mom. . . . Tell little Judy I love her," David wrote of his little sister in almost every letter. And though she was just shy of her fourth birthday when David joined the army, she continues to possess an uncanny memory of her brother. "I may not be able to remember where I put my keys today, but I have the most vivid memories of my brother, David."[14] David's letters frequently lamented that he missed one of several hometown girls—and most importantly, his prized guitar. Providing insight into David's persistent request to have his guitar shipped to him, Judy recalled, "He played the acoustic guitar, and he played it very well. I remember that he had a voice like an angel and he was so handsome, all the girls loved him."[15]

At a very early age, David was captivated with the idea of becoming a soldier. As his brothers returned from World War II, he solidified his plans. His younger sister, Judy, provided a somber account of the last time she saw her brother.

> He was always spoiling me with candy and ice cream. He had his Army uniform on, and we were all so proud of him. He put me up on his shoulders. He was always putting me up on his shoulders and I loved it. He said "How about taking my little Sis for a big ice cream cone?" You know, I've thought about it every day of my life. It takes the kindest of hearts to

help save a devastated people, as the Koreans were at the time, especially knowing that he could lose his life in doing so. He was wonderful, talented, funny, and a loving brother. I will never forget him. Never.[16]

Reading the handwritten words of my teenaged uncle nearly six decades later was at once deeply painful and incredibly informative, answering a lifetime of questions. Judging by their physical condition, they had clearly been opened and read on very few occasions. After reading them, I understood why.

For months, the words of the boy who so resembled my own son hauntingly occupied my every thought. From his letters, I studied the progression of David's mood from grand elation to despair. Like so many other fighting men in Korea, he was a typical American boy. They came from cities, farms, underprivileged and privileged families. They had dreams. "I have a chance to go to music school," David wrote to his mother.[17]

I observed the painful transformation from an innocent boy's belief that he would have time to play his guitar to the sorrowful realization of what lay in store, "Mom, please don't send my guitar if you get this letter in time. I won't need it in Korea. . . . Please try not to worry about me, Mom. Just pray for me."[18]

During the weeks of his basic training at Fort Ord and later at Camp Stoneman, California, there was simply no urgency for anyone to be forthright about his age. Family members began to wonder about the consequences of such action. Some of the elders in the family believed the U.S. Army would "make a man" out of David. Since it was a time of prosperity and peace in America, it might just be the best medicine for a boy who had been skipping school and missing time at his after-school job. The 146 days separating sixteen-year-old David's enlistment and the start of the Korean War would become a lifetime of guilt and torment, forever haunting members of his family.

On U.S. Army paper, underneath a gold-winged eagle, a proud sixteen-year-old penned a cheerful letter to his mother and father. The return address was "PVT David D. Steward, Company L, 8th Infantry Regiment."

Dearest Mom and Dad,

Sorry I haven't written sooner, but I've been a very busy little man. I just got off bivouac a week ago yesterday. Yesterday, I was promoted from the grade of recruit to Private. My orders also came into the orderly room and I'll start back to El Centro to spend about eleven days. . . . Mom, I won't be around after I spend my leave at home—for 2 and 1/2 years. I'll be in Japan. That's what my orders say. . . .

Lots of Love, (Tex) David[19]

Only days before the gates of hell were flung open on the Korean Peninsula, the homesick soldier once again wrote his parents, this time from Camp Stoneman, California, and Fox Company Replacement Battalion.

Dearest Mom and Dad,

How is everyone? . . . As for me, I'm o.k. except a little lonesome. I guess I'll be shipping out next week. . . . Mom, you and Blackie [David's eighteen-year-old friend] are the only ones I've heard from since I left. It really hurts my feelings. . . .

Kiss little Judy for me and tell her I still love her. Mom, if there's any possible way of shipping my guitar to me please do it as soon as possible and I can pay you back as soon as it arrives. . . . Don't worry about it, because if it hasn't gotten to me when I ship out, they'll send it to my new address. It's really too lonely here without my ol' faithful guitar. I decided I'd better wait until I get overseas to have the bonds taken out. Something might happen. . . .

All my love, Dave[20]

By the end of June 1950, the tone of David's letters had changed dramatically. Like his brother William, who became severely ill at basic training at Fort Francis, Wyoming, David reported to the infirmary with unusual symptoms.

Dearest Family,

Just received your letter a few minutes ago, just after I got off K.P. I am sure tired. I had a nervous breakdown the other day, and my temperature was 102. I was shaking like a leaf. Felt like I would die. I saw Blackie Saturday, I couldn't believe it when the nurse told me what kind of ward he was in. We were really glad to see each other. He told me that when there was no one left in the world left to trust, he could trust "Mom and Dave." I love him like a brother. Tell Sis [Helen] I'll do what she says—about marrying a girl I love. That is, if I can ever find one I can love and trust . . . I hope I can. I'm not on orders but I'll probably be shipping this weekend, but you can still write to me and I'll get my mail as always.

Love Always, Dave

P.S. I'm glad Dad liked the card I sent him![21]

Military camps, where large groups were assembled and housed in close quarters, remained problematic for the army. They created an ideal setting for the spread of infectious disease and particularly the epidemics of highly contagious streptococcal diseases and rheumatic fever. During World War II, the association of streptococcal disease with rheumatic fever was relatively unknown. Following Dr. Francis F. Schwentker's bacteriological studies at Fort Francis E. Warren during the war, the connection between streptococcal infections, rheumatic fever, and scarlet fever was better understood.

In an odd coincidence, David's brother William was included as a part of the Fort Warren studies since he had contracted streptococcal pneumonia and was unable to ship out to North Africa at the beginning of World War II. The army, however, did not have an official medical policy on follow-up for soldiers presenting with streptococcal infections. There was no follow-up of those with symptoms of rheumatic fever, especially those who were mobilized overseas.

In 1950, before antibiotics were commonly used to treat strep throat, more than 22,000 deaths occurred from rheumatic fever and the heart disease it caused.[22] During World War II, some air bases had incidence of rheumatic fever in excess of twenty-five per thousand troops, and one large post revealed rates in excess of one hundred per thousand troops. Later, when sulfonamides became readily available, troops had better protection, but "no mass protection was undertaken" for men stationed overseas.[23]

Rheumatic fever is a serious disease, which can lead to inflammation, weakening of the heart muscle, and death if untreated. Heart valves may be damaged and a condition known as Sydenham's chorea often occurs in untreated cases, manifested by uncontrolled twitching and body movements. More often, rheumatic fever symptoms include joint pain, swelling of the legs and arms, and resulting pain.

On July 3, eight days after the start of the Korean War and just before shipping out, David received his unit assignment. He would serve with the

29th Infantry Regiment, 29th Regimental Combat Team (RCT) stationed at Okinawa. He wrote his parents one last letter from American soil.

Dearest Mom and Dad,

Today is the 3rd and I leave the 5th. You can go ahead and send my guitar to my new address, and it will be waiting for me when I get there. . . . How's my little Judy? If she's been a good little girl, I'm going to send her something pretty from Okinawa. Mom . . . I've been havin' heart trouble or something, which has been making me pass out. My nerves are very bad. . . .

I love you all.

Love Always, David[24]

David likely developed rheumatic fever as a result of two bouts of streptococcal infection, the last being the most severe. Medical records from both Fort Ord and Camp Stoneman, along with corroboration from his personal letters, reveal that he suffered from nervous reaction, twitching, and some involuntary muscular movements. He returned several times to the base infirmary at Camp Stoneman and Okinawa—and army physicians at both suspected rheumatic fever.

The five major indicators of the Jones criteria for diagnosis of rheumatic fever are inflammation of the heart, arthritis, chorea (involuntary jerky movements of the body), rash/bumps under the skin, and itch. Minor indications are fever, joint pains, and a history of previous attacks of rheumatic fever. The presence of two major indicators—or just one major and two minor manifestations—signals the highest likelihood of rheumatic fever. David Steward's medical records, along with corroboration from his personal letters, reveal that he possessed four major and two minor indications of rheumatic fever before being shipped out to the misery of the Korean front.

David did not ask for special treatment for his illness—in fact, he did everything in his power to downplay it. Above all else, he wanted to be a soldier. In the calamitous first weeks of the Korean War, anyone who could march, hold a rifle, and fight was feverishly deployed.

For young Tex, like so many other American boys, he was in the wrong place at the worst possible time.

PART IV
THE TEMPEST

11

THE HERMIT KINGDOM

The wounded seldom cry—there's no one with time and emotion to listen.

—Marguerite Higgins,
Korean War combat correspondent

JUST FOUR DAYS after the hordes blasted across the 38th parallel into the Republic of Korea, sixteen-year-old citizen soldier David Steward wrote his parents from Camp Stoneman in California. For the first time, the return address read, "CO-F/29th Infantry Regiment."

Dearest Mom and Family,

. . . My destination is Okinawa! Got my orders today and I'll be leaving the 6th of July. If you're going to send my guitar, you can send it to my new address. That is if you haven't already sent it. If you have, the C.O. [commanding officer] will transfer it to me, so there's no need to worry. Mom, I'll be on Okinawa for 15 mon. That is, if the war ends in Korea soon. Don't you and Dad worry about me. I'll be alright, and besides, if I have to help fight this war, I'll be fighting for my family, and my country. I'm not afraid for myself. That is, not much, anyway. Ha! Kiss little Judy for me and tell Mickey and Donna and Earl and Bill and Rene to write to me or I will be awfully lonesome.

All My Love, Dave (Tex)[1]

For families of thousands of men who were killed, captured, and died in POW camps, the Korean War remains a hellish labyrinth, absent of understanding. Soldiers were shuffled from unit to unit as casualties mounted. In the early days of the war, they were sent to a unit only to witness its annihilation—and often sent on to another, becoming a part of the carnage themselves.

The circumstances leading to the Korean War began much earlier than the invasion of Communist aggressors in June 1950, perhaps centuries earlier, but most notably at the close of World War II.

The Korean Peninsula is bordered by China and Russia to the north, the East Sea (Sea of Japan) to the east, the Yellow Sea to the west, and the Korean Strait to the south. At 683 miles in length, the ancient "Land of the Morning Calm," or Chosun, is mountainous, with mountains covering almost 70 percent of the peninsula. Broad, steep valleys, lowlands, and terraced rice paddies separate towering mountains. While much of Korea is situated in the temperate climate zone, it is at times quite inhospitable. The monsoon season, from June to September, is hot and oppressively humid, and the winter is insufferably cold in northern regions.

During the middle of the nineteenth century, Korea was relatively unknown and somewhat isolated. The "Hermit Kingdom" was a befitting name. Protected by sea and mountainous terrain, the Korean people wished only for peace and to till the rice paddies in their ancient, misty valleys. Their wishes would not be granted; indeed, the Hermit Kingdom was ruled by foreign powers three times in modern history. And each time the impoverished Korean people paid a terrible price.

Between 1904 and 1905, the empires of Russia and Japan fought for imperial domination over Manchuria and Korea. Under the leadership of President Theodore Roosevelt, the United States was instrumental in negotiating peace between the two powers. The Treaty of Portsmouth was signed in New Hampshire in September 1905.[2] President Roosevelt was awarded the Nobel Peace Prize for his effort to foster world diplomacy. As part of the Treaty of Portsmouth, the freedom of Korea was agreed upon by all nations, but Japan's "paramount political, military, and economic interests in Korea" were both recognized and sanctioned. While scholars continue to debate the historical significance of the treaty, it undoubtedly transformed the balance of power in East Asia. To the Empire of Japan, it became a rubber stamp to dominate the Hermit Kingdom.

During the years leading up to World War II under Japanese colonial rule, the Korean culture was savaged. Ancient literature was burned, and Koreans were not allowed to pursue education. Japanese became the official language, and Korean language was neither taught in schools nor allowed in public.[3] Koreans were used as slaves in war factories and conscripted as front-line soldiers for the Imperial Japanese Army. Thousands of Koreans died in forced labor under the colonial occupation of the Hermit Kingdom.

The suffering of Koreans under colonial rule was not limited to conscripted males. Korean girls and women were also brutalized at the hands of their occupiers. Recently discovered documents revealed that thousands of girls and women were taken from their families and conscripted as "comfort women" for Japanese soldiers. While most of the women were from occupied nations, such as Korea, China, and the Philippines, many were of European origin, from the Netherlands and Australia.[4] The young women were taken "by force or entrapped by deception in many countries in and beyond Asia," but Korea, which was a Japanese colony, had large numbers of these young women.[5]

Held as sexual slaves for soldiers, the comfort women were subjected to daily rape, torture, and beatings. A clinical study revealed that sixty years later, high levels of PTSD existed among these surviving Korean women.[6] Ninety-two-year-old Kim Bok-dong and the few surviving Korean comfort women reluctantly came forward to tell their story.

> Because we were under Japanese rule, they could do whatever they wanted to with us. They even pulled male students out of school to fight as "student soldiers." Unfortunately, the boys weren't the only ones taken. We didn't want to go. They forced us. I was fourteen in Western age. It was during the time that all young Korean men were conscripted into the Japanese military.[7]

The comfort women were among millions of women who for centuries have been brutalized during wars fought around the globe. But not until recently was wartime sexual violence against women prosecuted. The United Nations International Criminal Tribunal for former Yugoslavia (ICTY) delivered landmark judgments advancing the cause of justice by labeling wartime sexual violence as a war crime.[8]

Victimized long before wartime sexual violence was labeled as a crime against humanity, comfort women around the globe were subjected to inhumane treatment, and thousands died. At the age of ninety-two, Kim Bok-dong made world news in a 2018 interview, declaring, "I decided that no matter what, we should live to tell what happened."[9]

For scholars and family members alike, an ever-elusive insight into the Korean War requires an understanding of the policies of World War II. At the end of 1943, President Franklin D. Roosevelt, British prime minister Winston Churchill, and Chiang Kai-shek of China met to restrain the aggression of

Imperial Japan. The outcome of the meeting between the "Three Great Allies" was the Cairo Declaration. Japan would be expelled from all territories stolen by "violence and greed." "The aforesaid three great powers, mindful of the enslavement of the people of Korea, are determined that in due course Korea shall become free and independent."[10]

Refinement of the Korea policy occurred in 1945, when the "Big Three"—Roosevelt, Churchill, and Soviet premier Joseph Stalin—met in Yalta. They concluded that Korea was to become an Allied trusteeship administered by the Big Four powers, including China. The trusteeship had many troublesome aspects, including the existing unrest in China and the industrial war machine created by Japanese occupiers.

Most industry in Korea existed in the northern regions, with most agriculture in the south. The arbitrary separation of the two Koreas at the 38th parallel led to economic chaos. Commerce, manufacturing, and trade were completely disrupted. Corruption was rampant, and poverty among Koreans was widespread and devastating. There were few roads, the terrain was difficult, almost no plumbing existed, and clean drinking water was scarce in rural areas. While thirty-five years of Japanese occupation provided some industrial development and urban growth to Korea, the division of the peninsula left a suffering Korean people in disarray, poverty, and misery.

As the guns fell silent from World War II, jubilant Americans celebrated the end of war and prepared for peace. But dreams of peace and prosperity were shattered as the coming months were transformed into one of the most perilous times in world history. It was during this time, in the shadows of the most destructive war in human history, that the Cold War began. It was the quintessential struggle between communism and democracy. The seeds were planted for the Korean War.

As World War II came to a close in August 1945, the Soviet Union declared war on Japan. Early that month, with more than a million soldiers, the Soviets invaded Japanese-controlled Manchuria in northeastern China. The Soviets then invaded northern Korea, and by August 26, they had reached the 38th parallel, sealing the demarcation line.

Americans believed the Soviets intended to seize control of the entire Korean Peninsula with the ultimate goal of proliferating the spread of Communism throughout East Asia. To restrain Soviet advances, Americans hurriedly responded by sending troops stationed in occupied Japan into southern Korea.

After a brief examination of a school map of Korea, a Pentagon army colonel proposed dividing the Korean Peninsula at the 38th parallel—and the

Soviets readily accepted the demarcation. The line that would separate north and south was drawn with little regard for trade, property ownership, terrain along the 38th, or existing communication lines. For over seven decades, the arbitrary line continues to separate the people of Korea.[11]

The Western world watched with disquieted alarm as the Soviets began to insidiously devour important regions of the world. In 1947, as a result of Soviet aggression, President Harry S. Truman presented the Truman Doctrine to Congress. It quickly became the basis of American Cold War policy throughout the world.

The Truman Doctrine sought to curtail Soviet geopolitical expansion and halt the spread of Communism. Truman believed it was the responsibility of the United States to support "free people who are resisting attempted subjugation by armed minorities or by outside pressures."[12] Truman reasoned that American financial aid would provide nations with the political and economic stability to contain Soviet Communism. As a result of the Truman Doctrine, nation-building became an integral, enduring tenet of American foreign policy.

Less than a year before the start of the Korean War, democracy suffered another resounding blow. In China, the U.S.-backed Nationalists fell to the Chinese Communist Party. The People's Republic of China was created—and American boys would later face its legions in insurmountable odds at a place forever immortalized as "Frozen Chosin" in Korea.

The Soviets installed a Communist regime in northern Korea, the Democratic People's Republic of Korea (DPRK), with Pyongyang as its capital city. The DPRK was deeply influenced by Communist China and heavily armed by the Soviets. Controlled by Americans, the Republic of Korea was established in the south, and in 1948, the United Nations held supervised elections. A devout anti-Communist authoritarian leader, Syngman Rhee had spent many years in the United States, receiving his master's degree from Harvard University and his PhD from Princeton. He would be elected president for three terms in the newly formed Republic of Korea.

• • •

The American public had its fill of war after World War II. After the surrender of Japan in 1945, Congress demanded rapid demobilization of U.S. forces along with harsh military budget cuts. In December 1945 alone, one million men received their military discharges. U.S. military forces were reduced nearly 90 percent between 1945 and 1947, when the World War II draft was terminated.[13]

Before the war ended in 1945, the number of active military personnel was more than 12 million—and by the start of the Korean War that number had dwindled to just over 1.5 million. The reduction delivered a devastating blow to military preparedness and gravely affected American foreign policy. Many military experts believed such drastic cuts "weakened the prestige of our national policy and endangered the security of the nation." Military scholars reported that the U.S. Army was reduced "to a state of near impotency," prior to the war in Korea.[14]

Truman had a contemptuous relationship with the military. His goal of attending West Point had been shattered when he was rejected as a result of poor eyesight. His only military option was to join a local National Guard unit, furthering his disdain for the regular army. As a U.S. senator, he conducted investigations into wasteful military spending and was lauded by the press. He publicly admonished and heaped scorn on generals, admirals, and professional military officers, referring to them as "dumb" and like "horses with blinders on." Highly accomplished in slashing and burning the world's mightiest military, Truman fell dangerously short in maintaining military readiness and American preparedness for war.

In a post–World War I letter to his wife, Truman displayed an almost vengeful bitterness toward the military: "I want to be where I can cuss 'em all when I please." He did just that—and much more. Under the president's direction prior to the Korean War, massive and crippling budget cuts were imposed on the Pentagon. The nation's reserve nuclear weapons deteriorated to a severely weakened state.

In his critically acclaimed book *The Forgotten War*, Clay Blair described Truman's gutting of the nation's military as, "the President's sins against the military."[15] In 1948, Army Chief of Staff Omar Bradley wrote that the United States Army was in a "shockingly deplorable state." Just three years earlier at the end of World War II, the army had a fighting force of six million men and nearly one hundred highly trained divisions, each equipped by America's vast arsenal of democracy. By March 1948, the greatest army on earth had been eviscerated, reduced to only 530,000 men. Bradley penned that it had "almost no combat effectiveness," and "could not fight its way out of a paper bag."[16] Under Truman, the world's mightiest navy and air force were equally savaged.

The Truman administration, especially Secretary of Defense Louis A. Johnson, forced severe cutbacks on the Marine Corps. As a former member of the National Guard, Truman had little use for the Marine Corps—in fact, he wanted to eliminate it: "The Marine Corps is the Navy's police force and as long as I remain President that's what it will remain. They have a propaganda machine that is almost equal to Stalin's."[17]

Marine expeditionary forces were slashed from 300,000 men in World War II to just over 27,000 men by the start of the Korean War. A large portion of marine landing craft and amphibious carriers were transferred to the army, and more were sold or scrapped. Ultimately, the United States Marine Corps fared no better than the army, navy, and air force during the Truman administration's military razing.

Truman turned to beloved five-star Gen. Dwight D. Eisenhower to soften the blow of his drastic military budget cuts. Eisenhower was to act as presiding officer for the Joint Chiefs of Staff during the tense and controversial budgetary negotiations. In his diary, General Eisenhower wrote, "We're suffering," referring to the plundering of the American military. Eisenhower had led the Allies to victory as Supreme Commander, Allied Expeditionary Force in the European theater of World War II. He understood that a fighting force must be prepared in number, equipment, and training—and ready to fight at all times.

Referring to his time as army chief of staff, Eisenhower lamented the political decisions that led to the dismantling of the army, "During 1946, 1947 and early 1948, I pleaded for a fifteen-billion-dollar budget. We never got it."[18]

While witnessing the carnage to America's military during the budgetary proceedings, Eisenhower became so distraught that he fell seriously ill. The loss of General Eisenhower as an advocate for the military proved even more devastating to American fighting forces prior to war on the Korean Peninsula.

Another serious problem for the U.S. Army was that it had been "civilianized" through the peacetime draft of 1948, 1949, and 1950. Many of these inexperienced soldiers never envisioned fighting a war. Because it was peacetime, most recent enlistees joined the army for a steady paycheck and to travel the world, as the recruiting posters promised. In an attempt to fill quotas, recruiters pointed to slogans like "Join the Army and See the World." Unlike the recruiting posters of World War II depicting a suffering Lady Liberty and the words, "It's up to you, Protect the nation's honor," Korean War recruiting posters portrayed soldiers having fun. Recruiters avoided imparting a sense of obligation to country or the harshness of training and combat. Gung ho enlistees were stirred into the pot of disgruntled peacetime draftees, weakening esprit de corps. Draftees and enlisted alike were in no manner combat-ready.

By 1948, post–World War II military budget cuts had a draconian effect on the army's training program. By the end of the war, army ground forces wisely adopted a new seventeen-week training program, which not only provided soldiers with standard thirteen weeks of basic training, but also four weeks of specialized unit skills. But during the years preceding the Korean War, the army's basic training program was again slashed from the standard thirteen to just eight weeks, delegating responsibility for additional training to the unit of attachment.

The severe military cutbacks of Congress, Truman, and Secretary of Defense Louis Johnson provided a fatal blow to American military preparedness—and to the green soldiers first cast onto the battlefields of Korea. Maj. Gen. Matthew Ridgeway, who later became commander of the Eighth U.S. Army in Korea, recalled, "We were, in short, in a state of shameful unreadiness."[19]

By the time war came to the Hermit Kingdom, America had only ten army divisions and nine regimental combat teams, eight of which were at 70 percent strength. Each regiment had only two battalions, rather than the customary three; each artillery battalion had only two instead of three battalions. The army's World War II–era equipment was worn out, and not a single division was adequately supplied with either equipment or weapons.

The underequipped, ill-prepared men who marched into battle in the early days of the Korean War had in many ways been deluded. T. R. Fehrenbach, a Korean War veteran and historian, described the carnage that befell American soldiers: "They were normal American youth, no better, no worse than the norm, who though they wore the uniform were mentally, morally, and physically unfit for combat, for orders to go out and die."[20]

As part of the occupational force of Japan, the 24th Infantry Division was stationed on Kyushu, the southernmost of Japan's four major islands. Just over 400 miles away lay the island of Okinawa, home of the 29th Infantry Regiment/29th Regimental Combat Team, attached to the 24th Division. These soldiers would become David Steward's new family—and they were among the first to enter the Korean War.

Okinawa and Japan were of strategic importance to the U.S. military due to their location near mainland China, the Korean Peninsula, and the Taiwan Strait. At the end of World War II, the U.S. military began its postwar occupation of Japan with famed Gen. Douglas MacArthur acting as Supreme Allied Commander. The Eighth U.S. Army, commanded by a native Texan, Lt. Gen. Walton H. Walker, was designated as the American occupation force in Japan. "Johnnie" Walker, so named for his favorite brand of Scotch whisky, was a pudgy, five-foot-five, hard-drinking hero of both world wars. So impressed was he with Walker's hard-as-nails leadership, Gen. George S. Patton personally pinned him with his three-star insignia.

General Walker commanded four understrength and poorly trained divisions in Japan at the outset of the Korean War—the 1st Cavalry Division, the 7th, 24th, and 25th Infantry Divisions. From these four divisions, the 24th Infantry Division was selected as the first to enter into battle in the Korean War. Unfortunately, the 24th was not at full strength and was the least combat-ready of the four divisions in the Eighth Army.

Initially, General Walker's troops were soft. The relaxed atmosphere of occupational duties and the severity of budget cuts left them underequipped and undertrained. Walker recognized the state of unreadiness in his troops; only 10 percent of his soldiers had combat experience. A few months prior to the start of the Korean War, General Walker began a rigid campaign of combat readiness training. But it was too little, too late for the green citizen soldiers of the Eighth Army—the closest fighting unit to the Korean War zone.

General MacArthur developed the idea of landing troops at Inchon only four days after the war began. Operation Bluehearts was the frenzied master plan hurriedly devised at general headquarters, under the direction of General MacArthur and his chief of staff, Maj. Gen. Edward "Ned" Almond. The plan called for the 24th Infantry Division to lead troops into battle since they were the closest to South Korea. They recklessly assumed that understrength, underequipped, and unprepared American soldiers would stop the North Korean People's Army (NKPA) in their tracks.

The plan called for the 25th Infantry Division to secure the center of Korea, followed by a 1st Cavalry landing at Inchon near the end of July. Finally, the 24th would drive north, entrapping the NKPA. From the ivory palace of general headquarters, it was a guaranteed victory. But for young soldiers hastily cast into fierce combat for which they were completely unprepared, it was a death sentence—and for some, it was far worse.

Operation Bluehearts was an impetuous and extremely risky plan that required a well-equipped, well-trained, combat-ready fighting force—none of which applied to Johnnie Walker's Eighth Army in the early days of the war. General Almond later conceded the army was only "40 percent combat effective."[21] Owing to early punishing blows of NKPA, it wasn't long before Operation Bluehearts was scrapped. General headquarters in Tokyo scrambled to devise a new strategy of redirecting the 1st Cavalry to Pusan, serving as reinforcements for the 24th and 25th Divisions.

In addition to questionable battle strategy and lack of combat readiness, the 24th Division had both an officer and equipment problem. Many officers did not have proper infantry troop training, and many were simply unqualified to lead men into combat. The 34th Regiment was using outdated World

War II antitank bazookas and lacked the army's new armor-piercing antitank ammo. They were short of mortars and mortar ammo. The mortar ammo they had was ancient and frequently defective—only 20 percent of the shells exploded.[22] Machine guns were worn out—and one officer reported that the equipment provided to soldiers was a "national disgrace." They were short on everything from trucks and jeeps to foxhole spades and combat boots. In the chaotic first days of the war, some soldiers of the greatest military on earth were shamefully "forced to wear tennis shoes" into battle.[23]

Elements of the 24th Infantry Division were first in combat on the Korean Peninsula. They would ultimately take the full brunt of a better-trained and Soviet-equipped fanatical NKPA, the Inmun Gun. The heedless mission of the American soldiers was simply to delay the advance of the NKPA until reinforcements from other divisions could arrive.

The flames of war were ignited by a fateful series of events—the Soviets' detonation of their first atomic bomb, an ever-changing balance of power, Western fear of Communist proliferation throughout East Asia, and the feckless actions of American politicians. A new "Robin Hood" policy of robbing military budgets for foreign aid and nation-building crippled the American military. There was almost no understanding of the severity of the American military's weakness or the extent to which it had been plundered—only the hubris of many, including a president who naively stated, "By God, I'm going to let them have it."[24]

Like a supercell creating its own fuel as it swept across the Korean Peninsula, the ominous clouds were seeded again and again by legion of ill-conceived actions. The U.S. military had been systematically gutted, and a war-weary American public consensually let down its guard.

The first American soldiers to arrive amid the fury of the monstrous storm were sacrificial lambs, sent into battle with no chance of winning. They were there simply to hold the line—for a few days or a few hours. The aftermath of the fierce storm would forever remain the grievous punishment of the Forgotten War.

12

LAND OF THE MORNING CALM

He sent them not to destroy the unholy, but merely to hold the line.

—T. R. Fehrenbach, Korean War veteran, historian

Dearest Mom and Dad,

I got your letter today and was really glad to hear from you. . . . Mom, please don't send my guitar if you get this letter in time. I won't need it in Korea. Please don't get worried about me, because I'll be ok. That is, if they issue us sharp enough shovels to dig in with, ha! No kidding, Mom, I'll be ok. You can just save the pictures for me too, until I get back. I might get them soiled in Korea. Ha!! I'm really homesick. I want someone to write me. I realize how long it takes for mail to get overseas. . . .

With Love Always,

Dave[1]

In the waning hours of darkness on June 25, 1950, the frenzied shrieks and horns of the North Korean People's Army (NKPA) pierced the bucolic morning calm. The unnatural line drawn on Korean ground was breached, and dreams of democracy for the people of South Korea were blasted away. The firestorm of fury would ultimately claim the lives of more than 5 million people, including 36,634 Americans.[2] As of September 2023 nearly 7,500 remain missing in action.[3] Over 103,000 Americans were wounded, and more than 7,100 were captured and subjected to brutal treatment at the hands of their North Korean captors. Some 2,700 of those POWs are known to have died during captivity.[4] While estimates for civilian deaths in the Korean War vary widely, most researchers believe between 1.5 and 2 million Korean civilians were killed.[5]

More than 90,000 soldiers of the NKPA poured across the 38th parallel, attacking in three columns.[6] Having served in both the Chinese and Soviet armies during World War II, they were tough and battle-hardened. Suddenly, the deafening rumble of Russian-built tanks, artillery, and small-arms fire silenced the screaming voices of the attacking Inmun Gun, or North Korean People's Army. In the ancient land of Chosun, exploding shells and violent flashes devoured the timid shadows of a radiant Korean dawn. The flames of war had been ignited and the Land of the Morning Calm was set ablaze. An end to battlefield hostilities would not return for more than three years.

On June 25, at 2:00 p.m. in an emergency meeting, the United Nations Security Council passed a resolution condemning the armed assault on the Republic of Korea (ROK). The resolution demanded the immediate withdrawal of North Korean forces behind the 38th parallel. The Russian delegate was not present for the vote. By June 27, with Communist nations clearly ignoring the resolution, a new resolution was passed, recommending assistance from all members of the United Nations to halt North Korean aggression. Once again, the Russian delegate remained absent from the vote.

President Harry S. Truman desperately wanted to contain Communism, and he believed all of Asia lay in the crosshairs. The United Nations breach of peace resolution now provided him with the moral and legal authority to send American troops to a foreign land—without congressional approval. On June 30, 1950, at the urging of Gen. Douglas MacArthur, President Truman sent in the boots.

The president initially ordered only two U.S. Army divisions to the battlefront, those stationed in Japan. Without the consent of Congress, he made his case to the American people. "If we let Korea down," the president said, "the Soviet[s] will keep right on going and swallow up one [place] after another."[7]

President Truman appointed General MacArthur as the Commander in Chief, United Nations Command. Less than five years after the deadliest war in history, the United States was once again at war. Back home, the press sought answers for a shaken public as they witnessed frantic and chaotic efforts to prepare American forces for deployment. Hoping to create calm, the president stated, "We are not at war."

A confused press asked the president if he could elaborate on his earlier statement. "Yes, I will allow you to use that," Truman emphatically declared. "We are not at war."

Reporters continued to question the president.

"Mr. President," a reporter asked, "would it be correct . . . to call this a police action under the United Nations?"

"Yes," replied the president. "That is exactly what it amounts to."

The regrettable, perhaps deceitful term "police action," as well as the United Nations cloak, would come back to haunt the president, military leaders, and most especially, those who fought under their command.[8]

The Inmun Gun had been well advised and armed by the Russians. They had an air force, which supported a well-trained and well-equipped army of nearly 150,000 men. They boasted one full armored division, a tank division, and ten infantry divisions. The North claimed to have 35 reconnaissance aircraft, over 100 attack bombers, and nearly 150 Yak fighter planes. They possessed a total of 274 T-34-85 Russian-built tanks and trucks, as well as Russian-built 122-millimeter howitzers and enormous artillery firepower.[9]

In stark contrast, the ROK Army had eight divisions armed with American M-1 rifles, few machine guns and mortars, and only five battalions of field artillery, which included junked howitzers from the United States. The ROK Army had no tanks, no heavy artillery, and not a single combat-ready aircraft. The defenders were no match for the well-equipped Inmun Gun, which swiftly steamrolled their way to Seoul, the capital of the Republic of Korea.

Seoul erupted into fear and chaos. American military advisors, civilians, and Department of State personnel, including the ambassador, began their evacuation. They abandoned food stores, gasoline, and almost 2,000 American vehicles—all left for the taking of the advancing Inmun Gun. Refugees were everywhere, and thousands of ROK soldiers fleeing the advancing tanks streamed into the capital.

Three divisions of ROK soldiers and equipment were now in Seoul with the Inmun Gun on their heels and expected to arrive in less than twenty-four hours. Long columns of refugees began to flee the city with only what they could carry on their backs. Legions of men, women, children, oxen, and soldiers scattered in every direction, most having no idea where to go. As the columns of frightened and downtrodden refugees began to grow, the Han River bridges were quickly clogged.

The ROK military planned to evacuate its troops and blow the Han River bridges behind them in an effort to create a natural barrier for the Inmun Gun. But in the ensuing panic and chaos, the order was given too quickly. The highway bridge exploded into a massive fireball, killing hundreds and hurling hundreds more to drown in the Han. Near Seoul, the Han is well over half a mile wide, so the costly mistake trapped more than 40,000 ROK soldiers and their lifesaving equipment on the north side of the river. Most simply disappeared.

Stunning the world from Seoul to Washington, the Inmun Gun smashed the border of sovereign Republic of Korea with dreadful force and lightning speed. Not only were ROK soldiers taken by surprise, the Truman administration and the U.S. military were caught completely off guard.

The troops most readily available to General MacArthur were those stationed in Okinawa and Japan. Although it was the least combat-ready of the four divisions available to General MacArthur, the 24th Infantry Division was chosen to lead American and United Nations forces into battle. The division was operating at only 65 percent.

The 24th Infantry Division was commanded by fifty-year-old Gen. William F. Dean, who was well aware that his division was not combat-ready. In the frenzy, soldiers were shuffled like playing cards from other divisions to bring the 24th up to a respectable fighting force—but in number only. The 1st Cavalry Division was stripped of 750 senior noncommissioned officers (NCOs), who are the backbone of fighting units.[10] These men, who generally included all grades of corporal and sergeant, were trained in both leadership and combat. The loss of these NCOs would later severely hamper the fighting capabilities of the 1st Cavalry Division, which engaged in some of the fiercest fighting of the Korean War.

The first weeks of the Korean War were filled with dark desperation. The 21st and 34th Regiments were the most readily available to General Dean, neither of which were combat-ready. Task Force Smith, a 406-man infantry force named for its commanding officer, thirty-four-year-old Lt. Col. Charles B. Smith, was the first to see combat in Korea. Due to severe budget cuts, only two dozen C-54s were on hand in Japan and most needed repair. Only six C-54s were available to the small, severely underequipped, and understrength force of the 21st Regiment, resulting in troop and supply delays. The monsoon rains further stalled deployment.

Getting men and equipment to the front line was a herculean task. Charles "Fritz" Mudgett, the 21st Regiment's executive officer, was charged with the hasty deployment of the entire 3rd Battalion—without aircraft. After commandeering three "filthy" Japanese freighters, which had been used to transport Russian-held Japanese prisoners of war, a disgusted Mudgett declared, "It was a hell of a way to go to war."[11]

Leaving desperately needed equipment and additional support behind, the men of Task Force Smith were hurriedly flown into Pusan under torrential rains. With limited transport, Lieutenant Colonel Smith was forced to leave nearly half of his firepower on the tarmac in Japan, including two critical recoilless rifle teams and two mortar teams. The 34th Regiment would dig in around Pyeongtaek and the village of Ansong [Anseong]. Elements of the 21st Regiment, supported by the 52nd Field Artillery Battalion, were to arrive by sea and reinforce the front line. Ordered by General MacArthur, the mission of Task Force Smith was to delay the advancing enemy from Seoul and "take the initial shock" of the advancing Inmun Gun.

Like David Daniel Steward, most of the soldiers of Task Force Smith were under the age of twenty. Only one in six had seen combat prior to the mission.[12] Most of these citizen soldiers were better schooled in the details of the 1949 World Series than the tactics of combat. They were told the NKPA lacked training and was severely underequipped. This dangerous misconception prevailed. "Just wait 'til [they] see an American uniform—they'll turn and run like hell!"[13] Only weeks earlier, Task Force Smith's soldiers had left their hometown baseball fields for the battlefields of Korea. And just as the New York Yankees won four out of five games over the Brooklyn Dodgers, the task force's soldiers were confident of an easy victory.

In a driving rain, Lieutenant Colonel Smith, a survivor of the horrors of Guadalcanal in World War II, stood before his men at Itazuke Air Base in Japan. His orders from headquarters were clear. The NKPA was to be brought to a dead stop, as far as possible from Pusan. In the words of General MacArthur, Task Force Smith was to be "an arrogant display of strength" that would incite fear and worry in the minds of the enemy. Instead, it became the embodiment of military unpreparedness, unveiling the reckless decimation of the American military during the interwar years.

They left Japan on July 1, 1950, and by July 5 they were dug in on the hills surrounding Osan. By the next night, their mission was over.

The men of Task Force Smith fought against insurmountable odds. They were provided with scant ammunition and two C-rations. Many soldiers ran out of ammunition or had weapons that wouldn't fire, and they were outmanned ten to one. With no effective antitank weapons, the task force was cannon fodder for nearly three dozen Russian-built T-34 tanks, followed by more than 5,000 NKPA infantry soldiers.

The task force was quickly outflanked and overrun. Colonel Smith ordered his surviving men to withdraw under constant heavy fire, leaving only the litter-bound wounded and the hero corpsman who refused to leave them. Heavy machine-gun fire savagely ripped into the disorganized troops as they attempted to withdraw. For those stragglers who managed to escape, the rice paddies became their point of egress. The lucky ones joined a small American convoy withdrawing from enemy fire. Covered with slime from a frenzied withdrawal through the paddies, most of the surviving Americans had no weapons, helmets, or even boots.

The soldiers of Task Force Smith managed to hold the line for seven hours, suffering horrendous casualties as they withdrew. More than 150 Task Force Smith soldiers were killed, wounded, or missing, accounting for 40 percent of the force. The many litter-bound wounded and the hero medic who refused to leave them were later found tied and executed by the brutal Inmun Gun. In the final analysis, there were sixty dead, twenty-one wounded, and eighty-two committed to the hell of North Korean capture. Thirty-two of them would die in brutal POW camps.[14]

From the moment sixteen-year-old David Steward and thousands of other ill-prepared men stepped onto Korean soil, there would be no calm—no mercy. A July 16, 1950, *New York Times* editorial depicted the woeful misfortune of inexperienced American troops thrust onto the battlefields in the early days of the Korean War.

> Our emotions as we watch our outnumbered, outweaponed soldiers in Korea must be a mingling of pity, sorrow, and admiration. This is the sacrifice we asked of them, justified only by the hope that what they are now doing will help to keep this war a small war, and that the death of a small number will prevent the slaughter of millions.[15]

After reading news of the defeat of American troops, David's worried mother and father attempted to locate him through a barrage of letters, which were waiting for him as he departed the ship. The sixteen-year-old responded immediately in a hurriedly written letter.

Dearest Family,

Arrived in Okinawa at noon today [July 20, 1950], and two hours later was alerted to go to the battlefront in Korea. I'll be here about 30 days. These pictures and the certificate I want you to keep for me until I return.

Please don't worry about me, because I'll be o.k. (I hope—ha!). At least I have a part in this war too. I must do all I can. Kiss little Judy for me and tell Dad for you and him not to worry about me.

All my love, David[16]

Lessons were rarely learned during the Korean War. The Inmun Gun was on the verge of devouring the entire peninsula. After the nightmare of Task Force Smith, the effort to halt the advance of the Inmun Gun became even more disordered. As if by prophecy, on the same day that David Steward made his entrance into the Korean War, United Nations forces suffered devastating losses.

On the day of David Steward's arrival on Okinawa, the effort to stop the onslaught of the Inmun Gun ended in disaster. As rumors and word of UN defeat began to spread through units awaiting frontline deployment, a desperate battle ensued to hold the city of Taejon. With little combat experience, forty-two-year-old Col. Charles E. Beauchamp was assigned to lead his 34th Regiment in the frantic attempt to hold the line at Taejon. At the time of his arrival, Beauchamp became the youngest regimental commander in Korea. During World War II, he had specialized in logistics, serving in "rear-area staff jobs." He had not served with a combat unit during the entire Second World War.[17]

Col. Guy "Stan" Meloy Jr., commander of the 19th Infantry, served as an infantry division chief of staff in World War II. Like Beauchamp, he had not previously commanded troops in combat.[18] The 19th Infantry, the "Rock of Chickamauga," had achieved fame for its stand in the Civil War battle at Chickamauga, Georgia. The men of the regiment proudly referred to themselves as "Chicks," a befitting moniker for the young and utterly green troops attempting to hold the line at Taejon.[19]

Encircled by two full divisions of the NKPA, the 34th Infantry and 2nd Battalion, 19th Infantry were overrun. The decimated Americans no longer existed as organized fighting units. Once again, small, disorganized handfuls of soldiers fought desperately to escape—to save themselves from the horrors of being captured by one of the most brutal enemies ever faced by American troops.

Desperately attempting to rescue Colonel Meloy and a few surviving wounded Chicks, the only light tank available was sent to the front. The tank's worn-out engine failed. The group of wounded soldiers and Meloy, himself badly wounded, destroyed the tank with a thermite grenade and watched from a ditch where they spent the night.

Risking his life, another brave officer commandeered a dilapidated truck and rescued Colonel Meloy and the few wounded who managed to survive. As fighting during the early days of the war continued, casualties among high-ranking officers were proportionally higher than at any time since the Civil War. In his brilliant book *The Coldest Winter*, David Halberstam described the brutality of July 1950: "One of the worst months in American military history . . . it was an army trying to buy time in precious increments with the most precious coin of all, the lives of its young men."[20]

Atrocities against American soldiers began to mount, and it soon became evident that surrender was not an option. As the few survivors of the 19th Infantry Chicks retreated against overwhelming odds, wounded men were scattered about the hillsides. One chaplain, Herman Felhoelter, refused to leave them. Watching through his field glasses, a sergeant witnessed the chaplain's execution as he knelt in prayer over his wounded soldiers.[21]

By the end of the battle for Taejon, nearly 1,000 American soldiers were killed, 228 were wounded, and nearly 2,400 men were missing in action.[22] Most of those captured and missing were executed by the NKPA.[23]

After the fall of Taejon, Maj. Gen. William Dean, the commander of David's 24th Infantry Division, was himself captured. Separated from his men, the general had wandered alone in the hills near Taejon for more than a month before he was taken prisoner. Emaciated and sick, he was placed in a four-foot cage in the village. He was the NKPA's highest-ranking American prisoner of war. The North Koreans kept General Dean's capture a secret, and American military leaders presumed he had been killed in action. General Dean was one of the lucky ones. He was finally repatriated on September 4, 1953, in Operation Big Switch.

Years later, Colonel Beauchamp, the commander of the 34th Infantry Regiment, attempted to articulate the desperation that faced his soldiers: "It was just criminal to send our troops into battle, manned and equipped the way they were. When I took over, the 34th's two battalions were down to about half strength, and many of these were green fillers. . . . It was just lucky that any of us got out of there alive."[24]

At noon on July 20—the day Taejon fell to the NKPA—sixteen-year-old David Steward arrived on Okinawa. Along with 400 hastily assembled U.S. Army recruits, David arrived aboard the USNS *Walker*.[25] In his letter home, David noted the battle alert was issued only two hours after disembarking their ship from the United States.

The following day, barely off the ship and before they could unpack, the freshly arrived recruits boarded transport for shipment to the battlefield in Korea. The "green fillers" were assigned to accompany two battalions of an equally green 29th Infantry Regiment—most of whose soldiers had no combat experience at all.

Both battalion commanders were West Pointers, new commanders with no prior combat experience. Both were advised the two battalions would first arrive in Japan for six weeks of field and combat training. So desperate was the situation on the front line, however, that the two green battalions were sent directly to Pusan on July 24, loaded on trucks, and sent to the front. They were sent as reinforcements for the beleaguered 19th Regiment's Chicks, who were nearly wiped out near Taejon.

On July 27, just seven days after transport from the United States and only three days after they arrived on the battlefront, an entire NKPA division, well armed and supported by tanks, summarily slaughtered the raw unprepared teenagers from David's Okinawa battalions. In a 2010 news story on the sixtieth anniversary of the Korean War, a seventy-eight-year-old survivor recalled the calamitous ordeal of the "Tragic 29th": "We were told they had pitchforks and sickles," Jesus Rodriguez said. "And as soon as they saw our uniforms, they'd turn and run. But it didn't work out that way."[26]

The 3rd Battalion, 29th Infantry suffered 50 percent casualties, and their company commander was captured. In an ambush at Hadong, one battalion suffered 495 casualties out of 700 men. On the same afternoon, another lost 214 men.

"We heard the others got wiped out," an emotional Rodriguez said. "I didn't ask too many questions because I was scared.... I was so scared, I was talking to the Lord all the time. What happened to my regiment was a tragedy. But at the same time, there were a lot of heroes that were never mentioned."[27]

Korean War historian Clay Blair described the misery that befell David's fellow soldiers in the 29th Infantry Regiment. "The decision to commit the two, utterly green Okinawa battalions for this purpose was unfortunate, even callous," Blair wrote. "Serving almost as cannon fodder, the two units had incurred a shocking 618 casualties in a single day to little purpose."[28]

Like so many units of the 24th Infantry Division, David's regiment was thrust into battle simply to buy time for the arrival of reinforcements. Distraught that he was unable to ship out with others of his regiment, "Tex" was instead sent to the dispensary to undergo tests to explain the swollen limbs and high fever he developed on the ship. David's rheumatic fever spared him the fate of the Tragic 29th.

The sense of urgency to reinforce the battlefront with manpower and equipment was palpable in the early days of the war. The mood of David's letters turned somber. Word of his regiment's tragedy had already begun to circulate among Okinawa's frontline soldiers-in-waiting. Like David, they likely wondered why they were spared the fate of their fellow soldiers, and perhaps more poignantly, when their turn would come.

Wading through endless army bureaucracy, David's parents received three earlier written letters from Okinawa in late August. The letters revealed the physical and psychological struggles of their son. Confined to his quarters with rheumatic fever, David had plenty of time to write. From an Okinawa army hospital bed, he penned a doleful song, "Blues in My Heart." His song laid bare the conflicted emotions of a boy whose dream of becoming a soldier was transformed into a hellish nightmare. Like fifteen-year-old Elisha Stockwell at the Civil War's Battle of Shiloh, David's letters shared the sentiment of another underage soldier who painfully lamented, "What a foolish boy I was to run away and get into such a mess as I was in." Another letter from David read:

Dear Mom & Dad,

. . . I don't think I'll have to go to Korea after all. I went (back) to the dispensary with my rheumatic fever today. My leg is swelled in a strut [sic]. The doctor told me he wasn't sure I had rheumatic fever or not, but he honestly believed I did. I'm going again in the morning for a complete check-up. From there I will probably go to the hospital. That might mean I'll get to come back to the U.S., but I don't really want out of the Army. But if my rheumatic fever shows up, I'll have to be discharged. Mom, if I were medically disabled for the Army, what would I do for a living? I'm very worried about it.

All my love,

(Tex) David

P.S. I love you![29]

Excerpt from "Blues in My Heart" by David (Tex) Steward:

Blues in my heart oh how it aches
Nobody knows the sorrow it takes . . .
I never dreamed we would ever part
I have those lonesome blues in my heart.
Gone is the love I couldn't hold
I feel like the Lamb that strayed from the fold.
What can I do, what can I say?
Blues in my heart has got me this way.
Rain falling down, down from the sky

Even the sun is beginning to cry.
Everything is wrong since we are apart
I wish I could lose these blues in my heart.[30]

By the following day, "Tex" Steward knew the dream was over. Like his buddies from the Okinawa battalions, he desperately wanted to do his part—but most of them had already been killed, wounded, or captured. He was certain army officials had received his mother's urgent letters advising them of his true age. He knew army physicians had discovered the rheumatic fever from which he had long suffered. Surely, they requested his medical records from Camp Stoneman. And as his symptoms worsened, he finally realized he was in no shape for combat.

Dearest Family,

. . . Mom, I'm trying to get to come home. I think I can because of my rheumatic fever. If I stay here much longer it will surely kill me. The doctor has confined me to quarters because of it. He doesn't realize at the present that it's rheumatic fever. He seems to think it's broken legaments [sic] in both my legs. I didn't let on like I knew a thing, but I'm going on sick call until he realizes what it really is.

All my love, Dave (Tex)[31]

As David's condition worsened, the situation on the ground in Korea became more desperate. He had trouble walking from his quarters to the dispensary, his legs remained swollen, and he experienced persistent joint pain. His dismal letters revealed a constant state of worry and inner conflict. Since he was treated for rheumatic fever at Camp Stoneman, he was sure of the problem, but he naively wondered if his condition would "clear up" once he arrived on the battlefield with his buddies. He was an expert rifleman, and he knew good riflemen were desperately needed on the front. But as his symptoms worsened, he resigned himself that he would be sent home.

Dearest Mom & Dad,

I'm going to the hospital (again) this afternoon, and be x-rayed. . . . I know it will show up. . . . I've been suffering a lot lately. I'll sign off right now, and finish this afternoon. . . .

> *Well, I just got back from the hospital and they said they would notify my company commander as soon as they had the x-ray ready. . . . I wish they would hurry and just get it over with . . . [it] is killing me.*

All my love, Tex[32]

Still confined to quarters, David awaited word from the army physicians. Originally assigned to the doomed 29th Regimental Combat Team on Okinawa, he finally received word of his fate. He was given his new assignment from the company commander. Just as David expected, he would be leaving Okinawa, but not for Texas—for the Korean battlefront. He was assigned to the 15th Replacement Battalion, attached to the beleaguered 1st Cavalry Division, sent to shore up the Pusan Perimeter and relieve the battered 24th Division.

To add to the chaos of the early weeks of the war, troops and supplies were delayed by the severity of the 1950 Pacific typhoon season. Typhoon Helene pummeled the Korean coastline until the end of July, which delayed the landing of elements of the 1st Cavalry and 82nd Field Artillery Battalion in Pusan. The Eighth Army's rations dropped to a one day's supply.[33]

David's original division was the first to be sent to the battlefields of Korea. The 24th Infantry Division had lost almost 30 percent of its troop strength, and nearly 2,400 of its men remained missing in action. The 1st Cavalry arrived on the battlefield near Taejon at noon on July 22, exactly two days after David landed on Okinawa. Like his brother William in World War II, David was assigned as a replacement in his new unit. Although he was proud to serve the "Black Horse" of the 1st Cavalry, he was well aware of the horrendous casualties they recently suffered.

United Nations forces were pushed into an ever-shrinking defensive line as the ruthless Inman Gun overran one unit after another. Surrounding the immensely important port of Pusan, the 140-mile-long defensive line was bordered to the west by the Naktong River and to the east by the East Sea, or Sea of Japan. The objective of the 1st Cavalry was to support the 24th Division as it fell back along the Naktong and to defend their ground at all cost. It was the last stand for the United Nations forces. For Americans, the battle for the Pusan Perimeter would become one of the bloodiest of the Korean War, with nearly 20,000 American casualties.[34]

Although still suffering from symptoms of rheumatic fever, David never returned to the medical dispensary. His test results were never revealed—and decades later, they were said to be lost.

Like the condemned in Dante's *Inferno*, the sons, fathers, brothers, and uncles of normal American citizens were hastily and sorrowfully cast through the gates of hell onto the Korean battlefront. They were sent into battle, not to destroy the demon but to delay him. And they, the first American soldiers to walk through the gates, would come to understand its inscription: "Abandon all hope, ye who enter here."

1. William H. Steward, 1945. 78th "Lightning" Division, 309th Infantry Regiment, World War II. 3rd Infantry Division, Korea. *U.S. Army photo.*

2. David Daniel Steward (January 29, 1934–September 21, 1950), KIA, Battle of Pusan Perimeter. *U.S. Army photo.*

3. William Steward, 3rd Infantry Division, on the Korean battlefront, 1951. *Photo from author's collection.*

16-Year-Old Missing in Korean War

Sixteen-year-old David D. Steward, son of Mr. and Mrs. W. H. Steward, La Casa Courts, El Centro, was reported missing in action in Korea since September 21, the secretary of the army informed his parents this week.

The youth, whose birth certificate had incorrectly listed his birth date as January 29, 1932, rather than 1934, his mother said, enlisted January 28 of this year, one day before his 16th birthday. He took basic training at Fort Ord and arrived in Korea August 31. He was reported missing three weeks later.

David's father is an employee of the Imperial Irrigation District.

Steward attended Central Union High School part of the 1948-1949 year and then withdrew. He has three brothers and two sisters.

4. *Imperial Valley Press*, October 1950. *Photo from author's collection.*

5. Steward family at the grave of Kenneth Carl Steward (August 3, 1940–April 13, 1941), Beech Creek Cemetery, Atlanta, Texas. L-R: Helen, William, David (arms folded), Earl Wayne, Delta Ray, Howard Neil, Aubrey Carroll, and William Henry Steward. *Photo from author's collection.*

6. Howard Neil Steward (October 9, 1937–March 13, 1946). *Photo from author's collection.*

7. Callie and William Steward on the day of David Daniel Steward's funeral in Atlanta, Texas, 1951. *Photo from author's collection.*

8. Ludendorff Bridge at Remagen on March 7, 1945, just before capture by American troops. *Photo courtesy of U.S. Army Signal Corps/National Archives, U.S. Army Center of Military History.*

9. Norman "Hob" Hobson and William Steward in Germany, 1945. 78th "Lightning" Division, 309th Infantry Regiment, K Company. *Photo from author's collection.*

10. William Steward reviewing enemy positions on Korean battlefront, 1951.
Photo from author's collection.

11. Maj. Harvey H. Storms, 7th Infantry Division, 31st Regimental Combat Team (RCT-31). Serving as the last commander of Task Force Faith, he was KIA at Chosin (Changjin) Reservoir but remained MIA for nearly 70 years. His remains were recovered in 2018 and identified in July 2019.
Photo courtesy of Sam Storms, son.

12. Joseph Roth Miller, USMC, KIA Chosin (Changjin) Reservoir, at Yudam-ni, November 28, 1950.
Photo courtesy of Jon (Miller) Kitts, son.

13. First Cavalry soldiers fire on an NKPA patrol on August 26, 1950. *Photo courtesy of U.S. Army Signal Corps, SFC Riley, #8A/ FEC-50-7043.*

14. A grief-stricken soldier is comforted when his buddy is KIA on August 28, 1950. In the background, a corpsman fills out the fallen soldier's casualty tag. *Photo courtesy of U.S. Army Signal Corps, SFC Al Chang. ARC identifier #531370, NARA File #080-SC-347-803.*

15. U.S. Marines move forward as F4U Corsairs flush out the enemy near Chosin (Changjin) Reservoir. *Photo courtesy of U.S. Military (USMC), Cpl. McDonald, December 26, 1950.*

16. Lt. Gen. Richard E. Carey, USMC, United States military 1945–1983. Carey served as a combat veteran of Korea and Vietnam. As a 2nd Lieutenant, he fought in the battles of Inchon Landing, Seoul, and Chosin (Changjin) Reservoir. In Vietnam, he flew 204 combat sorties and commanded a Fighter Attack Squadron, receiving the Distinguished Flying Cross and 16 Air Medals. In 1975 Carey led the largest helicopter evacuation of refugees in history. His awards also include the Silver Star, Legion of Merit (2), and the Purple Heart, among many others. *Photo courtesy of U.S. Military National Archives.*

17. Chinese Communist forces swarm up a snow-covered hill to overrun a UN position, November 1950. *U.S. Public domain tag on file, U.S. National Archives.*

18. UN troops fire on Communist-led North Korean forces in the streets of Seoul, September 20, 1950. *Photo courtesy of U.S. Army Signal Corps, National Archives (NARA) Identifier #531381.*

Former Spartan Killed In Action

David D. Steward, 16-year-old former C.U.H.S. student, has been listed as killed in action in Korea.

The boy had earlier been reported missing in action.

An incorrect birth statement allowed him to enlist in the Army on January 30.

Mr. and Mrs. Steward were informed two weeks ago that he had been missing since September 21. On Saturday they received a telegram from the defense department informing them that the young soldier had been killed.

David belonged to the Cadet Corps during the short time he was a member of the student body here at Central. He was more widely known among last year's freshmen as "Tex."

He had not completed his freshman year when he enlisted.

20. *Imperial Valley Press*, October 1950. *Photo from author's collection.*

AMERICAN RED CROSS

Sept. 1, 1950

Dearest Mom & Family,

I arrived in Korea yesterday. I haven't seen any action yet. Please try not to worry about me, Mom. Just pray for me.

Maybe this thing will clear up soon, and God will let me go home to my loved ones.

I received a letter from you and one from Sis when I boarded the ship. I was very glad to hear from my darling Mom and my Sweet Sis. I haven't heard from Daisy again yet

over

FORM 539A

19. Excerpt from David Daniel Steward's last letter before leaving for the battlefront near Taegu. Sixteen-year-old David entered battle on the day the NKPA launched their massive offensive on the Pusan Perimeter, September 1, 1950. The following two weeks were described by T. R. Fehrenbach as "the heaviest fighting and heaviest casualties of the Korean War." *Photo and letter from author's collection.*

21. David Daniel Steward, 1947. *Photo from author's collection.*

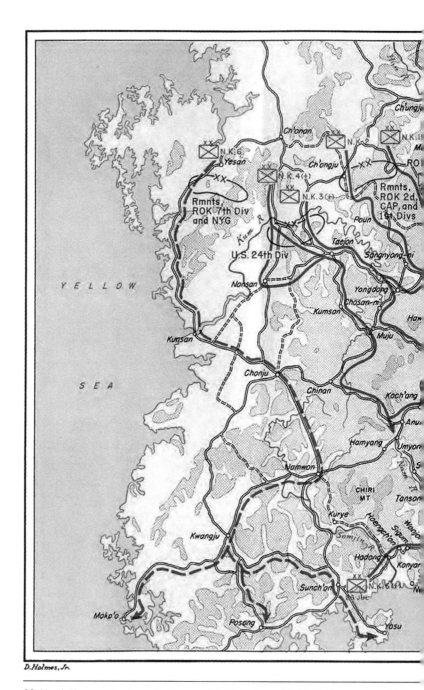

22. North Korean attacks on UN forces, July 14 to August 1, 1950. *Map courtesy of U.S. Army Center of Military History, D. Holmes, Jr.*

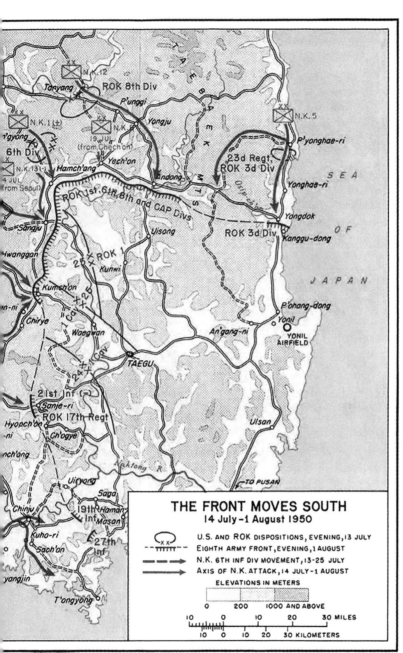

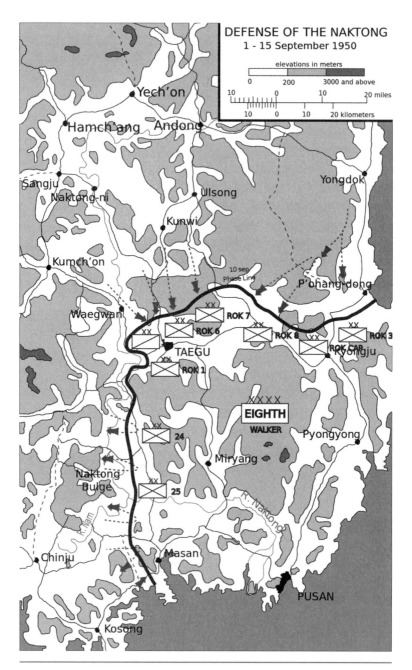

23. The Great Naktong Offensive, September 1–15, 1950. Arrows indicate NKPA attacks on the Pusan Perimeter beginning on September 1, David Steward's first day on the battlefront. *Map courtesy of U.S. Army Center of Military History.*

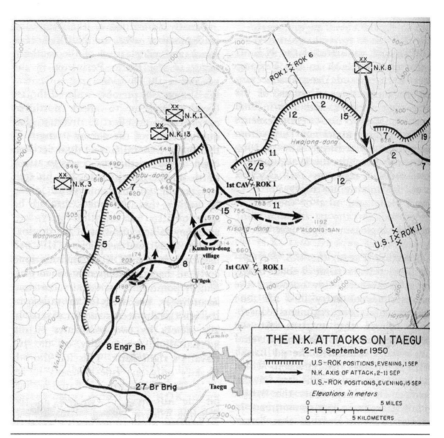

24. North Korean attacks on Taegu and First Cavalry Troopers, September 2–15, 1950. The location of David Steward's death, Kumhwa-dong village, on September 21, 1950, is listed. *Map courtesy of U.S. Army Center of Military History.*

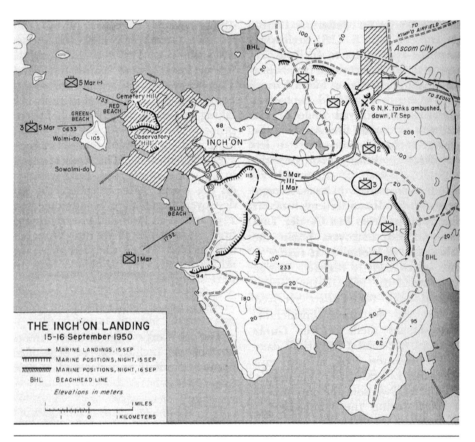

25. U.S. Marine Corps at the Inchon Landing, September 15, 1950. *Map courtesy of U.S. Military (USMC), Cpl. McDonald, December 26, 1950.*

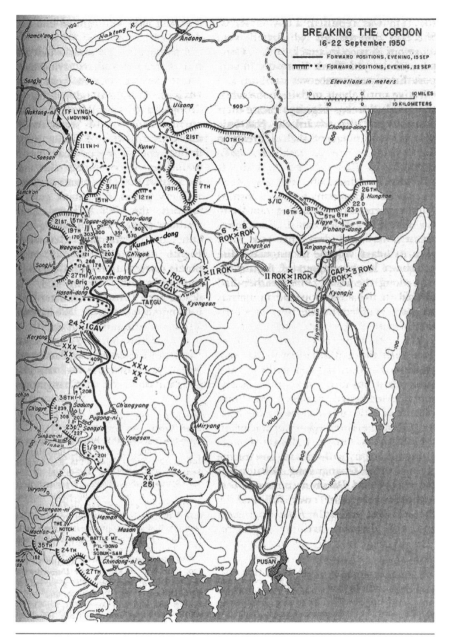

26. First Cavalry troop positions on September 16–22, 1950 at the time of David Steward's death. *Map courtesy of U.S. Army Center of Military History.*

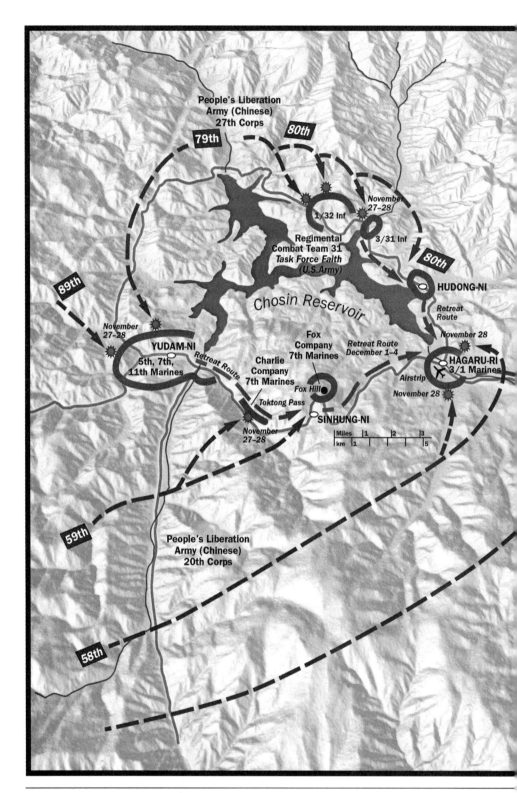

27. Chinese Communist forces attack on the Chosin (Changjin) Reservoir, November 1950. *Map design and artwork courtesy of Steve Walkowiak, SWmaps.*

13

STAND OR DIE

The God of Death himself hovered with heavy, beating wings . . .

—General Paik Sun-yup, Republic of Korea

Dearest Mom & Family,

I made out ten thousand dollars insurance today, and forty (dollar) allotment to you . . . if you need it all, don't hesitate to keep it all. If there's anyone I trust it's the ones I love so dearly, and that's you, Mom and Dad.

We were issued our weapons and field equipment today. We were also assigned our duty on the battle front. I'm a messenger, and I take with me one of the fastest, if not the fastest weapon on the field. It's a carbine, and can fire 750 to 755 rounds per min. That makes me pretty well protected. We go on maneuvers Tuesday, and learn to protect ourselves in combat. . . .

All my love,

Dave (Tex)[1]

By August 1950, replacements were arriving in Japan and Korea each day by air and sea—but it was not enough to replace the staggering number of casualties that occurred in the early weeks of the war. By the first week of August, more than 7,800 Americans had been killed or seriously wounded, and hundreds more were missing. For the men holding the line in the Pusan Perimeter, the situation remained grim. Gen. Walton H. Walker, Commander of the Eighth U.S. Army, told his troops to "stand or die."

There will be no more retreating, withdrawal or readjustment or any other term you choose. There is no line behind us to which we can retreat.... There will be no Dunkirk. There will be no Bataan. A retreat to Pusan would be one of the greatest butcheries in history. We must fight until the end.... We will fight as a team. If some of us must die, we will die fighting together.... I want everybody to understand we are going to hold this line.[2]

As the battles raged in the summer of 1950, a severe drought inflicted even more punishment on beleaguered troops attempting to hold the line at Pusan Perimeter. Only five inches of rain fell, rather than the normal twenty or more. Temperatures were far above average, routinely reaching between ninety and one hundred degrees Fahrenheit, with humidity levels often reaching 90 percent.[3]

Lack of clean drinking water was a serious problem, and as American soldiers scrambled across steep mountainous terrain, the blistering heat resulted in dehydration and heat exhaustion. With no other source of water, they drank from the rice paddies—which were fertilized with human waste. Adding to the casualty toll, dysentery became a significant problem for the outnumbered and outgunned soldiers, deepening the misery of all who endured the Forgotten War.

David's medical condition at the time he entered the battlefront will likely remain as it has for more than seventy years: a haunting conundrum. According to the army, his Okinawa medical records remain lost, and his hurriedly written last letter made no mention of his condition. Less than three weeks before arriving on the battlefront, while waiting for test results to confirm his original diagnosis of acute rheumatic fever, he wrote from the Okinawa base hospital, "I've been suffering a lot lately." One week later, still confined to quarters, he penned one of his last letters.

My Dearest Family,

The reports on my heart x-ray haven't returned yet, but I'm expecting them this afternoon.... I'll be seeing you soon.... Don't forget, Mom, I love you all. I love you very much....

All my love,

David "Tex"[4]

Just ten days before landing in Korea, the anxious teenager wrote to his mother and father. "I still haven't heard from the reports of my tests yet. I wish I could hurry up and find out what's going to happen to me."

There is no definitive diagnostic test for rheumatic fever, only the Jones criteria. At Camp Stoneman, California, David scored "highly positive" for rheumatic fever. "The doctor told me he wasn't sure I had rheumatic fever . . . but he honestly believed I did," David later wrote to his parents. Just two days before shipping out to Okinawa during the first week of the war, David again wrote his mother. "Mom . . . I've been havin' heart trouble or something, which has been making me pass out. My nerves are very bad."

For Tex, like so many other men in Korea, "The cogs miss, the wheels turn . . . it was a terrible bit of timing."[5] In the chaos and confusion of the first weeks of the war—and as the casualty count mounted—it is unlikely that his medical records from Camp Stoneman were ever retrieved. Whether he still suffered symptoms of acute rheumatic fever after arriving on the battlefront in Korea remains unknown. Only the desperate need for replacements in defense of the Pusan Perimeter is known.

Capt. Frank Munoz, a commander in the embattled 9th Infantry/2nd Infantry Division at the Naktong Bulge, arrived early in the war like David. He answered a haunting question: how did David Steward go directly from the base hospital in Okinawa to the battlefields of Korea in a matter of days?

At the start of the war, Munoz's 2nd Division stood at 50 percent of its original strength. Munoz described the army's desperation in filling the ranks. "We turned the vacuum cleaner on," he said. "It sucked up men from everywhere, behind desks, out of hospitals, from depots. We filled up fast."[6]

The timing of David Steward's arrival on the battlefields of Korea could not have been worse. The last NKPA offensive against the Pusan Perimeter was massive. Kim Il-sung, the ill-educated and brooding premier of North Korea, demanded complete victory over United Nations forces by September 1, 1950. The offensive began on the night of August 31, the same day sixteen-year-old David Steward first touched Korean soil. NKPA orders were to mount a five-pronged "do-or-die" attack against UN forces in the Pusan Perimeter.

The NKPA sought to penetrate the perimeter at several geographical areas of weakness. The Naktong Bulge was an area in which the wide Naktong River bowed to the west, near the town of Yongsan. The NKPA quickly deemed the Taegu corridor another possible route of penetration into the Pusan Perimeter. United Nations forces were thinly stretched and underequipped along the entire length of western boundary of the perimeter, marked by the Naktong River. Characterized by bitter and chaotic fighting, the battles in these areas resulted in massive American casualties.

With hurried pencil strokes on American Red Cross stationery, young Tex scribbled a last letter to his mother and family on September 1, 1950. Afterward, he and his group of quickly assembled replacements marched toward the savage fighting near Taegu.

Dearest Mom & Family,

I arrived in Korea yesterday [August 31]. I haven't seen any action yet. Please try not to worry about me, Mom. Just pray for me.

Maybe this thing will clear up soon, and God will let me go home to my loved ones. . . .

All my love,

Tex[7]

The NKPA planned "the great crossing" of the Naktong River on the day David made his unfortunate arrival on the Korean Peninsula. On September 1, David's first full day in Korea, the NKPA launched their massive strike on the Pusan Perimeter. The NKPA offensive involved thirteen infantry divisions, an armored division, and two armored brigades. Over 100 new Russian-built T-34 tanks and more than 98,000 North Korean soldiers joined the offensive.[8] Lt. Col. T. R. Fehrenbach, a Korean War veteran and historian, labeled the first two weeks of September "the heaviest fighting and heaviest casualties of the Korean War."[9]

By September 3, the enemy had made important gains in the mountainous country north of Taegu. As the second battle of the Naktong Bulge raged, the NKPA inflicted heavy casualties on the newly arrived 2nd Division defenders of the Bulge. North of Taegu, the 1st Cavalry "Troopers" were engaged in fierce combat and forced to pull back close to the city. By the third day of the NKPA offensive, the U.S. 2nd and 25th Infantry Divisions were on the brink of disaster.

On the nights of September 5 and 6, David's green 15th Replacement Battalion was greeted with cooling rain that rapidly became a torrential downpour. As they marched off to join the battle-weary and severely understrength 1st Cavalry soldiers, their packs were soaked and their boots stuck in the sludge. Wheeled and tracked vehicles bogged down as they slipped and slogged through heavy rain and knee-deep mud.[10] As if to welcome the fledgling replacements to Korea, the rain finally subsided and oppressive heat and humidity quickly ensued. Casualties in the 1st Cavalry were staggering.

Without reinforcements, the Troopers were in grave danger of being annihilated. The green replacements trudged on, anxiously awaiting their baptism of fire.

Just ten days after arriving in Korea, against a fanatical Inmun Gun, David's 1st Cavalry Division dug in to hold the city of Taegu in a desperate last stand. Fighting along the nearly forty-mile Taegu front would become some of the most vicious of the Korean War. As American reinforcements began to arrive elsewhere in the Pusan Perimeter, the Inmun Gun repositioned. At the Naktong Bulge, and along the 1st Cavalry front in the steep hills and valleys near Taegu, the fighting raged with renewed savagery.

Infamous Hill 314, a key position in the battle for Taegu, exemplified the bitter fighting endured by David's 1st Cavalry Division. At just over a thousand feet high, Hill 314 was used by the NKPA to observe all 1st Cavalry movements and pound them with mortar fire. A new order was issued from General Walker: the 1st Cavalry and the ROK 1st Division were to take the hill at all cost. Under heavy mortar fire, the Troopers were repelled twice. On the third attempt, as hand-to-hand fighting raged on the steep slopes of the hill, the battle was over and the 1st Cavalry seized all-important Hill 314.

The cost was terrible. One battalion had 229 casualties in just two hours, most of their officers were dead, and the Troopers witnessed some of the worst atrocities of the war against their fellow soldiers. Hundreds of enemy dead were carrying American rifles and wearing American uniforms. The Troopers found their friends bound, bayoneted, and shot. One officer had been bound, doused with gasoline, and set afire before the brutal NKPA retreated.[11]

With battlefield atrocities becoming more evident, Gen. Douglas MacArthur warned the North Korean High Command of criminal accountability for war crimes. As the 1st Cavalry defended the Naktong River and took another high point on Hill 303, they discovered the bodies of twenty-six mortar men who had been executed.[12] Lying in rows, they were bound and shot in the back of the head. The Hill 303 massacre ultimately resulted in the murder of forty-one U.S. soldiers. Other American soldiers were not as lucky. The barbarous NKPA began to torture captured Americans in hopes of instilling fear among United Nations troops. A United States Senate Subcommittee on Korean War Atrocities later reported that "two-thirds of all American prisoners of war in Korea died as a result of war crimes."[13]

As 1st Cavalry took hill after hill, only to find fellow Troopers bound and tortured—they stiffened in their hatred of the enemy. The green young men of the 1st Cavalry began to fight with a new ferocity. They became soldiers.

During his first week on the battlefield, sixteen-year-old David received his baptism of fire as a rifleman with L Company/8th Cavalry Regiment, 1st Cavalry Division. Growing up hunting in the East Texas piney woods, he was an excellent rifleman. On Okinawa, he was originally given the assignment of messenger, but as casualties mounted, he quickly received his new assignment as a rifleman with the 1st Rifle Platoon. During the Korean War, riflemen did as much as 90 percent of the fighting, especially during the early months of the war. During the intense combat of the first three months, many rifle companies were down to 25 percent strength. David's 3rd Battalion/8th Cavalry Regiment suffered a staggering 400 casualties out of 700 during the first two weeks of September.[14]

It was during this time, army historians later penned, that the 1st Cavalry was in a "fight for its very existence."[15] Like ants, thousands of the NKPA swarmed the hills and steep valleys amid sweltering heat and knee-deep mud when rain finally came. Hills were conquered and lost, sometimes changing hands more than five times. Day after never-ending day, the fighting went on. David and his 1st Cavalry Troopers suffered blistering heat while scrambling up and down the steep mountains near Taegu. Food and water were in short supply. And with thousands of enemy soldiers crawling the hills and ravines, sleep was unthinkable. Desperate for rest, soldiers dared not close their eyes.

By September 14, the 1st Cavalry and the ROK 1st Division were in deadly gridlock with three divisions of NKPA. Against the onslaught of the entire NKPA 13th Division, David's 8th Cavalry Regiment took the full brunt of bitter fighting. Only eight miles from Taegu, each foot of mountainous ground proved costly for David and his beleaguered 8th Cavalry friends.

On September 15, just two weeks after arriving in Korea, David's 3rd Battalion/8th Cavalry Regiment captured an important hill in the battle to save Taegu. Sustaining many casualties, David's L Company assaulted Hill 401 where the NKPA occupied the high ground. Fierce fighting ensued in capturing the hill. After taking command of the remaining men in his platoon and capturing Hill 401, Sgt. 1st Cl. Earl R. Baxter was mortally wounded. Sergeant Baxter posthumously received the Distinguished Service Cross for Valor on Hill 401.[16]

On the same day, Marines made a historic landing at Inchon, ultimately altering the course of the war. The Inchon landing was planned, replanned, and carried out in the utmost secrecy. Originally scheduled for the end of July as Operation Bluehearts, the plan was revised and postponed due to the early walloping from NKPA forces. At Tokyo General Headquarters in late

August 1950, top U.S. military leaders convened to discuss the Inchon landing. Many believed the plan was a foolhardy scheme that would drain even more resources from the bloody Pusan Perimeter, resulting in complete failure. MacArthur's words rang true.

> The only alternative to a stroke such as I propose will be the continuation of the savage sacrifice we are making at Pusan, with no hope of relief in sight. Are you content to let our troops stay in that bloody perimeter like beef cattle in the slaughterhouse? Who will take the responsibility for such a tragedy? Certainly, I will not.[17]

A new landing force, X (Tenth) Corps, was assembled for the amphibious landing. X Corps was commanded by Lt. Gen. Edward "Ned" Almond. X Corps originally included the 1st and 7th Marines of the 1st Marine Division, along with the army's 7th Infantry Division. But the marines demanded the 5th Marines be pulled from the fierce fighting of the Pusan Perimeter to join the invasion. The 1st Marine Division commander, Maj. Gen. Oliver P. Smith, had his way and the 70,000 men of Tenth Corps readied themselves for a mid-September D-Day at Inchon.

The largest amphibious assault since the Normandy invasion of World War II, the Inchon landing, called Operation Chromite, was bold and risky. The tidal range at Inchon is one of the largest in the world. Extensive mudflats and seasonal tidal variations created another problem, leaving a meager three-day window for troop landing—September 15–18. The duration of spring tides above a minimum level for landing troops was less than four hours. This provided a narrow window for landing as many troops and supplies as possible before the next high tide. The harbor was defended by enemy batteries and protected by two islands, Sowolmi-do and a larger island, Wolmi-do. Wolmi-do had to be seized first, followed by the larger invasion at Inchon.

Lt. Gen. Richard E. Carey, serving as a second lieutenant during the Inchon landing, recalled his baptism of fire during one of the most famous amphibious landings in history.

> I was concerned by the heavy smoke created by the intense shelling. As it turned out, my concern was legitimate as our units' landing crafts were somewhat disoriented, resulting in hitting the beach at unplanned locations.... My platoon was driven into a creek's seawall opening. So, rather than going by ladders over the seawall we exited our craft into a creek bed opening which was surrounded on both sides by heavy

concertina barbed wire.... I was rapidly moving back and forth behind my men encouraging them in the wire cutting when at one point I stopped in order to better observe behind the wire. At this time a sniper's bullet hit me over the right shoulder, breaking the shoulder strap on my PC536 radio, which fell to the ground. As I reached down to pick it up, a second round was fired, hitting the marine directly in front of me. My platoon scout sniper saw the enemy sniper and took him out. This was to be the first of many close calls for me![18]

As marines landed under heavy mortar and machine-gun fire, the enemy was quickly neutralized by nightfall on September 15. Marines entered the city of Inchon on the morning of September 16, and by September 18, the critically important Kimpo airfield was secured. General Almond's Tenth Corps casualties were low: 20 men killed, 174 wounded, and one man missing in action. General MacArthur's Inchon landing was a stunning success.

The recapture of South Korea's capital city proved to be lengthier and much more difficult. Almond wanted the capture of Seoul by September 25, on the three-month anniversary of North Korea's invasion. While both MacArthur and Almond declared the liberation of Seoul on September 26, marines continued to be engaged in vicious urban warfare until September 28.

General Carey remembered a legendary incident involving MacArthur. As then–Second Lieutenant Carey and his men moved rapidly toward Seoul, they encountered resistance and a firefight ensued. Carey recounted the tale of his battlefield meeting with MacArthur.

I was behind a hooch [small hut-like dwelling] at the side of the road briefing my squad leaders and platoon sergeant on our next move ... when my platoon sergeant said, "Lieutenant, look what's coming up the road!" To my utter amazement, coming up the center of the road, with his aides and staffers dodging and weaving the bullets hitting the buildings and road ... was Gen. Douglas MacArthur! He was in his full regalia.... peaked hat, sunglasses, khakis, and his corncob pipe! When he came abreast of where I was, I ran out and jerked him with me behind the building ... in the process he fell to the ground. I quickly reached out and helped him to his feet apologizing profusely. While brushing himself off and with a frown he asked, "What the hell do you think you're doing, Lieutenant?" "Sir," I stated, "we're in a firefight and I'm trying to save your ass!" With a smile and a chuckle he replied, "Lieutenant, the bullet isn't made that can kill me!"[19]

Amid considerable pageantry and cheers from hundreds of Seoul's citizens, MacArthur arrived into a city of rubble. As fighting continued on the outskirts of Seoul, Gen. Oliver P. Smith believed his 1st Marine Division men should be fighting, rather than serving as security for such a dangerous and frivolous event.

Before being routed from Seoul, brutal Communist forces committed numerous war crimes, killing women, children, and family members of ROK soldiers. Any and all suspected of being pro-American were killed. Liberating UN forces found the remains of thousands of tortured and executed civilians in houses, on streets, and in mass graves.

The people of Seoul were joyous at the arrival of American troops and lined the streets as MacArthur's motorcade rolled into the devastated city. In a dramatic ceremony, MacArthur personally returned the capital city of Seoul to seventy-five-year-old Syngman Rhee, president of the Republic of Korea. Rhee's trembling hands, mangled from Japanese torture, held MacArthur's hands as he spoke.[20] "We admire you," he said to MacArthur. "We love you.... How can I ever explain to you my own underlying gratitude and that of the Korean people?"[21]

MacArthur was bolstered by the success of Inchon and the capture of Seoul. Officials in Washington, including the secretary of state and President Truman, began to see the possibility of erasing the arbitrary and unnatural line that separated the people of Korea. Secretary of Defense George C. Marshall issued a communiqué providing the Supreme Commander with permission "to proceed north of the 38th parallel."[22] The move north to the Yalu River bordering China was inevitable. It was quickly approved by President Truman.

Back in the Taegu corridor, the daring landing at Inchon provided little relief to the embattled soldiers of the 1st Cavalry Division. Both men and supplies were hurriedly stripped away from the Pusan Perimeter to support the Inchon landing. Roads and villages were clogged with refugees—and infiltrators dressed as refugees and farmers. They constantly wreaked chaos upon freshly arrived American soldiers as they fought for their lives in a new kind of hell.

On the battlefield, "dead" Inmun Gun inflicted as many last-chance casualties as possible, shooting and blowing up advancing Americans. Each day, the sun scorched and flooded the battlefield with fiery intensity, but for men of the 1st Cavalry, the Pusan Perimeter was the darkest place on earth.

By September 19, David's 8th Cavalry Regiment was on the move but had already sustained extensive casualties. Many were out of ammunition, most were out of food and water, and they were deeply imperiled. They were reinforced with the 3rd/7th Cavalry in hopes of capturing Tabu-dong on the same day—but the NKPA 13th Division again stopped them with fanatical resistance. On September 20, at least seven tanks of the 70th Tank Battalion were lost. Machine-gun crossfire and heavy mortar and artillery fire resulted in staggering casualties for David's 8th Cavalry Regiment.

With 3,441 Americans killed in action, September proved costly in American treasure. In one day alone—David's first day in Korea—386 Americans were killed in action. By the following week, there were nearly a thousand more battle deaths. For American troops, September was the deadliest month of the war, bringing the highest number of casualties than any other time in the Korean War. By the end of September, American battle casualties totaled nearly 20,000.[23]

The U.S. Air Force did not escape the carnage of September 1950. A B-26 and ten of its crew were lost, along with three F-51s and the same number of F-80s. Within the next few days, two B-29s went down with all sixteen crew members. In the four-day span of September 10–14, there were more than 350 battle deaths, most of which occurred as the 1st Cavalry's attempted to hold the line at Taegu.[24] Finally on September 20, slogging through a heavy morning fog, the 24th Infantry Division began crossing the Naktong River near Taegu. The NKPA was in retreat.

Early the next day, September 21, the morning sunlight caught the polished brass medals adorning the full dress uniform of a high-ranking NKPA officer. Proudly wearing his Russian pistol and slowly walking into the small village held by the 8th Cavalry, he surrendered to two men of David's regiment. Col. Lee Hak-ku led the division that killed, maimed, and tortured so many of David's 8th Cavalry buddies.[25] Claiming a loss of faith in Communism, he was the highest-ranking NKPA officer to be taken prisoner during the war, and he readily provided valuable intelligence to Americans.

By nightfall, the NKPA had collapsed. On that same day, an 8th Cavalry Regimental radio called out, "This is skirmish Red. Don't fire."[26] First Cavalry Gen. Hap Gay and David's 8th Cavalry commander, Raymond Palmer, congratulated their battle-weary men for accomplishing their mission to encircle the enemy and save Taegu. At 6:50 p.m., Sargeant First Class Goodrow of the 7th Cavalry shook hands with members of David's 8th Cavalry Regiment as the two regiments finally met up.[27] The enemy was disintegrating, retreating in disarray.

Finally, after the slaughter of Task Force Smith, the massacre of David's ill-fated Tragic 29th, and fighting hand-to-hand and hill-to-hill, the beleaguered soldiers of the Eighth U.S. Army began to believe in themselves. Recklessly hurled through the gates of hell, the men of the 1st Cavalry Division had accomplished their mission at unfathomable cost. And for a brief moment, the sound of boyhood laughter echoed through an ancient valley in the Land of the Morning Calm.

For David Daniel Steward, there would be no celebration, no handshaking, no victory. On that day—a rare day on which his 8th Cavalry buddies dared to smile—young Tex lay at the brink of a steep ravine near the village of Kumhwa-dong, just north of Taegu. On September 21, 1950—just nineteen days after arriving on the Korean front line, David "Tex" Steward was killed in action. He was sixteen years old.

On the day he died, U.S. Air Force T-6 Mosquitoes located large numbers of NKPA tanks maneuvering for position to ambush and annihilate the 24th Infantry. The flyboys and ground artillery were called in, destroying at least fourteen of the NKPA tanks as the remainder fled the carnage. For the first time since the brutal Inmun Gun had breached the 38th parallel, the inescapable darkness was pierced by an evanescent ray of light. The breakout of the Pusan Perimeter had begun.

A hapless child of the Dirty Thirties, David Daniel Steward traded his Depression-era relief overalls for the proudly worn uniform of the U.S. Army—finally becoming the soldier he dreamed of being. Paying a dreadful price for every inch of ground held, he and his 1st Cavalry Troopers contributed heroically in the early effort to break out of the Pusan Perimeter.

For young Tex, the war was over. But for the weary soldiers who somehow managed to survive, it was just beginning. The survivors who gallantly fought through the early days of the Forgotten War and the bloody Pusan Perimeter were now committed to one of the most dismal chapters of American military history. They were on the move—north to the Yalu River.

14

A MILLION MILES FROM HOME

> *I pray that our Heavenly Father may assuage the anguish of your bereavement, and leave you only the cherished memory of the loved and lost, and the solemn pride that must be yours to have laid so costly a sacrifice upon the altar of Freedom.*
>
> —President Abraham Lincoln, letter to Mrs. Bixby

October 2, 1950

Dear Mr. and Mrs. Steward,

I regret that I must confirm my recent telegram in which you were informed that your son, Private David D. Steward, Infantry, has been reported missing in action in Korea since 21 September 1950. I know that added distress is caused by failure to receive more information or details. Therefore, I wish to assure you that at any time additional information is received it will be transmitted to you without delay.

The term "missing in action" is used only to indicate that the whereabouts or status of an individual is not immediately known. It is not intended to convey the impression that the case is closed. I wish to emphasize that every effort is exerted continuously to clear up the status of our personnel. Under battle conditions this is a difficult task as you must readily realize. Experience has shown that many persons reported missing in action are subsequently reported as returned to duty or being hospitalized for injuries....

Permit me to extend to you my heartfelt sympathy during this period of uncertainty.

Sincerely yours,

Edward F. Witsell Major General, USA
The Adjutant General of the Army[1]

Less than five years before receiving David's missing-in-action telegram, eight-year-old brother Howard Neil Steward died in a tragic accident. Five years earlier, baby Kenneth succumbed to bilateral bronchial pneumonia. And just weeks after David Steward landed in Korea, the War Department dispatched insufferable news to his parents—their blond-haired, emerald-eyed baby boy was missing in action. During the Korean War, such a pronouncement was and continues to be a tortuous sentence for families. Americans captured by the North Korean People's Army endured death marches, torture, and execution by the thousands. War crimes against POWs were well documented. More than 40 percent of these men died in captivity due to inhumane and brutal treatment from their NKPA captors.

William Steward was serving at Fort MacArthur in San Pedro, California. Just after receiving his alert for deployment to Korea, he received his father's telegram notifying him of David's missing-in-action status. When William last spoke to his mother only three weeks earlier, she told him she received a letter from David regarding his rheumatic fever. In his letter, David revealed that his doctor would "notify my commanding officer," and that he was sure to be discharged and sent home. But the devastation on the battlefields of Korea called for every able-bodied man to halt the advancing Inmun Gun. After being certain that David would be home soon, the entire family now feared the worst. Eight days later, another telegram and letter confirmed their deepest angst.

Dear Mr. and Mrs. Steward,

It is with regret that I confirm the recent telegram informing you of the death of your son, Private David D. Steward, Infantry, who was previously reported missing in action on 21 September 1950 in Korea. If additional information is received it will be transmitted to you promptly.

An official message has now been received which states that he was killed in action on the date he was previously reported missing in action....

I realize the burden of anxiety that has been yours since he was first reported missing in action and deeply regret the sorrow this later report brings you. May the knowledge that he made the supreme sacrifice for his home and country be a source of sustaining comfort. My sympathy is with you in this period of great sorrow.

Sincerely yours,

Edward F. Witsell Major General, USA
The Adjutant General of the Army[2]

The days following David's death were filled with heartache and despair for the Steward family. Newspapers from El Centro, California, to Dallas, Texas, were requesting interviews from the parents of the "boy soldier." In the two weeks after David's parents received the notification of his death, they received constant telephone calls, requests for interviews, and reporters at their door. Did he falsify his birth record? Did they notify army officials that he was only sixteen? When will his body be returned? Will he be buried in El Centro or Texas? For David's grieving parents and family, there was no respite.

Surrounded by the dark shadows of depression, William spiraled into a black hole of self-deprecation and blame for his younger brother's death. "Now I've killed two of my little brothers," he told his sister, Helen.[3]

David had wanted more than anything to be a soldier like his hero and big brother, William. In happier times, as his brother entered Central Union Cadet Corps, William playfully pinned him with his own World War II Combat Infantryman Badge, proclaiming, "You're a fine soldier, son." Awash with pride, David stood at attention as his brother saluted and presented him with every infantryman's most prized medal.

After all the horror William had witnessed in combat, he simply could not reconcile his actions—or his lack of action—as his underage brother joined the army. David's death opened a festering sore full of sorrowful guilt for every member of the family, but most especially for William.

As his recruiter promised, William's perfectly executed plan to serve out his peacetime hitch "on the beaches of California" was about to be realized. He made some money, married the love of his life, and had a baby son named Michael. He was in the best shape of his life, he was writing and playing music in his spare time, and most importantly, he had only a few months left on his U.S. Army hitch. But like the sovereign border of the Republic of Korea, blasted to pieces in the early morning darkness of June 25, 1950, William's hopes and dreams were faithlessly shattered. At last, William had found peace and happiness with Callie and his new baby son—but it was fleeting.

David's death was the first of a tragic sequence of events that would transform William's life into a grim nightmare. The situation in Korea was dire, and only after thousands of Americans were sacrificed at the altar of military unpreparedness did President Truman and the Eighty-First Congress take action to successfully prosecute the war. With or without their consent, the president ordered members of the National Guard and Army Reserve to active duty for twenty-one months. The draft law was extended for one year. The president and Congress authorized a one-year involuntary extension of service for all current enlistments. Public Law 624 was quickly signed into law.

The die was cast—William Steward was in the midst of calamity. Still reeling from his brother's death, he was once again preparing for war. He would leave behind his one-year-old son, Michael, and his pregnant wife, Callie. While William served his country for the second time in combat, his wife delivered a baby daughter, Linda. He missed her first step, her first words, and months later, she would not recognize her father at all.

Unlike his combat days of World War II, William would serve in an undeclared war under a flag that was not his own. The solemn covenant that he would never return to combat—that his country would be better served by his experience and ability to train new recruits—was simply a forsaken promise. He had served his country with honor but was cast into the very chaos and horror that took the life of his baby brother—into a war that could not be called a war.

Delta Ray Steward had seven sons. By the age of forty-eight, she was down to three. Born in 1902, she had experienced more than her share of heartache, beginning as a small child. When she fell from an old farmhouse porch as a toddler, her tiny hip was shattered, leaving her gravely injured. Unaware of little Ray's pluck, doctors informed her father that she would never walk. But even as a child, she refused the custom-made wooden wheelchair and learned to walk, a gritty feat for a small girl whose right leg was a full five inches shorter than the left. And although she spent the remainder of her life seriously handicapped, she proudly strutted about like a banty rooster. She studied theology and attended junior college, a rarity for women in the early 1900s. She was not the typical woman of her day, and her opinions—solicited and unsolicited alike—were widely known by all who knew her.

Delta Ray was not a timid woman. As an ordained minister, she loved and revered the pulpit. She spoke of her God of love and mercy but had a penchant for preaching a gospel full of fire and brimstone. Sinners in her midst were admonished and put on notice: sooner or later they would "drink the wine of God's wrath." She did not tolerate foolishness, and when she set her mind to something, it almost always happened.

From the moment she received the letter notifying her of David's death, she set out with fervent resolve to bring him back to the old homeplace in Texas. She wanted him to be laid to rest with his brothers. It mattered not that the Korean War was still raging in the area where David was killed, or that logistics and identification would be problematic for the U.S. Army. Delta Ray Steward wanted her baby back—and she demanded that her eldest son William, now in Tokyo awaiting shipment to the front line, serve as special escort for his beloved baby brother David.

> To Colonel James R. Clearwater, 2 M.C. Memorial Division, Washington, D.C.:
>
> *Dear Sir:*
>
> *In reference to . . . the letter concerning our request for the return of our son's remains to the U.S.A.*
>
> *I have another son [deployed] to Korea. . . . He knows the exact course to follow in carrying out our wishes, and also the route to travel in order to make things more convenient for both the War Department and our family. Sergeant Steward is married and has two small children. He is a combat veteran of World War II, was wounded and has the Purple Heart, Bronze Star, and other citations. He should not have been sent to Korea to fight in this undeclared war in the first place. I have another son, Sergeant Earl Wayne Steward, who served in the Navy during WWII and now in the Air Force. My husband was in the Third "Rock of the Marne" Division in World War I and was wounded in the Argonne Forest.*
>
> *I think we have contributed largely to the wars and service of our country. The government has never granted one request for me in the course of three wars. I am making this final appeal . . . to grant my son, Billy, the privilege of escorting the body of his beloved brother to his final resting place. He is strong and fully capable of carrying out this assignment.*
>
> *They told Billy he would not have to go to war again, that he could remain in the States and train recruits, and he faithfully served for a long time. . . . Then Billy was shipped [overseas] immediately and at a time when he was needed at home badly. We are overwhelmed with sorrow over the death of our youngest son, David.*
>
> *In summary, please give your fullest attention to the identification of my son, David and let me hear from you concerning this request as it is convenient for you, Sir.*
>
> *Respectfully,*
>
> *Mr. and Mrs. William Henry Steward*[4]

On the day following receipt of the telegram that notified her of her son's death, Delta Ray began writing letters to the War Department, her local and national veterans' service offices, congressmen, and the president of the United States.

Astonishingly, many of her photocopied letters, accompanied by copies of typewritten responses from government and military officials, were included in the Individual Personnel File (IDPF) for David Daniel Steward. Included in David's IDPF, along with his mother's photocopied letters, were numerous field reports including exact coordinates of the location of his body. Battlefield reports included personal effects found on his body, field autopsy reports, details of identification of remains, and reports from the decorated 8204th Graves Registration Army unit. Many of the reports were typed on ancient typewriters from field command posts.

Fearing the circumstances of David's death would be lost upon the death of my father, I requested my Uncle David's IDPF. With no way of knowing the file's contents or the haunting burden I would forever shoulder, I received the file in 1999. Safely tucked away in their protective case, the documents, letters, and field reports were examined hundreds of times—always with sobering reverence. Without the detailed reports, notes of his many attachments from one unit to the next, and photocopied letters from my grandmother, his death would have likely remained a mystery. Like the words on his cracked and yellowed letters, the story of the boy soldier would have waned into oblivion.

After writing the War Department several times, Delta Ray determined that a response had not arrived in a timely manner. Having given her baby boy, she expected and demanded a response from the army. Knowing the pen is mightier than the sword, she wrote again, this time forewarning of that to come:

> *Dear Sir:*
>
> *. . . Do not underestimate a grieving mother at whose side stands the Almighty himself. I will write every politician in California, the President, the War Department . . . and I will notify every local newspaper, every single day until my request is honored.*[5]

And she did.

As of September 2023 there were nearly 7,500 Korean War heroes who remained unaccounted for.[6] These brave warriors simply vanished from the earth. As one eighty-year-old sister tearfully described, they were left "a million miles from home." For the families of these men, each day ends with thoughts of their lost loved ones and dreadful rumination of their ultimate fate. The families will have no peace, no closure, until their boys once again return home to touch American soil. Unfathomable to most Americans, their pain and sorrow is never-ending, an eternal wound that never heals.

Like thousands of young men who served and died in the Forgotten War, the body of David Daniel Steward—precious son, brother, and uncle—lay in the frozen Korean ground where he gallantly made his last stand.

15

LOST BATTALION

> *I don't know if I will live through the day or night. We are close to heaven, but really we are . . . in hell.*
>
> —Father Emil Kapaun, Army Chaplain,
> 8th Cavalry Regiment

AS DELTA RAY STEWARD continued the daily campaign to bring her boys back to Texas, the Korean War took another savage turn—and a new enemy emerged with violent ferocity. The dreadful sacrifice made in the Pusan Perimeter seemed futile. The ancient Land of the Morning Calm once again became a killing field. For Delta Ray, the fall and winter of 1950 were blurred by the death of her youngest son and her eldest son's order back to the front. As she immersed her body and soul into getting her sons back, the war in Korea became even more ghastly.

After the U.S. Marines' successful amphibious assault at Inchon on September 15 and the subsequent recapture of Seoul, United Nations forces made significant advances. During the week of David's death, UN forces were successful in breaking out of the Pusan Perimeter. The weakened North Korean People's Army began retreating northward with UN forces on their heels.

Many politicians and military leaders erroneously believed a United Nations victory was imminent, and when wrong—as they had been so many times in Korea—the former were not reelected and the latter were fired. But for soldiers fighting on the ground, these miscalculations were a death sentence. Once again, a failure to understand the enemy and the hubris of political and military leadership resulted in the horrific loss of more American treasure.

Refusing to accept the notion of Chinese intervention, Gen. Douglas MacArthur remained unconvinced that China would enter the war. MacArthur willingly accepted the inaccurate reports of his personal intelligence advisor. His discountenance of commanders on the ground emerged as one of the greatest military blunders in modern history. The inevitable storm was brewing. In reality, Chinese leadership had already agreed to intervene with the backing and military support of the Soviets.

As Supreme Commander for the Allied Powers, MacArthur wanted total control of the war and its execution, including all intelligence operations on the Korean Peninsula. He renounced outside interference from meddling politicians at the Pentagon, as well as the president. At the time of the invasion of South Korea, the Central Intelligence Agency (CIA) was a fledgling organization created by the 1947 National Security Act. The entire agency had no more than 5,000 employees worldwide and only three officers in Korea.[1]

Critics of the CIA later condemned its failure to report dangerous developments on the Korean Peninsula, but in 1949 the CIA reported that removal of U.S. troops from Korea would "likely lead to war." Just five months prior to the invasion, the CIA warned of civilian evacuations and a massive buildup of North Korean forces, tanks, and heavy artillery along the 38th parallel.[2]

Unwilling to relinquish full power to prosecute the war, MacArthur minimized CIA reports early in the war. He had his own intelligence chief, who was eager to tell him exactly what he wanted to hear. Maj. Gen. Charles Willoughby had a lengthy relationship with MacArthur, meeting him in an officer's training center in Fort Leavenworth, Kansas, prior to World War II, and serving as MacArthur's intelligence expert in the Philippines in 1940. Willoughby had MacArthur's ear.

Charles Willoughby did everything in his power to downplay the notion of Chinese intervention, assuring MacArthur that hundreds of captured Chinese were simply "advisors" and in no way full-strength fighting units. Even after interrogated prisoners revealed they were a part of hundreds of thousands of Chinese Communist forces, Willoughby continued to dismiss them as volunteers and stragglers. Willoughby knew MacArthur's greatest goal was to reach the Yalu River. And his intelligence was shaped, even fabricated, in order to get him there.[3]

Tenth Corps Chief of Operations Lt. Col. John Chiles, elucidated the menacing actions of Charles Willoughby. "MacArthur did not want the Chinese to enter the war in Korea," Chiles said. "Anything MacArthur wanted, Willoughby produced intelligence for. . . . In this case, Willoughby falsified intelligence reports. . . . He should have gone to jail."[4]

On October 15, 1950, Truman and MacArthur met on Wake Island in the Pacific. Truman was already alarmed by the possibility of Soviet and Chinese intervention in Korea. The president's first words to MacArthur were straightforward: "All of our intelligence indicates that the Chinese are about to intervene."[5]

MacArthur immediately and emphatically assured the president that the war would be over by Christmas. When the president inquired as to the possibility of Chinese intervention, MacArthur reiterated his belief that it would not happen—assuring the president that even if they did intervene, they could only muster 50,000 to 60,000 soldiers. Neither Truman nor his staff had the stomach to ask the tough questions that should have been asked. In his book *The Coldest Winter*, David Halberstam described the fateful decision to move north: "Of the American military miscalculations of the twentieth century, Douglas MacArthur's decision to send his troops all the way to the Yalu stands alone."[6]

In fact, Chairman Mao Zedong of China had already reorganized the Chinese military. As the NKPA collapsed and United Nations troops advanced toward the Chinese border, Mao restructured his army for intervention in Korea. He created the People's Volunteer Army (PVA) in an effort to evade an "official" war with the more modernized forces of the United States. Mao authorized the Chinese First Phase campaign, intending to limit the early offensive to South Korean forces.[7]

After David Steward's death, the men of his 1st Cavalry Division continued to move north. In one of the Korean War's major battles, the 1st Cavalry captured the North Korean capital of Pyongyang on October 19. A feeling of optimism swept over the bone-weary Troopers as talk of a Tokyo victory parade echoed among the men. Having survived the bitter early months of the Korean War, they began to believe in the possibility of going home.

After arriving in Pyongyang, MacArthur himself flew from Tokyo to congratulate the 1st Cavalry Troopers. This reassured hopeful troops of the war's end. MacArthur, who spent not a single night in Korea during his command, stayed only a few hours in the capital city before returning to Tokyo. Later, on the Troopers' last evening in Pyongyang, Bob Hope arrived to entertain the troops. Hope's USO show was a morale booster for the exhausted Troopers—the laughter and dancing girls were medicine for soldiers, but the good feeling was ephemeral.

The next morning they received orders to advance north to shore up the stalled ROK 1st Division, which was marching toward the Yalu River bordering North Korea and China.[8] Reports indicated the South Koreans were involved in a skirmish and taking heavy fire in the village of Unsan. The 8th Cavalry Regiment was to move toward the village of Unsan to support the ROK 1st Division.[9]

Under intense secrecy, on the day the 1st Cavalry captured the North Korean capital city of Pyongyang, Chinese forces entered Korea. The Korean War was at once transformed. By the end of November, nearly 300,000 Chinese troops crossed the Yalu and streamed into North Korea. The number of Chinese in Korea would eventually swell to well over two million by the end of the war.[10]

By November 1, the Troopers were within fifty miles of the Chinese border. The substantial flow of ground intelligence was a warning shot aimed toward a well-coordinated intervention by the Chinese, and it deeply alarmed commanders on the ground. They were certain that Chinese forces were present in vast numbers. One of the most respected South Korean commanders, Gen. Paik Sun-yup, had been one of the first officers to warn of Chinese intervention. He was apprehensive as his men marched north through empty and desolate landscapes that were normally filled with columns of refugees. Adding to his uneasiness, temperatures were quickly dropping.

General Paik was not the only one with a sinking feeling of dread on the march north to the Yalu. First Cavalry commander Hap Gay, who served as George Patton's chief of staff during World War II, had witnessed his share of the Korean War's calamity. The high command lived in a "dream world," he said, constantly making reckless decisions for men on battlefield.[11] Like General Paik, Gay sensed his Troopers were not alone, and when a spotter plane reported large columns of enemy moving toward Unsan, he immediately requested that his 8th Cavalry Regiment be given permission to fall back. His request was doggedly denied by First Corps headquarters.

Ultimately, the sense of foreboding that gripped General Paik and Hap Gay was frighteningly accurate. Their men had walked into a well-laid trap. ROK survivors were forced to withdraw, with a captured Chinese prisoner in tow. The prisoner informed Paik, who personally conducted the interrogation, that "many, many thousands" of Chinese Communist forces were holed up in the surrounding mountains. But this and all other field intelligence was routinely dismissed by the American high command. Even the Eighth Army's commander, Gen. Walton Walker, rejected the notion of intervention by the Chinese, stating that "We should not assume that Chinese Communists are committed in force. After all, a lot of Mexicans live in Texas."[12]

The "skirmish" in which the ROK 1st Division was engaged was actually a desperate battle to hold the line. With many casualties, the ROK Army broke down and the 8th Cavalry took up the attack, with the 5th Cavalry protecting its rear and only the ROK 15th Regiment protecting the east.

On November 1, the Chinese set a trap for the U.S. 8th Cavalry Regiment. With superior numbers, the phantom enemy broke through and cut off the withdrawal route for the regiment. Two of the regiment's battalions suffered heavy losses, yet many soldiers managed to escape. By November 2, the 3rd Battalion was encircled and trapped by over 10,000 Chinese soldiers. Enduring savage nighttime attacks, their defensive perimeter shrunk to less than 200 yards.[13]

The 5th Cavalry Regiment sustained over 350 casualties in gallant attempts to rescue their fellow Troopers, but Chinese Communist forces crashed in on them in overwhelming numbers. L Company, the company with which David Steward had fought, was savaged, and most were killed or wounded and captured. Overrun and out of ammunition, the men of the 3rd Battalion fought to the end with bayonets and in hand-to-hand combat. When the battle was over, the once elite 2,400-man regiment had lost nearly half its strength and more than 1,000 men were listed as MIA.

Over the next several days, nearly 400 dazed and wounded men were able to return to friendly lines. For the ill-fated 3rd Battalion, the unit with whom David Steward made his last stand during the breakout of the Pusan Perimeter, only 200 men survived out of the original 800.[14] Two days later, the "Lost Battalion of Unsan" ceased to exist as a fighting unit.

Among the 3rd Battalion casualties were many wounded and nearly 300 captured, sentenced to the hell of enemy prisoner-of-war camps. Capt. Emil Kapaun embodied the grievous saga of Unsan. A Catholic chaplain from Kansas, Father Kapaun ran from foxhole to foxhole, dragging wounded soldiers to cover and tending their wounds. Amid the noise and confusion, exposing himself to enemy fire, he administered last rites to dying soldiers and heard battlefield confessions.

Beloved by the men of the 8th Cavalry Regiment, Father Kapaun saved the lives of many wounded, including Sgt. 1st Cl. Herbert "Pappy" Miller, who had served in combat with the 42nd Division in World War II. As Miller lay in a ditch, wounded from shrapnel that shattered his ankle, a Chinese soldier placed his rifle to Sergeant Miller's head. As the stunned Chinese soldier and American captives looked on, the unarmed Father Kapaun walked forward and calmly brushed the rifle away from Miller's head.

"Let me help you up," said Father Kapaun.

"He [the would-be executioner] didn't know what to do," Miller later recalled. "Father Kapaun had that kind of effect on those guys."

Father Kapaun and the survivors were captured, stripped of their boots and jackets, and marched over eighty miles in subfreezing temperatures.

Knowing the Chinese executed many of those who were unable to walk during the Death March, Father Kapaun carried Sergeant Miller on his back.[15] They arrived at a hellish cluster of Chinese POW camps, the first known as Death Valley, and were later marched to a remote camp at Pyoktong, North Korea.

Father Kapaun immediately became an expert at secretly raiding the camp's food supply. Risking certain death, he courageously stole food for fellow prisoners who had been starved and tortured. He is credited with saving many men by administering aid to the sick, digging latrines, smuggling dysentery drugs, and raising the morale of the starving, disheartened American prisoners.

Infuriating the barbaric guards who both hated and feared him, Father Kapaun assembled the men for nightly prayers and daringly conducted a sunrise Easter Sunday service on March 25, 1951. The filthy, lice-covered prisoners gathered around the bone-thin chaplain, who held a crucifix made of broken sticks. He described the torture and condemnation of Christ to men who had themselves endured months of torment, mockery, and beatings. The brutal guards glared with contempt.[16]

Although the guards had long wanted to kill Father Kapaun, they held back to avoid an uprising from fellow captives. And according to surviving prisoners, they feared the mysterious Almighty from whom the chaplain derived his courage, strength, and protection. Father Kapaun constantly gave his own meager rations to others, and as he starved, he developed a blood clot and became sick with pneumonia. As Father Kapaun fell gravely ill, the guards came to take him away, taunting him in front of the other prisoners. "Where is your God now?" they mocked in perfect English as they led the emaciated chaplain away.

Rising in protest, the barely standing skeletal men of all faiths—and those of no faith—demanded, "Leave him! Let us take care of him!"[17] But the threatening armed guards refused. The sobbing men watched as Father Kapaun was led away to the "hospital," a death house where prisoners were left to die alone without food or water. And although he was painfully aware of the fate awaiting him, the chaplain saved his last consoling words for the emaciated and heartbroken men he loved.

"You should be happy for me," Father Kapaun said. "I'm going where I always wanted to go."[18]

Father Emil Kapaun was originally thought to be buried in a mass grave near the Yalu River, but on March 2, 2021, the Defense POW/MIA Accounting Agency (DPAA) announced that he had been accounted for. Kapaun's unidentified remains had unknowingly been returned to the United States as part of Operation GLORY in 1953. In 1956, the army had declared his remains, as well as those of 848 unidentified others, as nonrecoverable.[19] One of those remains, listed as X-14550, was disinterred and transferred to the DPAA Laboratory at Joint Base Pearl Harbor-Hickam in Hawaii. Utilizing mitochondrial DNA analysis, dental and anthropological evidence, Father Kapaun was positively identified and later buried near his home in Wichita, Kansas, on September 29, 2021.[20]

The chaplain who served in both World War II and Korea was thirty-five years old. In a 2013 White House Medal of Honor ceremony, among other guests was one of the men Father Kapaun saved from execution, Sgt. 1st Cl. Herbert Miller. Father Emil Kapaun was posthumously awarded the Medal of Honor and is currently under consideration for canonization as a saint in the Catholic Church.

16

CHANGJIN

The world will know that free men stood against a tyrant, that few stood against many.

—King Leonidas of Sparta

THE BLOODY DEFEAT of the 1st Cavalry at Unsan, along with the staggering casualties and misery that ensued, was an egregious warning for top military leadership. A new and powerful force had entered the war, but General MacArthur and many of his staff continued to underestimate the Chinese Communists. Even after the slaughter at Unsan, MacArthur held to the tenet that there would be no full-scale Chinese intervention against United Nations forces. He ordered X (Tenth) Corps and other elements of UN forces to lead the northern assault to Yalu River on the border of North Korea and China. In late November, he assured Maj. Gen. John B. Coulter of the campaign's soundness. "You tell the boys that when they get to the Yalu [River] they are going home," he said. "I want to make good on my statement that they are going to eat Christmas dinner at home."[1]

X Corps, including the 1st Marine Division, elements of the army's 7th Infantry Division, and 57th Field Artillery Battalion were ordered to carry out General MacArthur's assault to the Yalu. Lt. Gen. Edward "Ned" Almond was handpicked by MacArthur to command the X Corps at Inchon. As X Corps commander, he was now in command of the controversial offensive to the Yalu River.

Disliked by several battle-hardened commanders, Gen. Almond managed to disperse the animus to commanding officers of both the 1st Marine Division and the Eighth Army. Wearing two hats, Almond achieved the momentary spotlight as he became both the new commander of X Corps, as well as General MacArthur's chief of staff. As one of MacArthur's most trusted advisors, Almond was also a personal friend. Near the end of October 1950, Almond was featured on the cover of *Time* magazine, adding to his confidence of the war's impending end.

While Almond was often accused of being egocentric and overly aggressive at the expense of his men, he was also hailed by General Eisenhower as one of the most promising men in the U.S. Army at the end of World War II. In the end, his service to country during both World War I and II, along with his ceaseless homage to MacArthur, likely garnered him plenty of favor with the Supreme Commander.

Decorated war veteran Maj. Gen. Oliver P. Smith commanded the 1st Marine Division. "O.P." Smith served in some of the Pacific's fiercest battles during World War II. He believed the plan to drive north to the Yalu River was extremely risky, if not foolhardy. He saw the mountainous terrain with its narrow entrance and exits as a looming trap for his marines. Just short of being insubordinate, General Smith is credited with intentionally slowing the march of his men northward. He wisely established supply points and an airfield, which later allowed for the harrowing but successful fighting withdrawal of X Corps through infamous Hell Fire Valley and on to the port of Hungnam—and likely saved the 1st Marine Division from annihilation.

For the marines and the army's 7th Infantry Division soldiers, General MacArthur's plans for Christmas dinner at home were tragically foiled. Thousands would never see home again—many of those who were captured and killed there would never be returned to American soil. The reckless decision to continue north to the Chinese border resulted in one of the most epic battles in American military history, the Battle of Changjin—remembered by Americans as the Battle of Chosin Reservoir.

General MacArthur's Home-by-Christmas offensive was an ill-conceived plan to advance north to the Yalu River bordering China. Tactical obstacles on the ground, such as extreme winter weather, mountainous terrain, and exit strategies were carelessly abandoned. With feckless miscalculation of the enemy, the plan was billed as the way to end the war. And for thousands of Americans, the Battle of Chosin Reservoir was indeed the end of their war. Warnings of Chinese intervention were plentiful, but the advice was not heeded. By the last week of November, the Chinese launched their massive Second Phase offensive of some 300,000 men.[2]

Between November 27 and December 13, 1950, those who fought at the Chosin Reservoir endured constant attacks by overwhelming numbers of Chinese forces. Enemy commanders prepared a strategy of surprise and entrapment of United Nations troops, ordering their armies to travel at night to avoid

UN reconnaissance aircraft. But Chinese forces were even less adequately prepared for the arctic cold than UN troops. Relying mainly on quilted uniforms, few enemy soldiers had gloves, and most wore inadequate shoes made of canvas and rubber. Food and firearms were limited, and some divisions marched more than 280 miles in less than three weeks before arriving at the Chosin battlefield.

Conditions were not much better for UN troops. Lt. Gen. Richard E. Carey was a second lieutenant when he fought to defend Hagaru-ri—the only way out of Chosin. S. Sgt. Watson Crumbie fought his way from Yudam-ni on the west side of the frozen Chosin. Both men lived the epic saga of Chosin Reservoir, considered by military historians to be one of the most brutal battles in American military history.

As UN forces marched toward the Chosin Reservoir, a Siberian cold front slammed into North Korea. Temperatures plummeted to historic lows of minus thirty-eight degrees Fahrenheit. Although wind chill factors were not measurable at the time, current estimates suggest that nighttime wind chill at Chosin reached as low as seventy degrees below zero.[3]

The innersoles of the marines' infamous shoepac boots froze as nighttime temperatures plummeted, resulting in devastating frostbite. Medics had to defrost frozen vials of morphine in their mouths. Frozen blood plasma was rendered useless in administering aid to wounded soldiers. Vehicle batteries lost their charge and weapons jammed as the lubricant froze. The battle would forever be christened the Frozen Chosin—and survivors were dubbed the Chosin Few.

Adding to the misery of the weather, the Battle of Chosin was fought on some of the roughest terrain of the Korean War. More problematic was the lack of roads in and out. General Carey explained the strategic disadvantages. "You only had one road, one point of entry and egress on each side of the reservoir," General Carey said. "And up to the reservoir, a dirt road was flanked by the hills on either side. A nightmare, an absolute nightmare."[4]

Gen. Ned Almond's X Corps troops were widely dispersed along a 400-mile front.[5] His orders perilously isolated units of the Army's 7th Infantry Division. Even more dangerous was the separation of the 7th Infantry and the marines.[6] On the main supply road was Koto-ri to the south and Hagaru-ri, the northern boundary of the main supply road. At Hagaru the road split—going west of the reservoir through Toktong Pass and fourteen miles north to Yudam-ni.

The 5th and 7th Marine Regiments, as well as heavy artillery of the 11th, occupied the northernmost sector of the reservoir's west side near Yudam-ni.[7]

The 1st Marine Regiment, including then 2nd Lt. Richard Carey's 3rd Battalion, occupied the important egress area of Hagaru, where General Smith had judiciously established a C-47 capable airfield. The 245 men of Fox Company/7th Marines protected one of most vital areas at Chosin, the important road between Hagaru and Yudam-ni. Although UN troops had a combined effective strength of 25,473, the U.S. Marines occupying the perimeter of the reservoir numbered only 12,000.[8]

Occupying the east side of the frozen reservoir were elements of the army's 7th Infantry Division. The understrength and hastily formed Regimental Combat Team 31 (RCT-31)—later called Task Force Faith—consisted of 2,500 Americans and approximately 700 KATUSA soldiers (Korean Augmentation to the United States Army). Two decorated World War II heroes, Col. Allan D. MacLean and Lt. Col. Don Carlos Faith, originally commanded the unit. Thirty-two-year-old Colonel Faith had served with the 82nd Airborne, jumping into Normandy on D-Day. Serving as the third and final commander of RCT-31, Texas Aggie Maj. Harvey H. Storms fought with Patton's 3rd Division in World War II. In letters to his wife, Helen, Storms described the difficulties that he and his men faced as they made their way to the east side of Chosin. "The news sounds good . . . then it sounds bad." Storms echoed the deep concerns of many commanders regarding only one point of entry and egress. "Supply—with no routes over which it can be moved quickly. . . . There are just no good roads here in this part of Korea—in fact, there are just no roads."[9]

Storms, who remained in excellent physical condition throughout his army career, relayed the extreme physical demands on the journey to the Chosin Reservoir.

> I'm so tired in body and mind. . . . I've been up and down mountains starting from a lowland elevation of about 5,280 feet and climbing steep inclines to about 8–9,000 ft. There are so many things I'd love to tell you about, but feel that it might endanger lives. . . . This war can't end too soon to suit any of us.[10]

By November 27, 1950, Col. Allan MacLean's RCT-31 advanced to within a few miles of the Yalu River. Dangerously split into two separate positions along a ten-mile stretch east of Chosin Reservoir, their unit faced temperatures of thirty degrees below Fahrenheit. In one of many letters to his wife, Major Storms described the desperation of the 31st Infantry Regiment.

All units of the 7th, because of severity ... have been so widely spread out, that if the enemy knew just how far, they could have walked right through us and have wiped us out. The 17th [Infantry Regiment] has been the only unit of the 7th Div. which has operated closely as a unit. ... Darling, the Lord is going to see me thru for you. Just pray for the Chinese and Russians to get sense enough to see the folly of their ways and cease hostilities.[11]

Helen, like most loved ones, immersed herself in the daily news of the unfolding tragedy. "I just had to cry as I was reading," she replied in a letter to her husband. "The news reports tell that even the gasoline is freezing."[12]

Inflicting heavy casualties, a massive Chinese force attacked Task Force Faith on the night of November 27. Reinforcements of a tank company and additional infantry battalion were promised but never arrived. The following morning, General Almond arrived by helicopter at Task Force Faith Command Post to reinforce General MacArthur's battle plan. Colonel Faith attempted to brief Almond on the gravity of the situation, informing him that two full Chinese divisions were on the verge of annihilating them. General Almond remained stoic.

"There aren't two Chinese divisions in all of North Korea!" Almond said in his orders to Faith. "The enemy who is delaying you for the moment is nothing more than remnants of Chinese divisions fleeing north. We're still attacking and we're going all the way to the Yalu. Don't let a bunch of Chinese laundrymen stop you."[13]

After hurriedly and unceremoniously awarding the Silver Star to Colonel Faith and two men "of his choosing," General Almond returned to the safety of his helicopter and headquarters. Knowing that his men were likely to be overrun, a thoroughly disgusted Colonel Faith ripped off the Silver Star and threw it in the snow. The tragic reality revealed that more than 120,000 Chinese Communist forces had encircled X Corps, and as many as 200,000 Chinese attacked to the west.[14]

On November 29, an entire division of Chinese Communist forces attacked Task Force Faith. The next morning, spotting a column of troops he believed to be his promised reinforcements, Colonel MacLean rushed forward onto the frozen reservoir calling for his men to stop firing. The column of troops, who were actually Chinese forces, opened fire on the colonel. He fell and stood up four times before Chinese troops dragged him into the bushes. Surviving POWs stated that MacLean died four days later of his wounds while enroute to a POW camp.[15]

Colonel Faith became commander of Task Force Faith. That night, Chinese forces launched another massive attack, capturing and killing hundreds of American soldiers and leaving 600 wounded. There would be no rescue attempts. Task Force Faith was surrounded and on its own. On Thanksgiving, Helen Storms put her children to bed and penned a frantic letter to her husband, Harvey Storms.

Thanksgiving, 1950:

Precious Angel . . . I have lived in darkness. The news says the enemy have you trapped. Our lives from now on will be so sealed together that no power on earth can take that unity away from me.[16]

Colonel Faith led a fighting withdrawal in a convoy of more than thirty trucks loaded with large numbers of wounded soldiers. Blocking the only road out, the Chinese stalled the convoy of wounded Americans attempting to withdraw. Refusing to leave the wounded, Faith and his men were overwhelmed by tens of thousands of Chinese soldiers. The men of Task Force Faith made a desperate last stand in hand-to-hand combat.

Faith led a daring attack, firing his pistol and throwing grenades until he fell, mortally wounded. Posthumously awarded the Medal of Honor, Lt. Col. Don Faith was hit by enemy grenade and rifle fire and died of his wounds. With more than two-thirds of Task Force Faith's 3,200 soldiers killed, wounded, or captured, Maj. Harvey Storms, highly respected by his men, became the last commander of the task force.

Storms attempted to lead an attack up Hill 1221, well-entrenched with enemy who were firing down at Task Force Faith's convoy and truckloads of wounded men. During the attack, Storms was wounded several times and was seen sliding down the hill with multiple bullet holes in his field jacket. Sgt. Bill Rowland, of Item Company in the 31st Infantry Regiment, reported seeing Storms as he made his way down Hill 1221. The sergeant later reported that he and another soldier loaded Major Storms on a truck with the wounded.[17]

Many survivors and officers of the 3rd Battalion believed that Storms should have received the Medal of Honor for his valor on December 1. In his book *East of Chosin*, Lt. Col. Roy Appleman described the heroism of the last commander of Task Force Faith. After leading an attack at the first blown bridge, the Texas Aggie engineer "was wounded, kept on going, and was wounded again."[18] In a written statement, a survivor and commander of Love Company, 3rd Battalion, stated that "Although wounded several times, he [Storms] insisted on walking. We finally got him to ride near the last road block after we rode along those railroad tracks."[19] While there are varying reports of exactly how and where he was lost, Maj. Harvey Storms died fighting—with his men.

Witnessing the carnage from above, marine air support watched in horror as thousands of Chinese ambushed and swarmed the convoy, burning and killing most of the wounded by hurling phosphorous grenades into the trucks full of badly wounded men. The severely wounded who remained alive were executed by Chinese soldiers in the trucks. In a last-ditch attempt to save the few remaining American soldiers, marine air support dropped napalm canisters, but the lead plane accidentally hit the front of the column, killing and severely burning dozens of surviving men.[20]

The surviving men of Task Force Faith, many of whom were burned and badly wounded, set off in small groups in a desperate attempt to make it back to Hagaru. Most were killed, captured, or died of wounds. Over the next three days, small groups of disoriented and wounded survivors stumbled into the U.S. Marines perimeter at Hagaru. Many of the battered men of the 7th Infantry Division slid and staggered across the frozen Chosin Reservoir to reach marine positions south of the reservoir. Some 300 severely frostbitten and wounded men were picked up by a marine rescue mission in jeeps.

In joining the marines at Hagaru, the battle-worthy survivors believed they had survived against all odds. But their fight was just beginning. Along with other 7th Infantry Division soldiers, they were organized into a provisional battalion attached to the 7th Marines. They would join the 1st Marine Division's historic seventy-mile breakout from Hagaru to the port city of Hungnam. Over mountainous terrain and along an icy single-lane road, the breakout was treacherous. For the men who managed to live through Task Force Faith, survival was once again dubious.

Of the 2,500 Americans of Task Force Faith, only 385 men were left to stand and fight their way out of Hagaru. Suffering nearly 90 percent casualties, over 1,500 men were wounded. More than 800 men were missing or killed in action, with 180 confirmed prisoners of war.[21]

RCT-31 was nearly annihilated east of Chosin Reservoir, but their delaying actions stalled the Chinese for five critical days. The men of Task Force Faith paid in blood for every hour of their gallant last stand east of Chosin Reservoir. By engaging Chinese Communist forces, RCT-31 ultimately contributed to the successful withdrawal of marines and X Corps from North Korea.[22]

The marines were facing their own nightmare—the Chinese relentlessly attacked at night and in the early morning darkness. Piercing the blackness of November 27, huge flares suddenly illuminated the ghastly, frozen landscape. Sounding like "a witches' conference," frightening screams, whistles, and horns announced the next terrifying human wave.[23] Marines at Yudam-ni were surrounded and attacked by two Chinese divisions while a third division blocked the vital road at Toktong Pass.

Wave after wave of Chinese soldiers attacked and infiltrated the 5th and 7th Marine positions, but the enemy suffered staggering casualties in their attempt to destroy the entire Marine garrison. Paying a heavy price, the Marines held the line. S. Sgt. Watson Crumbie witnessed the carnage at Yudam-ni.

> Our marines were in their sleeping bags and they found out their breath had frozen their zippers—they couldn't get out of their sleeping bags... some of them were bayoneted in their sleeping bags. The cold was so bad, your brain doesn't function, you couldn't even count to ten. There was no water, no food. You had no sleep, you would literally fall asleep while you were walking. And yet you had to fight thousands of Chinese.[24]

Toktong Pass was a narrow gorge along the main supply route and the only exit road leading to Hagaru. It was of critical importance in preventing Chinese Communist forces from cutting the 1st Marine Division in two. Just beyond the pass at 5,454 feet high, Toktong-san remained the highest spot surrounding Chosin Reservoir. The battle for "Fox Hill" would become one of the most legendary battles in Marine Corps history.

Capt. William Earl Barber was a Kentucky farm boy whose family farmed a plot of land near the 300-mile Licking River. By the age of thirty, Captain Barber had received a Purple Heart and Silver Star for his bravery on Iwo Jima. Wise beyond his age, he studied ancient Chinese philosophy and war strategy, a subject in which he excelled. As company commander of Fox Company, 2nd Battalion, 7th Marine Regiment, Barber received the unimaginable task of defending Toktong Pass against hordes of Chinese infantrymen. It was the only way out for the outnumbered marines at Yudam-ni.

By dusk, the 245 men of Fox Company were hurriedly digging in on Fox Hill. By 2:00 a.m., they were fighting for their lives against what seemed like the entire Chinese Army. The hill was aglow with flares, tracers, and thick smoke. Attacking enemy soldiers appeared as ghoulish silhouettes as they charged and fell in heaps around the men of Fox Company. As dawn lit the hellish landscape, the bloodstained snow revealed hundreds of grotesquely frozen corpses amid the stifling smell of phosphorus and Chinese garlic. Twenty-four marines were dead, more than fifty were wounded, and three were missing in action. Nearly one-third of Fox Company had become casualties of the first night, including Captain Barber, who received a bullet wound in his leg.[25] For the enemy, the first night on Fox Hill was even worse, with approximately 450 killed and hundreds more wounded.[26]

Marine command quickly realized that Captain Barber and the severely outnumbered men of Fox Company could no longer defend their position and would be massacred. The wounded Barber was ordered to withdraw from Fox Hill—but leaving the mountain pass undefended would entrap 8,000 marines at Yudam-ni. Captain Barber and his men decided to make a stand. Fox Hill was to be held at all costs.

Through sheer numbers, the Chinese had blocked the road at Toktong Pass. Captain Barber and his men were completely cut, off with no replacements or relief. After four days of savage attacks, Fox Company was surrounded by thousands of Chinese, and the marine perimeter had shrunk dramatically. Three-fourths of Barber's men had become casualties—annihilation seemed certain.

As Fox Company fought for their lives, the 8,000 battered and wounded marines from Yudam-ni attempted a fighting breakout for Hagaru. They would have to fight their way through the gauntlet of Chinese who now held the high ground along the only road out. On December 1, an ingenious but risky plan was hatched to rescue Fox Company. The off-road sneak attack would serve to rescue the besieged men of Fox Company in addition to capturing the high ground and securing Toktong Pass for the withdrawal. Col. Raymond Davis from Georgia and his 1st Battalion would travel stealthily over steep ridges and hills to reach Fox Hill. They would march under the cover of darkness to reach Barber and his remaining men, and sneak behind enemy lines to capture the pass. Colonel Davis's men received a new nickname, the Ridgerunners, which they proudly accepted as a badge of courage.

After enduring bitter cold and an intense firefight, the Ridgerunners finally reached Fox Company, a sight that those who witnessed would never forget. One of Davis's men described the scene. "We stood in wonder. Men bowed their heads in prayer. Some fell to their knees . . . as they witnessed this place of suffering and courage."[27]

Fox Company had been surrounded against insurmountable odds, sustaining continuous attacks for five days and nights. They emerged from their foxholes bloodied, barely able to stand or walk. Lying on a stretcher, Captain Barber hobbled to his feet with the help of a tree limb he had fashioned into a cane. He shook the hand of Colonel Davis. Surrounded by the frozen bodies of brave marines and more than a thousand fallen enemy soldiers, the two leaders were overwhelmed with emotion and unable to speak.

Captain Barber and the 245 men of Fox Company sustained 118 casualties. Collecting wounded and dead marines, the 1st Battalion and Fox Company set out for Hagaru. The dead and wounded were crammed together into battered vehicles. On December 3, the ragged and wounded column of men from Yudam-ni and Fox Hill began to trickle into Hagaru. Those who were seriously wounded were taken to the airstrip for evacuation. Of the eighty-two men of Fox Company who were able to walk, those who could still fight would join in the critical defense of Hagaru.

The marines at Hagaru were outnumbered in some units as much as ten to one. Surrounded on three sides with Chinese cutting off the withdrawal route, General Smith was concerned that Hagaru would not hold. General Carey described the Chinese battle organization.

> The only way they could overwhelm us was with sheer force of numbers. The first wave would all have weapons. The second wave would not all have weapons. They would pick up weapons from the first wave [of dead]. The third wave would be commissars with burp guns. Nobody retreats.[28]

General Carey knew what was coming.

> They [the Chinese] recognized the fact that East Hill was the key. We were halfway up the hill—and not with infantry—we had engineers, artillerymen, cooks, and bakers, whoever we could gather. You have to do it. You have to hold it.[29]

Carey described the desperate attempt to hold East Hill at Hagaru. He was given command of two reinforcing platoons. Their task was to hold off attacking Chinese Communist forces as they attempted to take the all-important hill. General Carey made the decision to occupy a foxhole with the wounded 2nd Platoon sergeant. The sergeant had been hit with grenade shrapnel, which damaged his eyesight.

Lt. Gen. Richard E. Carey and the battle for East Hill are immortalized on the Chosin Reservoir Battle Monument at the National Museum of the Marine Corps at Quantico, Virginia. One side of the bronze relief depicts a young Second Lieutenant Carey lobbing grenades at Chinese attackers. General Carey described the scene at East Hill near Hagaru at Chosin Reservoir.

No sooner had I entered the foxhole when the banzai charges began in earnest. Well, I threw three cases of grenades over the next several hours. I was encouraged by one of the best platoon sergeants in the Corps.... We held the hill in spite of the enemy's intention to annihilate us. A bloody night for all ... especially the enemy![30]

Newspapers back in the United States told the nightmare of Task Force Faith and of the 1st Marines being surrounded. Many suggested the entire 1st Marine Division would be annihilated and the only hope was a bitter fighting withdrawal. When *Time* magazine suggested that it was unlike the U.S. Marines to retreat, General Smith bristled, "Retreat, hell! We're not retreating, we're just advancing in another direction."[31]

At Hagaru-ri, 4,500 seriously wounded marines and army soldiers were evacuated on C-47s. Many of the dead, along with the letters of 10,000 troops, were flown out on the last flight out of Hagaru. "Every man became a rifleman," explained General Carey. They fought through the gauntlet of thousands of Chinese forces—nearly seventy miles to the port of Hungnam. "The hardest thing I ever did in my life was picking up bodies of the frozen marines who had been killed there," Watson Crumbie said of their departure.[32]

On December 6, the marines began the breakout from Hagaru-ri to Koto-ri through the infamous Hell Fire Valley. In an attempt to cut off the marine breakout, Chinese forces blew the one-lane treadway bridge over the thousand-foot chasm at Funchilin Pass. In one of military history's most amazing feats of engineering, eight C-119 Flying Boxcars dropped sections of a new bridge by parachutes, one section at a time. The last UN forces left Funchilin Pass on December 11.

There were 10,495 battle casualties at the Chosin Reservoir. Among the casualties were 4,385 U.S. Marines, 3,163 U.S. Army soldiers, 2,812 ROK soldiers, and seventy-eight British Royal Marines.[33] In addition, the 1st Marine Division suffered 7,338 nonbattle casualties, most of which were severe frostbite. Those who fought at Chosin Reservoir will never forget. For most, the lingering effect of crippling frostbite will forever remind them of the Frozen Chosin.

On Christmas Eve 1950, the battle-weary and wounded survivors of Chosin departed the port of Hungnam in a 193-ship armada. They were not alone. In the greatest humanitarian mass evacuation in history, Americans transported over 100,000 Korean civilians desperately fleeing the brutality of oncoming Communist forces. Two of those refugees were the parents of Moon

Jae-in, who in 2017 became president of the free and prosperous Republic of Korea.

Back home in Texas, the tragedies of the early days of the Korean War filled the news. Helen Storms, seven months pregnant with a son who would never know his father, scoured the *Valley Morning News*. One week after her husband went missing at Chosin, she wrote a desperate letter of hope that would be returned, marked "undeliverable."

December 7, 1950:

My Precious Husband:

Somewhere, I feel you are still living, still breathing, still wanting to be here with us. . . . For days I have failed to write you. I have not failed to think of you, cry for you, and pray for you.[34]

In far East Texas, another mother would grieve for her missing son. Some simply vanished from the earth, while others lay strewn across the frozen hillsides and deep valleys of North Korea. But those who loved them never abandoned hope. With unwavering resolve they awaited the return of their fathers, brothers, husbands, and sons to American soil—for years, decades, and for some, eternity. Delta Ray Steward was one of them.

PART V

HOME

17

GRAVE 182

It was on the ridges and sides of the mountain, and in the rice paddies of the valleys that the battles were fought and men died.

—Lieutenant Colonel John C. Cook, Q.M.C.

Dear Mrs. Steward,

This is in response to your communication concerning the disposition of the remains of your son, the late Private David D. Steward. Up to the present time, a report of burial and identification for the remains of your son has not been received in this office. In view of conditions existing in battle areas, there is sometimes considerable delay in the routing of information. . . . As burial information pertaining to your son is received from the overseas command, you will be notified.

It is the policy of the Department of the Army to carry out the wishes of the next of kin in making final disposition of the remains of our honored dead. Your request for the return of your son's remains to Atlanta, Texas has been noted in his file; however until such time as a report of burial and identification is received and pending the stabilization of conditions in Korea, I regret that it is not possible to comply with your request.

Sincerely,

James B. Clearwater Colonel, QMC Chief, Memorial Division[1]

Collecting the remains of soldiers killed on the battlefield, as well as those seriously wounded, proved a monumental task in Korea. The terrain made medical evacuations of wounded soldiers especially difficult. Evacuating wounded soldiers required navigating primitive road systems across punishing terrain to Mobile Army Surgical Hospitals (MASH units). The army purchased its first helicopter in 1941, but their use had been limited. The Korean War marked the first large-scale operational use of the helicopter in combat. Dubbed the "Angel of Mercy," helicopters transported more than 18,000 battle casualties to MASH units. The tactical use of helicopters was greatly successful in reducing the death rate of evacuated soldiers from 4.5 percent in World War II to 2.5 percent in the Korean War.[2]

During the Korean War, collection of fallen soldiers was infinitely slower and more difficult. Collecting remains from battlefields where intense combat continued made recovery extremely dangerous. Communications were inadequate, highways were almost nonexistent, and rugged terrain and unexploded ordnance presented a tremendous problem for Graves Registration units. Lt. Col. John C. Cook, whose name appeared on several letters in David's Individual Deceased Personnel File, described the difficulty of locating, transferring, and identifying bodies of fallen American soldiers from the battlefields of Korea.

> It was on the ridges and sides of the mountain, and in the rice paddies of the valleys that the battles were fought and men died. The removal of the dead to distant United Nations military cemeteries was a difficult and laborious undertaking. Such remains as could not be moved because of the exigencies of battle were hastily interred in foxholes, shell holes, or any area of soft earth which permitted a quick burial. These isolated graves were not always marked.[3]

Included in David's Individual Deceased Personnel File were copies of numerous documents, many typed by noncommissioned officers from battlefield positions. One such report was dated February 5, 1951, and titled "Investigation of Remains."

> At 1845 hours, 4 February 1951, a Corporal Harter contacted the 114th QM Graves Registration Collecting Point at Taegu, Korea and reported the remains believed to be an American.
> At 1100 hours Sgt. Charles E. Wilson of the 114th QM Graves Reg. Co. Collecting point at Taegu, Korea contacted SFC [Sergeant First Class] Shelton of the 1st Platoon, Co. A. . . . SFC Shelton gave Sgt. Wilson some papers and pictures. SFC Shelton received these papers and pictures from Cp. Buckman [sic] and Cpl. Dziecialowski who in turn received them

from a lieutenant. The papers consisted of some names and addresses, a birth certificate, an immunization record, and a social security card. All the papers, except the names and addresses, had the name "Steward, David D." printed on them.

SFC Shelton then directed Sgt. Wilson to a "Check Point" approximately 1-mile north of the village of Kumhwa-Dong, Korea; there Sgt. Wilson contacted Cpl. Claude Bachman and Cpl. Dziecialowski. Both men signed a statement stating how they knew of the remains and how they received the papers and pictures of the remains and the disposition of the papers and pictures. The half-sheltered remains were located at the top of a steep ravine near Kumhwa-dong, a small village north of Taegu.... [Sgt. Wilson] found 2 (two) identification tags on the remains. The tags were imprinted with the name and serial number, Steward, David D.

SGT. Charles E. Wilson[4]

After almost fifty years, Sergeant Wilson's report provided many answers—but many more questions. After four months of savage Korean winter, David's body was finally located, but verification of his identity was made under battlefield conditions.

According to the Defense Casualty Analysis System summary in September 2023, there were 33,739 American battle deaths in the Korean War (this figure does not include all in-theater casualties or missing presumed dead).[5] During the early months of fighting in the Korean War, battle deaths began to mount into the thousands. The task of removing and identifying Americans killed on the battlefield was extremely difficult, especially since battles were still raging amid constantly changing battle lines.

A few days after Sgt. Charles Wilson reported finding David's remains, Delta Ray received a letter from the Quartermaster General's office. She immediately sent a letter to William, awaiting transport to the front, notifying him that David's body had been found. In an odd twist of fate, one brother was finally leaving the bloody Korean War as the other was being cast into it.

Dear Mr. and Mrs. Steward,

This is in response to your letter ... concerning your son, the late Private David D. Steward. A copy of your letter has been forwarded to the Adjutant General, Washington, D.C., since matters pertaining to escorts come under the jurisdiction of that office.

> *The Office of the Quartermaster General has received a report from the Far East Command that remains tentatively identified as those of your son were temporarily interred in the United Nations Military Cemetery near Tanggok, Korea....*
>
> *The identification of your son's remains was made under combat conditions and is subject to verification. When military conditions permit, the remains of our service men temporarily interred in Korea are evacuated to Japan where carefully trained personnel endeavor to effect final determination of identity. Until verification of the original battlefield identification is made in Japan, no action for the final disposition of the remains will be made. This procedure was established to insure that remains returned to the next of kin would be those of their loved ones. At such time as additional information concerning your son becomes available, you will be notified.*
>
> *Sincerely yours, James B. Clearwater Colonel, QMC Chief, Memorial Division*[6]

Only after thorough identification and proper processing were remains returned to the United States in accordance with the wishes of next of kin. The American Graves Registration Service Group at Camp Kokura, Japan, was established in an effort to accomplish the tedious task. Although David's remains were found on February 4, 1951, along with dog tags and identifying papers, there would be no official identification until many months later.

As battles raged, fallen soldiers were interred in temporary United Nations cemeteries and collecting points, such as Taegu, until they could be transported to the central United Nations Tanggok Cemetery in Pusan. Personal effects found on the bodies were transferred to the Army Effects Bureau—and due to the large numbers of American casualties and battlefield conditions, fallen soldiers and their identifying personal effects were sometimes separated and mismatched. This resulted in further confusion in the identification process. In such cases, men were temporarily interred with grave markers stating their presumed identities.

Like many soldiers recovered in Korea, David's personal effects were separated from his remains on the battlefield. The identities of David Steward and "Unknown Soldier X-5000" were now blurred. In a letter from the Far East Command, and in response to the many inquiries from David's mother, clarifications on the effects found on her son's remains were officially requested.

FROM: Far East Command Personal Effects Bureau
TO: Chief, Army Effects Bureau, Kansas City 1, Missouri

FOR THE COMMANDING OFFICER

This depot has been advised that the remains from which the property listed ... was removed, has not been positively identified due to a discrepancy in physical characteristics. Therefore, the remains have been designated Unknown X-5000 pending further identification.

R. J. Provost Major, QMC Administrative Officer[7]

A later inquiry from the commanding officer addressed the identification of Unknown Soldier X-5000 and David D. Steward.

Subject: Change in Identification of Effects RE: Steward, David D.
Army Effects Bureau

Kansas City 1, Missouri

TO: Commanding Officer, Far East Command, Personal Effects Depot ... San Francisco

    1. Upon receipt here of shipment number fifty-two, piece one, package one hundred three was inventoried. An examination of the contents of the package revealed that a Social Security card, a birth certificate, and a photo bearing Private David D. Steward's name were included in this package. Therefore, the property has been inventoried under the name of Private Steward.

    2. It is requested that this Bureau be advised whether or not your depot still believes this property belongs to Unknown X-5000, Taegu Cemetery # 1.

S. Zablocki Captain, QMC Commanding Officer[8]

David's remains were first removed from the battlefield, then to a temporary cemetery in Taegu, near the location of his death. His remains were then transported to the United Nations Tanggok Cemetery in Pusan—all before official identification was made months later at Camp Kokura, Japan. And although mistakes were made, the Korean War marked the first time in American history in which a mass evacuation of remains occurred during hostilities. In previous wars, remains of the fallen were left in battlefield locations until hostilities ceased. The efforts of Camp Kokura's 8204th American Graves Registration made it possible for fallen soldiers to be returned to their families as quickly as possible, with little doubt that the returned remains were correctly identified. David's mother wrote dozens of letters, each receiving the same reply.

Dear Mrs. Steward:

We regret that we are unable at this time to complete the identification of your son's remains. . . . It is the policy of the Department of the Army to comply with the wishes of the next of kin in making final disposition of remains. However, it is not possible at present to foretell the time when your son's remains can be returned to the United States since their return is not only dependent on existing military conditions but also on the verification of the battlefield identification.

Sincerely yours,

James B. Clearwater Colonel QMC[9]

Delta Ray Steward did not give up easily. She was the essence of every fallen hero's grieving mother, and she simply could not let it go. Unable to abandon the fight to retrieve her son's remains, she continued her daily quest of getting him back, month after endless month. Neither she nor any member of the Steward family was ever aware of the discrepancies that existed in identifying her son's remains. Until David's Individual Deceased Personnel File was recovered, no family member was aware of Unknown Soldier X-5000. No family member saw the intercommand letters revealing the separation of David's personal effects and his battlefield remains. Until I received the Individual Deceased Personnel File in 1999, no one had seen David's field autopsy report or knew of the exact location or detailed circumstances of his death.

After nearly fifty years of ambivalence, the reports of my uncle's death provided me with a sense of closure, albeit a painful one. Unfortunately, that closure has been accompanied by the difficult decision to privately bear the burden of many disturbing details. Seven decades later, thousands of families continue their quest to unravel the tangled labyrinth of details regarding the death or whereabouts of their fallen loved ones. They search for answers in hopes of understanding and closure. And like David's mother, they will never abandon hope.

The recent return of remains of fallen Korean War soldiers illustrates the difficulty of identifying remains—especially in a war that occurred more than seventy years ago. Even with modern scientific DNA forensics, the task of identifying remains is painstakingly slow.

Forensic anthropology utilizing DNA was unknown during the Korean War. It wasn't until the end of the Korean War, in 1953, that James Watson and Francis Crick first identified the molecular structure of DNA. The first generation/practical sequencing of DNA did not occur until 1975, at the end of the Vietnam War.[10]

In simplified terms, DNA can be thought of as a highly accurate fingerprint. It is a powerful tool in identifying individuals, including ancient human remains. In all nucleated human cells, or those with a nucleus, there are two types of DNA. Nuclear DNA is found in the nucleus of cells. Mitochondrial DNA is found in small energy-producing cell organelles called mitochondria. Both types of DNA can be utilized as highly accurate identification tools for identifying human remains—resulting in a near perfect match depending upon the quality control of the sample.

Nuclear DNA exists as a linear copy in nucleated cells. It is made up of twenty-three pairs of chromosomes, or bundles of genetic information. In nuclear DNA, one chromosome of each pair is inherited from the mother and one from the father. Mitochondrial DNA is inherited from the mother. Because there are hundreds and even thousands of mitochondria in cells, mitochondrial DNA is much more plentiful.[11]

Both types of DNA degrade due to environmental and other conditions, especially when remains have been exposed to the elements for decades.[12] Because mitochondrial DNA is often more plentiful in remains and can be found in teeth and bone, it is especially beneficial in analysis of remains that have endured the elements. Since mitochondrial DNA is inherited from the mother, samples are donated from family members who are maternally related to the unidentified soldier. These samples are then compared to the DNA of the unidentified fallen soldier for a match.

Recent identification of remains from World War II and Korea are indeed rare; nevertheless, success stories exist—often representing a lifetime pursuit for living family members. One such success was the identification of Army Lt. Col. Don C. Faith Jr., killed in action on the east side of Chosin Reservoir on December 2, 1950.

Thirty-two-year-old Colonel Faith, commander of Task Force Faith, served with the 82nd Airborne in World War II and with the 1st Battalion, 32nd Infantry Regiment, 7th Infantry Division in Korea. As a result of Colonel

Faith's heroic actions at Chosin Reservoir, he received the Medal of Honor, posthumously accepted by his daughter, Barbara Broyles. Only four years old when her father left for Korea, "Bobbie" Broyles remembered her father well. "What I recall most about my father was that he was happy. I still can hear him laughing."[13]

Colonel Faith, originally listed as missing in action, was later designated as killed in action, but for sixty-two years Faith remained unaccounted for. In 2004, the Joint Prisoners of War/Missing in Action Accounting Command (JPAC) recovered commingled remains near Chosin Reservoir. The remains were sent to the Central Identification Lab at Pearl/Hickam, Hawaii, for identification. In 2012, after years of forensic work, Colonel Faith's remains were positively matched and identified with DNA obtained from his daughter and his brother. On April 17, 2013, Lt. Col. Don C. Faith Jr., one of the Korean War's greatest heroes, was laid to rest in Arlington National Cemetery, Virginia. After more than sixty-two years, Bobbie was presented with the folded flag from his casket.[14] More than 82,000 remain missing from World War II, Korea, and Vietnam through present-day conflicts.[15]

During the Korean War, although no such DNA fingerprinting existed, forensic anthropologists were employed to assist in identification of thousands of remains. Factors such as biological profile, age, race, and stature were considered, as well as the location of the body, personal effects found, and medical and dental records.

The first remains of fallen Americans in the Korean War arrived at Camp Kokura, Japan, on January 3, 1951. By January 30, nearly 5,000 remains were removed from cemeteries in Taegu and Tanggok where David was interred, and ultimately transferred to Camp Kokura.[16] Under difficult and unsettling conditions, the men of Camp Kokura's 8204th American Graves Registration worked long hours. In three-member teams, they identified, processed, and prepared soldiers for their journey home. Remains were shipped only when identity was determined beyond a shadow of doubt. Once the remains were ready, a formal dockside ceremony was held and a band played as the flag-draped caskets were loaded onto ships.

The 8204th adopted an intensely formal atmosphere of respect and honor for each fallen service member. Team members, including forensic anthropologists, army physicians, chaplains, and auxiliary personnel, were trained in the psychology of preparing remains. They were trained to avoid personalization of remains or to question the circumstances of death—treating them with the respect and honor deserving a hero who gave his life in the service of his country.

Robert Emmett Cassidy, a member of the 8204th, described his experience at Camp Kokura: "Even today I have flashbacks in the middle of the night thinking of processing all those fallen heroes from Korea. I wake up in a cold sweat."[17]

As of April 1952, remains of over 16,000 U.S. servicemen were processed and returned to next of kin in the United States. In 1955, President Dwight D. Eisenhower awarded a Meritorious Unit Citation to the men of the 8204th for their "significant contributions in returning the remains of fallen heroes to their loved ones."

Beginning each day after her morning prayers, Delta Ray voraciously read the news of Korea. She was deeply fearful that her eldest son, William, would also become a casualty of the dire situation on the Korean battlefront. William promised his mother he would not enter the Korean battlefield seeking revenge for David's death. Just before his arrival on the Korean battlefront, William wrote an emotional letter to Callie.

My Darling Wife,

Honey, tell Mom I'm going to look for David's grave [at Tanggok Cemetery] when I arrive in Pusan. I'm going to put my Combat Infantry Badge on it, remember, he always wanted it. Tell her she was right, I won't go into action with revenge in my heart. I will try to do what is right so I can come back.[18]

On his way to the front, William was allowed to visit his brother's grave at the United Nations Cemetery. Unable at first to find David's grave, he found a chaplain who directed him to the correct area of the massive Tanggok Cemetery. Walking row after perfect row, he finally arrived at the place he would never forget—plot C, row two, grave 182—the grave of his beloved baby brother.

William carefully placed his Combat Infantryman's Badge on the marker of grave 182, recalling the time he pinned it on his brother's shirt upon acceptance as a Central Union High School Cadet. He remembered Davy's beaming face as his big brother-hero saluted him. William's mind was flooded with thoughts of his wife and babies, of his mother and father, and the terrible pain they were now and forever condemned to suffer. He pondered his own fate in Korea, wondering if he would soon join his brother, but remaining oddly unshaken at the thought.

As William kneeled with head in hands at grave 182, the chaplain approached him, softly placed his hand on his shoulder, and offered his comforting words, "For he shall give his angels charge over thee, to keep thee in all thy ways." As the chaplain whispered the familiar passage from Psalms, William was overcome with emotion, recalling the day his darling Callie spoke those same words as his family left for the promised land of California.[19] Etched in his memory was the image of the old Ford pulling away from the piney woods he so loved—with little Davy sitting by his side.

As the battle-hardened combat veteran of World War II turned and walked away from grave 182, his tears turned to hollow desolation. He would soon report back to his unit, serving in his father's Rock of the Marne 3rd Division as a scout and machine-gun sergeant. William's job was to provide protection for the Forward Observation Team, Battery A, 955th Field Artillery Battalion.

In a few days he was back on the front line, once again a combat infantryman. But this was a different kind of war. In the lingo of politicians, this was a "police action" to be fought under a flag not his own. This war, unlike the last he fought, was a "limited war" with a new enemy and battle lines that were both changing and static. This "conflict" sent young Americans into battle not with the vast arsenal of democracy at their backs, but ill-equipped to fight an enemy in overwhelming numbers. In this war that was not a war, the price of every hill and valley was paid in blood—only to be lost, fought, and paid for again in the name of "conditional victory."

18

FINDING DAVY

I have given my baby boy. . . . Now that he has laid down his life in Korea, I ask that his brother be returned to us with the privilege of escorting the body of his beloved brother.

—Delta Ray Steward

BEFORE LEAVING FOR KOREA, William Steward asked his father to take care of his family in the event of his death on the battlefield. Reflecting on his days in Europe—the bitter house-to-house fighting in Schmidt and Kommerscheidt, the battle at Remagen, and the Rock Quarry—he realized he had been blessed with luck. And he knew it wouldn't last forever. He confided in his father that he would "never make it home again," feeling exactly as Bill Mauldin's Willy and Joe declared, "I'm a fugitive from the law of averages."[1]

William arrived on the Korean battlefront as he had in World War II, amid fierce combat and during one of the coldest winters on record. His baptism of fire in Korea was much like that in Europe, but he always held that the enemies he fought were vastly different. Communist forces in Korea seemed to have less regard for life of all kinds. In his first week on the battlefield William witnessed more than his share of savage atrocities committed against soldiers, innocent civilians, and even a small child in a captured village. To William, the enemy seemed accustomed to torture. Ingrained in their culture of war for centuries, torture was simply a brutal fact of warfare.

United Nations forces were fighting in areas they had previously secured at horrendous cost. It was a new kind of war for many reasons, most importantly due to the intervention of hundreds of thousands of Soviet-backed Chinese. As a result of Chinese intervention, the battle map was radically changed. On December 23, before William's arrival on the battlefront, the

Eighth Army's Gen. Walton "Johnny" Walker was killed in a jeep accident. He was replaced by Lt. Gen. Matthew Ridgeway—who famously led the 82nd Airborne in the D-Day assault at Normandy—jumping in with his division.

Upon entrance to the Korean War, William contracted dysentery during his first weeks of combat. Dysentery has been a continuous and well-documented problem for armies since the Crusades. During the American Civil War, soldiers were ravaged by dysentery, which accounted for more than 21,000 deaths.[2] In the Korean War, dysentery remained a significant problem for troops scrambling over steep, mountainous terrain. Without water, desperate soldiers drank from highly contaminated streams, or even worse, the rice paddies.

The success at Inchon and the difficult urban fighting to capture South Korea's capital city now seemed fruitless. The enemy once again controlled Seoul, and William arrived just in time for the massive Fourth Phase offensive of Communist forces. Entrapping American soldiers in a winding, narrow valley, Chinese forces inflicted massive casualties at Hoengseong. The well-preserved bodies of hundreds of Americans lay on the freezing ground, stripped of their boots and winter clothing, with their hands tied behind their backs, shot in the head. Almost one month later, marines marched past the dead Americans and bitterly posted a sign: "Massacre Valley, Scene of Harry S. Truman's Police Action. Nice Going, Harry!"[3]

The U.S. 2nd Division/23rd Regimental Combat Team, along with the French Battalion and South Korean forces, fought what is widely considered the Gettysburg of the Korean War, at Chipyong-ni, North Korea. Nearly 25,000 Chinese soldiers cut off and surrounded the 5,600-man United Nations force, which fought fiercely to drive off repeated human waves of attacking Chinese. The battle-hardened soldiers were now combat-wise, having cut their teeth in places like the first breakout of the Pusan Perimeter, Unsan, and the Chosin Reservoir. Stopping wave after wave of Chinese assault, United Nations forces stood firm. The Eighth U.S. Army, mauled in the early days of the war, "had risen from its own bitter ashes."[4] In the vicious combat leading to March 17, 1951, the Eighth Army and the ROK 1st Division once again expelled Communist forces from Seoul—marking the fourth time the capital city had changed hands.[5]

The Korean War became a back-and-forth political battle, with soldiers on the ground often serving as sacrificial pawns. Adding to the chaos and confusion, South Korea was teeming with guerrillas and Communist sympathizers, making it difficult for United Nations troops to distinguish friend from foe. In April 1951, Communist forces launched new attacks with more than 700,000 troops in the Chinese Spring offensive. William described the changing battle lines and onslaught of thousands of Chinese soldiers in his letters to Callie.

My Darling Wife & Babies,

... A few lines to let you know that I am ok. We finally stopped them but had to go all the way back to the Han River to do it. I thought for a while they were going to chase us clear out of Korea. They had me a little worried for a while. U.N. forces killed and wounded thousands of them before we could stop them. Honey, I don't see how they can keep on, every day. The U.N. forces kill thousands of them, but yet they keep on coming. . . . I love you with all my heart. Kiss my little darlings for me. I love you.

Your Bill[6]

The Korean War was characterized by political miscalculation and intrigue. None was more stunning than the president's action in April 1951. Amid public outrage and political controversy, Truman fired his Commander-in-Chief, Far East, Gen. Douglas MacArthur. Within forty-eight hours, the White House had received more than 5,000 telegrams in protest. On April 11, facing a political firestorm, the president addressed the nation, "Our aim is to avoid the spread of the conflict. . . . I believe that we must try to limit the war to Korea."[7]

Privately, Truman despised MacArthur for failing to respect the president's authority. When the two met on Wake Island, following his disastrous miscalculations on Chinese intervention, MacArthur shook the president's hand rather than salute him. Sadly, it was the men serving under them who suffered most from their arrogance and the bitter animosity between the two.

Public fallout from Truman's dismissal of MacArthur was enormous. Truman's approval ratings plummeted, and as the Korean War dragged on, he gave up his bid to run for reelection. MacArthur returned to the United States a hero, honored in parades throughout the nation. In New York City, General MacArthur was given one of the largest ticker tape parades in history. He famously addressed Congress in his "Old Soldiers Never Die" speech. "War's very object is victory, not prolonged indecision. In war there can be no substitute for victory," MacArthur defiantly proclaimed.[8]

Years later, Harry Truman's contempt of MacArthur and military leaders resurfaced when asked his reason for relieving General MacArthur of his command. A December 3, 1973, *Time* magazine article reported that in the 1960s

Truman had made an off-the-record comment about the firing. "I fired him because he wouldn't respect the authority of the President," Truman reportedly said. "I didn't fire him because he was a dumb son of a bitch, although he was, but that's not against the law for generals. If it was, half to three-quarters of them would be in jail."[9]

Truman's concept of "limited war" rather than unconditional victory quickly became the standard for American Cold War policy. The early months of the Korean War were marked by drastic changes on the battlefront. In the new limited war, battlefronts became more static. And after historic peace talks in war-scarred Kaesong on July 10, 1951, a stalemate quickly ensued. As warring parties held negotiations around the conference table, soldiers continued to fight and die on the battlefield for two brutally long years.

Hoping for peace agreements, the war dragged on, and men continued to fight and wait. At times when they lay in foxholes or during the lulls that existed later in the war, the soldiers shared their dreams and constantly talked of family. Sharing letters from home with their buddies, they proudly displayed crumpled photos of wives, babies, and family pets.

"Bill" was a young soldier in William's platoon. Too young to have his own wife and children, he was touched by William's letters and family photos. In one photo, baby "Mikie" sat on the ground playing with William's framed army photo, "Talking to Daddy." In a letter home, William referred to the soldier in his platoon as "not much older than Dave." William's letters to Callie revealed his genuine affection and concern for the inexperienced boy he had taken under his wing. "He's not a good soldier," he wrote. "He's always doing things that could get him killed. But I'm trying my best to teach him how to be a soldier and stay alive."[10]

Shortly before he was killed in action, the teenager Bill penned a poem on four small pieces of lined note paper. The poem was written for the baby son William so often spoke of. Decades later, in one of my father's frontline letters, I was astonished to find the poem, neatly written by the soldier known only as "Bill."

Daddy

Mikie, Daddy's here in Korea tonight, fighting under a bright moon.
But don't cry, he's alright. He'll be home soon.
He misses you—like you miss him all through the day.
He said to me after reading his mail, "I hope he's ok."
Daddy misses Linda and Momie too.

But remember his thoughts are on you the nights and days through.
When he comes home, you'll crawl up in his lap
And no more will you cry for daddy while taking a nap.
He knows that when you say your prayers, you mention his name.
Please dear God, keep my daddy the same.
I believe God has answered your prayers in more ways than one.
Just keep them up and daddy will be home soon
For his family and Mikie, his only son.
But just don't say them for him,
Say some for the boys and also remember me.
And we'll be home to our family and folks,
Safe too. You'll see . . .

—Written especially for Mikie
From a friend of "Daddy." Korea, 1951[11]

Every man was needed on the front line. And they continued to fight, sweat, freeze, to suffer dysentery and malaria, and to witness the horror of the Forgotten War. William's 135-pound frame quickly dwindled to 115 pounds and his letters home grew more disturbing and desperately dark. His mother knew he was running out of time. Her greatest fear was that both of her precious sons would never again return home.

Delta Ray Steward was a wise woman and a formidable piece of work. Bringing her son home for burial on American soil had been her singular mission. But now there was a new mission and a new sense of urgency. Without intervention, she feared the worst for William, who was fighting just north of the bloody Pusan Perimeter where his brother was killed. With die-hard resolve, she relentlessly attempted to rescue her eldest son from the jaws of death that took her baby. Delta Ray wrote to Colonel Clearwater, Chief of Memorial Division, twice each week. And each time, he responded.

The United States Army did not discount the letters and requests of Gold Star mothers. And while requests could not always be honored, each letter received a response from army leadership. In her front window, Delta Ray proudly displayed a Gold Star banner with one star, and a Blue Star banner with two stars. The banners represented a mother's loss of one son in service to country and two sons serving their country. Bereaved and obsessed by the loss of her son, she continued to fight her own battles, wielding her pen as a mighty sword. Her words exemplified the heartache and desperation of a mother's anguish.

Dear Sir,

Some time ago I wrote in regard to the return of my son's body. I also requested that his brother . . . be permitted to escort the body. . . . Now due to circumstances, I am writing in regard to the return of my son, Sgt. William Steward, as it seems my other request is impossible at present. Sgt. Steward is seriously ill. His enlistment period was up . . . but he was sent back into battle. He was in World War II. His family (wife and two small children) is in desperate need of him, . . .

All my sons are in service except David, who was killed. . . . I have given my baby boy, he was my only source of help and comfort. Now that he has laid down his life in Korea, I ask that his brother, Sgt. Steward, be returned to us as soon as he recovers. He has already done his part, his health is gone. He was wounded in World War II and has the Purple Heart, Bronze Star, and other medals. He was an outstanding and brave soldier. Please send him home at once. Please, Sir, as we need him. . . .

Respectfully, Mrs. W. H. Steward[12]

Reading my grandmother's letters and the frontline letters of my uncle and father was a sobering reminder of the Forgotten War's brutality. Her letters embodied the tormented soul of war's forgotten casualties—the mothers, fathers, siblings, and children of those killed and missing in the savage fighting. And while the suffering of war was not limited to the battlefield, my father's letters lay bare the thoughts and emotions of a combat veteran at the breaking point. The human misery, cruelty, and horrific atrocities of the Korean War would forever be ingrained in the souls of all those who endured it.

My Darling Wife & Babies,

. . . I am okay. Honey, we are moving north . . . we are now about 30 miles north of the 38th parallel. There are lots of rumors that we are going to go back . . . and wait for . . . a peace treaty, I sure hope that's right.

It seems like every time we move into another area we find a bunch of dead [civilians]. . . . Yesterday the first Sgt. told me to [arrange] a detail of 3 men to bury the dead ones. . . . There was a little boy . . . and an old man . . . the old man had been shot in the back by the Chinese soldiers . . . and down in the house there was a woman who had been shot . . . but there was nothing I could do for her. One of our boys was digging . . .

and dug into a Chinese soldier who had been buried there, they are everywhere.

It sure isn't any fun this crazy war. I've seen all of it I want to see. . . . It gets a guy to wondering sometimes, all these people over here are killing each other . . . over nothing, I am so tired of this sort of life . . . all men of earth should be friends and try to help each other. I have been thinking the last couple of days, I only want you and the babies. . . . I want my people and to be left alone and let me live a free life like a man has the right to. . . .

My son will never go to war if I can help it, that is a promise I'll keep to you, my Darling. Honey, if anything happens to me, I want you to tell little Mike what war is like, there is nothing glorious about it. It is nothing but one long nightmare of death and destruction. Also tell him how a man dies on the battlefield, even though he is a hero, he doesn't die like one, he has to die . . . with his face in the mud . . . they don't even get a decent funeral, they just dig a hole in the ground and roll him in it.

I guess you are wondering why I am telling you all of this. I am telling you all of this because I never want Mike to go to war. If anything happens to me, I want you to promise me that you will tell him what I have said.

I love you,

Your Bill[13]

As William's letters grew darker and more disturbing, the tenacity of his grieving mother finally paid off. After dozens of letters, David's remains were exhumed and shipped from Tanggok Cemetery in Pusan to Camp Kokura Japan for official identification. The identities of Unknown X-5000 and David Daniel Steward were finally determined to be one and the same. On August 3, 1951, at Camp Kokura Japan, a physician with the 8204th, Yukinari Kohara, confirmed the identity of David Daniel Steward.[14]

In late August 1951, William's commanding officer handed him a letter with instructions to report to command post. The letter stated that his brother's remains had been officially identified. At his mother's request, he was to serve as special escort for his brother's remains to Texas for interment. Overcome with emotion, William steadied himself and saluted the officer.

One week later, on August 27, Delta Ray Steward received the urgent notification for which she had prayed. Order Number 8-1079-C came directly from Colonel Broderick and was signed by John Nuzzo, the assistant attorney general.

> Sgt William Steward, 955th FA Bn, APO 301.
>
> Classification: URGENT
>
> EM [enlisted man] is ordered to report this Replacement Cen, and by air o/a 28 Aug 51 to US. EM is placed on TDY [temporary duty] w/6010th ASU, Oakland Army Base for the amount of time necessary to escort remains of brother, PVT DAVID D. STEWARD to place of final interment. Upon completion of leave EM will report . . . as directed for return to parent organization.
>
> BY ORDER OF COLONEL BRODERICK.[15]

Although he wanted more than anything to see his family and escape the horrors of the battlefield, William had tremendous anxiety about serving as special escort for his brother's remains. He knew his current emotional state was fragile. Uncontrollable symptoms came out of nowhere—panic attacks, insufferable insomnia, alternating rage and crying fits, and episodes of violent shaking. He had witnessed the death of his friends and heroes in two wars, agonizing over the dishonorable manner in which they were hastily covered and left so far from home. He wanted to bring his teenage brother home in a dignified manner, and for him to be treated with the honor and respect of a soldier who made the supreme sacrifice for his country.

As instructed, William reported to Tokyo, where he was issued clean uniforms and paid for the first time in months. For the remainder of his life, he was haunted by the smallest details of escorting his brother's body back to Texas, forever recalling that his name was called fourth among those waiting in line. After receiving flight information and orders for the civilian flight to Travis Air Base in California, he pinned his service ribbons onto a newly issued uniform that revealed his emaciated frame.

The plane made two stops, at Wake Island and Honolulu. Finally, on the third day of his trip, he saw a landmass through the window and called the flight attendant to his seat. His hands shaking badly, he placed his fingers on the window to still them.

"Is that California, ma'am?" he quietly asked.

She gently placed her hand on his shoulder and whispered, "Yes, Sergeant, welcome home." He placed his head on the window to calm his shaking body and disguise the tears flooding his weary soul.[16] William Steward and the boy soldier were going home.

19

PINEY WOOD HOME

Mom, I'm trying to come home . . . if I stay here much longer it will surely kill me.

—David Daniel Steward,
letter from Okinawa, August 1950

IN 1947, THE U.S. ARMY Transportation Corps established a program to repatriate the remains of nearly 172,000 fallen World War II heroes. The army's repatriation program was originally scheduled for completion in under five years—but just over four years later, American boys were coming home from Korea on mortuary ships that transported as many as 8,000 remains.

After arriving in the United States, remains were transferred to civilian passenger trains equipped with specialized army mortuary cars that listed their precious load as "Deceased Passengers" rather than cargo. The fallen heroes were delivered to fifteen distribution centers. Entire trains often consisted of one mortuary car after another, with sleeper cars for special escorts.[1] From coast to coast, these somber trains whined across the plains, providing everyday Americans with a sobering reminder of the price of freedom.

Nearly sixty years later, William's memories of bringing Davy home were vivid and precise.

> I looked at my orders once more to assure myself . . . I was not having some kind of bad dream. My orders were real. I was to report to Oakland, California. From there I would serve as military escort for David back home to Texas. One positive of my orders was that I would soon see my wife and my two children. When I left for Korea my son, Michael, was fourteen months old and my wife was pregnant with our daughter,

Linda. She was born while I was on the front line in Korea, [and now she was] walking and talking, but I had never seen her.[2]

David's remains, along with those of 603 other soldiers killed in action in Korea, arrived in Oakland aboard the SS *Valdosta Victory*. After arriving at Travis Air Force Base, William was driven to Oakland Army Base Repatriation Headquarters. After days of traveling, he finally arrived at the office of Maj. P. F. Hazelbaker to be briefed on his duty as special escort. William was provided with three days leave to see his family in Southern California while his brother's body was prepared for transport home. During his leave, he was to instruct his family on protocol for the full military funeral to be held in their hometown of Atlanta, Texas. He described the emotion-filled reunion with his family.

> My father's car pulled up at the main gate and I was waiting in full dress uniform. With my father was my mother, my sister, my wife and two children. Everyone was crying, even Dad. It just really got to me to see him cry so hard and I could hardly understand him when he asked me, "Where is David, son?" I told him the major requested more time to get him ready for transfer. My mother and sister were sobbing, and my wife was holding little Mike by the hand and Linda in her arms. My son recognized me right away and came wobbling to me, yelling, "Daddy, Daddy." But my new daughter was understandably upset and would have nothing to do with the strange man in uniform. Linda and I were seeing each other for the first time. The reunion was very emotional.[3]

Three days later, his family began their journey back to the East Texas town of Atlanta and William returned to Oakland Army Base to begin the solemn duty of escorting his brother's remains to Texas. Only two other soldiers were with him in the barracks that night—also escorting their brothers home. Decades later William described his feelings: "As I slid into my bunk a feeling of loneliness and fear swept over me. . . . I just lay there staring into the darkness."

While the army does not forbid special escort duty by immediate family members, it is no longer encouraged due to the psychological strain of escorting a loved one. Before the Vietnam War and especially during World War II and Korea, it was not uncommon for immediate family members to serve as escorts. But escorting the remains of fallen soldiers is intensely emotional, even when the soldier is unknown to the escort. For immediate family members, it can lead to lasting emotional trauma.

Army Sgt. Bill Daigneault, a Vietnam veteran who served as escort for the remains of nearly seventy fallen soldiers, conveyed the difficulties of escorting remains. "I had to hold back my emotions. I had to. It was real hard. Sometimes at the hotel, you'd just let it go. But you had to hold it. Somebody had to stand there and be brave enough to take everything."[4]

Returning to Major Hazelbaker's office, William received instructions for receiving his brother's remains.

> "You will be driven to a receiving warehouse where you will receive your brother's remains. Your belongings will be placed in your stateroom aboard the train, and you will be given final instructions by an officer who will meet you at the warehouse. Sergeant, I have always believed that any man who dies for his country is a hero. Your brother is a hero, take him home as one, Sergeant."[5]

"I will, sir," replied William, as he saluted the major and thanked him for his kindness.

On September 14, 1951, William signed a Receipt of Remains document for beloved son and brother David Daniel Steward. He was issued a briefcase containing an instruction notebook, six pairs of white gloves, three black armbands, white laces for his trooper boots, and an American flag. His family, already en route to Texas, would finally reunite with their two sons at the train station in East Texas.

William never forgot the Oakland Army Base warehouse and seeing David's flag-draped coffin for the first time.

> It was wide and as long as a football field . . . as clean as any building I have ever seen. The floor was made of polished concrete, shined to a high gloss. An aisle had been marked off in the center of the floor with two white lines about four feet apart. On each side . . . was a double row of flag-draped coffins. There must have been 500 of them . . . lined up in perfectly straight rows. The blue fields and white stars of the flags covered the hearts of the soldiers. In front of the door lay a coffin on a silver handled funeral cart. . . . The coffin . . . had a more square appearance than the others. I guessed it to be David's coffin in a shipping box all ready to go.[6]

William reported to a lieutenant who issued final instructions.

> "The deceased will ride all modes of transportation feetfirst. At such times as he is moved by funeral cart, he will be moved slowly and with respect and you will walk at attention by the blue field of the flag covering the coffin. The funeral home in your hometown has been notified; and at your request, your brother, Sergeant Earl Wayne Steward, has been placed on leave to assist you. At the funeral home you will remove the shipping box . . . and cover the coffin with the new burial flag. You will supervise a full military funeral . . . and at graveside you and your brother will fold and present the flag to the next of kin listed on your orders. No one else is to receive the flag. Are there any questions, Sergeant?"[7]

An army jeep with flashing lights led the slowly moving military hearse across the Oakland Bay Bridge to Southern Pacific Train No. 58. Standing still as the hearse passed by, people removed their hats and placed their hands over their hearts. William was deeply moved and grateful for the public reaction honoring his brother.

Months after the frozen ground of Korea thawed, William Steward was finally bringing his kid brother home to the old Beech Creek Cemetery in the small southern town of Atlanta, Texas. Dressed in his army best, his duty was to escort Davy's flag-draped coffin from Oakland, California, to their East Texas home. The boy soldier and his brother made two stops before arriving home; first in El Paso, followed by Fort Worth. In downtown Fort Worth, David's coffin was transferred to train No. 4 at the Texas & Pacific Railway Station.

For the remainder of his life William had a special, endearing love for the city.

> I was greeted at the Texas & Pacific Railway Station in Fort Worth by the passenger agent. He wore a blue suit with a black armband on his left sleeve and I was kinda surprised to see this. He told a station employee to take my gear, then walked with me to the baggage coach for the unloading of David's coffin.[8] I'll never forget as David was unloaded, the passenger agent stood with his hand placed over his heart.[9]

Well into his eighties, William remembered how the good people of Fort Worth stood in silence, with cowboy hats and hands over their hearts as the train pulled into the station. He spoke of a kind woman who offered to press his uniform before the final journey home and how so many had come to honor the fallen boy soldier. Just before David was loaded onto the final train in Fort Worth, William fought to hold back his tears. He placed his white-gloved hand on the flag-draped coffin and whispered, "We're going home, little brother. We're going home."[10]

Long into the night, the crowd of farmers, sawmill employees, and families gathered at the old railway station in tiny Atlanta, Texas. Still dressed in their work overalls, they dutifully awaited the return of the boy soldier and his brother. William remembered the scene as the train slowly pulled into his hometown. "Finally, the train began to slow and the lights of my hometown came into view. When the train came to a stop, I stepped out the coach door and onto the railway platform. I was shocked at the size of the crowd. . . . I could see my family waiting on the loading platform."[11]

Amid the quiet sobs and flashes of light from news cameras, David Steward's flag-draped coffin was unloaded onto the train platform. He was one of their own, still only a child—the semblance of their own children. Their faces lined with life and worry, many of the small-town citizens likely pondered the fate of their own boys as the war in Korea dragged on. Fighting to keep their emotions in check, David's two brothers slowly saluted as pallbearers loaded the hometown soldier into the hearse.

"I could hear sobs coming from the throng of people, and there were more flashes of light from the popping flashbulbs," William recalled. "I walked by the blue field on the flag and Bo [brother, Earl] walked one pace to my left. I suddenly found my emotions near the breaking point."[12]

As customary in the Deep South at the time, David was taken to his grandfather's farm to lie in state until the funeral. It was there, in the place he loved, that David had fished in the bountiful creeks and played his beloved guitar on his grandfather's front porch. And it was there, to his piney wood home, that sixteen-year-old David returned—wearing the uniform of the United States Army, pinned with his Purple Heart and the Combat Infantryman Badge he always dreamed of earning. With a twenty-one-gun salute and full military honors, David Daniel Steward received a hero's send-off. His soldier brothers folded the flag, which William presented to their heartbroken mother.

In the darkness of September 18, 1951, amid a large and solemn crowd, the boy soldier made his final journey home, his hero brother at his side. Some four years earlier, a child of the 1934 millennial drought, the Dust Bowl, and the Dirty Thirties, left his Texas home for the promised land of California. His sister remembered, "He was wearing his hand-me-down government relief overalls . . . and he had tears in his eyes. Little Dave just turned around for a last glimpse of our piney wood home."[13]

Nearly seven decades later, Helen recalled the day vividly. "I have seen that sad and beautiful little face in my dreams for so long, Bug. I don't think he ever really wanted to leave the old homeplace."[14]

Unlike so many Americans still scattered about the Korean Peninsula in unmarked and mass graves, young "Tex" finally returned home to a hero's welcome. He was laid to rest among his piney woods on September 21, 1951—exactly one year after he made his last stand on the battlefields of Korea. Eternally at his side lay his beloved brothers, eight-year-old Howard Neil and baby Kenneth.

For more than seventy years, David's official army records and the American Battle Monuments Commission continue to list him as nineteen years of age at the time of his death. And while his official birth certificate and Cass County Census records acknowledge his true age of sixteen, like thousands of underage soldiers, his army records were never contested or changed.

Like thousands of Americans who gave their lives "to defend a country they never knew and a people they never met," David's sacrifice in the Forgotten War was far too unbearable to remember. But nearly three decades after he was laid to rest, his brother's daughter, the niece he never knew—would not forget him. I had a towheaded baby boy and named him David. And like his Uncle Davy, endowed with the gift of music, when life allows he sits on the porch and plays his treasured Martin guitar.

PART VI
FORGOTTEN

20

THE ABYSS

A second's action would end everything. A few drops of desperation.

—Winston Churchill

AFTER BURYING HIS BROTHER DAVID, William Steward found little peace.

> I had nightmares. And boy, they were horrible nightmares, just like I was really there. I'd wake up and I'd be dripping with sweat. I had some bad headaches, and of course my shoulder hurt all the time where I got hit in Germany. I really wondered if that might be causing all of this. Every now and then I would be talking to someone and just start shaking for no reason at all. I figured it was natural for me to be sad after bringing David all that way home, seeing how bad it was for my family and all. But it felt like something more. I just didn't know what was wrong with me. It really put the fear of God in me though, because I thought I might be going off the deep end. I heard a lot of guys ended up that way, everyone called them "psychos." After the funeral, I went to Granddad Wood's house, then we drove back to California. I don't remember much at all about what happened. I guess I just blocked that all out of my mind. But I do remember we stopped at the Grand Canyon on the way back. It was the most beautiful place I'd ever seen. But it scared me to death standing out there on the edge. I was afraid I would just jump right off into it.[1]

During the highest intensity combat in Korea from June 1950 to the end of 1951, battle casualties skyrocketed to 460 per thousand—along with the incidence of psychiatric casualties. During this time, psychiatric casualties in

Korea were much higher than those recorded in Vietnam and equal to those seen in the highest intensity combat of World War II.[2]

For those who served in extended combat of both World War II and Korea, there was a new problem. Still untreated for the horrendous combat they endured in World War II, thousands of men found themselves once again on the battlefields of Korea—this time in a barbaric police action, characterized by quickly shifting front lines and horrific atrocities.

These battle-hardened soldiers were fighting a different war. Korea, they were told, was not a war—but a conflict that nevertheless took thousands of American lives. Unlike World War II, in which the objective was to defeat the tyrannical enemy at all costs, many American soldiers in Korea could not comprehend the rules of engagement, or for that matter, for whom they were fighting and dying. One 1st Cavalry infantryman from David's unit wrote his mother, "Mom, we don't even know what we are fighting for."

Psychological trauma deepened, especially for infantrymen who experienced sustained combat in both World War II and Korea. Since PTSD remained largely unknown until Vietnam, many untreated Korean War combat veterans were returning with symptoms of what is now recognized as complex PTSD.

Complex PTSD (C-PTSD) is differentiated from PTSD in that the psychological trauma is prolonged and repeated over months or years. Prisoners of war who have endured prolonged captivity and children who have been abused or neglected over several years have been diagnosed with complex PTSD. While not included as a separate classification in the *Diagnostic and Statistical Manual of Mental Disorders*, it is believed that individuals suffering from complex PTSD exhibit symptoms of PTSD in addition to other unique symptoms.

Complex PTSD is a relatively new concept in which there is a great deal of symptom overlap. Over 90 percent of patients with complex PTSD have identical symptoms of PTSD, such as nightmares, flashbacks, insomnia, or reacting adversely to loud noises. But patients diagnosed with complex PTSD also tend to develop a debilitating sense of despair about the world. They may isolate themselves due to negative self-perception, guilt, or shame, and they often develop an intense lack of emotional regulation leading to extreme sadness and explosive anger.

Treatment of PTSD in combat veterans has improved dramatically since the Vietnam War. But scientific research remains woefully inadequate for aging veterans who experienced sustained combat over several years—especially among World War II, Korean War, and Vietnam veterans.

William's duty to his country was to end in July 1951, two months prior to serving as special escort to his brother's remains. But the involuntary extension of his service required that he return to the Korean battlefront just two weeks after his brother's funeral. The days and weeks that followed were simply lost—other than his letters, no written record exists.

After David's funeral, his family returned to California. William and Callie rode with brother Mickey and his wife Donna. The family desperately wanted William to have a break after escorting David's body back to Texas. In just a few weeks he was to be back on the front lines of Korea, so the family decided to stop at one of America's most beautiful sites, the Grand Canyon. Over six decades later, Donna reluctantly described the side trip.

> Bill was just not the same person, he was on edge the whole time and he . . . well, he just didn't seem right. We tried to make conversation, we just tried to make the best out of the situation after David's funeral and have a good time before Bill had to go back. And of course, we were all just worried to death about him going back to Korea, so many boys were getting killed over there. We had perfect weather and the Grand Canyon was so beautiful, and I thought he would have a good time. But he kept looking off into that deep canyon, then he'd turn around and come back so fast, white as a sheet and shaking like a leaf. He told Mickey not to let him get too close to the edge.[3]

William was not the first or last troubled soul to feel the beguiling lure of the canyon; indeed, it holds the macabre record of claiming more suicide victims than any other National Park. Experiencing a lifelong battle with the "black dog" of depression, British prime minister Winston Churchill knew well the lure and terror of the abyss. Although he helped transform the course of human history, Churchill aptly described the turmoil of soul-crushing depression and standing on the edge of existence.

> I don't like standing near the edge of a platform when an express train is passing through. I like to stand right back and if possible get a pillar between me and the train. I don't like to stand by the side of a ship and look down into the water. A second's action would end everything. A few drops of desperation.[4]

Seeing the Grand Canyon for the first or the tenth time can be life changing. The ageless siren and her deep chasms have mesmerized millions—and devoured more than 700 enchanted but hapless souls. Something happened to William at the great abyss. In less than a week he was to return to Oakland Army Base before heading back to the Korean front—and neither he nor Callie believed they would ever see each other again. But after arriving in El Centro, William told Callie to "get the babies, we are leaving here."[5]

The next few days and weeks were a blur of Route 66 souvenir shops, boiling hot coffee, and nickel peanut patties—a cheap, energy-filled, rosy round brimming with sugar and peanuts. But as always, William sought his grandfather's wisdom and calming presence.

After wandering through Texas and Louisiana to "see my friends and family one last time," and spending time with his grandfather, William called his worried mother. He reassured her that he was on the way back to California to return to Oakland Army Base—but as he, Callie, and the two babies arrived, a military police car was waiting for him. Emaciated and tormented, William was handcuffed and whisked away as his sobbing family watched in horror. Years later, Callie tearfully recalled the scene, "Lord, he just looked so pitiful, even the MPs [military police] felt sorry for him."[6]

Unauthorized absence, even after burying your brother, is a serious offense in the United States Army. While many factors determine a soldier's punishment, on the thirty-first day of absence, the offense is considered serious and resolved through pretrial confinement and a military court-martial. In a letter to Callie, William expressed his fears.

> I am here at Camp Cooke, I don't know what will happen next. . . . Maybe someday all of this will be over . . . and we will never have to be apart again. Kiss the babies for me. . . . I love you forever.
> Your Bill[7]

After spending several days in solitary confinement, William was marched into an office where he crisply saluted and stood at attention in the presence of a hardened, by-the-book, middle-aged commanding officer. The room was filled with an eerie silence, broken only by the sound of shuffling papers as the major silently scanned William's file. After what seemed an eternity, the major lifted his head and quietly spoke the words William never forgot.

> I see you were in the 78th. Hell of an outfit. Hürtgen Forest, Remagen. Those boys were tough. . . . OK. The Purple Heart, Bronze Star, and some rough action in Korea with the 3rd. Sergeant, I see you've been on leave and I want you to know I am very sorry about your brother. But

that can never excuse your actions, Sergeant. What were you thinking? You know what it's like in Korea. You've been a good soldier in the U.S. Army for a long time. You have proudly served your country with great men, heroes. You had to know you couldn't overstay your leave like this, especially with young men dying every day over there. What happens to you, Sergeant, is not up to me. Son, you are in a lot of trouble."[8]

With his head down, staring a thousand yards into the polished concrete floor, William was at the lowest point of his life. As the officer motioned for the military guard to escort him to a new cell, William noticed a folded letter and photos on the desk next to his wallet and file. Before being led away, still staring at the floor, a disheartened William made a barely audible request: "Sir, may I keep the letter and the photos from my wallet, sir?"

After an excruciatingly long pause, the major replied to William's request. "Sergeant Steward, don't worry about the letter. I am aware of its contents. The letter will be in safekeeping for you and your family, but unfortunately, I cannot return it to you. That is the policy of this facility and the United States Army. You may keep the photos, Sergeant." Speaking to the waiting guard, he directed the corporal to remove the photos, "Once you reach his quarters, you may return them to Sergeant Steward."[9]

William was led away by the same tall and cocky young guard who had remained just outside the door during his time with the officer. "Here's your brand-new home for a few days, Mr. World War II hero," said the guard, who appeared barely out of his teens. With a sadistic grin, he flipped through the four photos as he pushed William into the cell. In a display meant for everyone in earshot, he loudly questioned William. "Who the hell is this beautiful dame? Think I'll try to look her up while you're doing time in here. I'm pretty sure she doesn't want to be with a no-account coward like you."

As William tried to control his rage, the insolent guard continued, pausing at David's army photo while reading the back of the snapshot. "Yeah, a great looking dame like that will never give a psycho like you the time of day again, pal." Sitting on the sheetless cot, the guard continued to taunt William, holding up David's photo. "A big World War II hero like you, back here in California while his friends are dying in those rice paddies over there. I guess you let your brother do the fighting for you."[10]

With the full force of his 115-pound frame, William rushed the guard in a fit of rage but was quickly subdued by two more guards who had gathered for the entertainment. His hands cuffed behind his back, he was pummeled into the concrete wall and finally fell to the floor. The next morning, still cuffed,

William had an egg-sized lump on his throbbing head and knife-like pain in his shoulder. He was quickly labeled a "psych case."

Under military law during both World War II and Korea, Army Regulation (AR) 615–360 was specific in provisions for soldiers who returned from the battlefield with combat neurosis.

> The court or any one of the personnel of the court, prosecution or defense, has the right to inquire into the existing mental condition of the accused . . . in the interest of justice.[11]

Under the provisions of section II, a neuropsychiatrist was often appointed as one of the medical officers in determining proper disposition of the accused soldier, especially in cases where combat fatigue or combat neurosis was suspected. Findings of the neuropsychiatrist were paramount in determining whether the soldier's combat neurosis was the result of his "line of duty." Additionally, the diagnosis of the neuropsychiatrist was presented to the board to determine whether the soldier's disposition would be accomplished by medical discharge.

Along with his worsening shoulder injury, William exhibited symptoms of what is now regarded as full-blown PTSD—and he immediately captured the attention of an army physician who specialized in neuropsychiatry.

The circumstances of William's unauthorized absence, along with his past performance as a decorated soldier, allowed for special leniency by the military court. S. Sgt. William Steward fought his way from the Normandy coast to the Rhine River, where he received the Bronze Star. He received a Purple Heart fighting in the Ruhr Pocket of Germany, still carrying a piece of shrapnel deeply embedded in his shoulder—and he fought against overwhelming odds on the battlefields of Korea. But after serving as special escort for his teenaged brother's body, twenty-eight-year-old William was busted from staff sergeant to private and sent to Camp Chaffee, Arkansas, to serve ninety days of confinement. This time, along with the lengthy period of preconfinement, was considered "lost time," after which he would immediately return to the front line of Korea to make up for his lost time. Although the sentence was lenient and later commuted, for the combat soldier who had proudly served in both World War II and Korea, it seemed like a death sentence.

William rapidly lost more weight, he was barely able to raise his arm, and his letters home, always reviewed by army staff, revealed suicidal tendencies. His symptoms included nightmares, severe depression, and withdrawal. He isolated himself and spoke only to the Camp Chaffee chaplain and the army neuropsychiatrist who gained his trust. Remembering him as "the army doctor who saved my life," he developed a deep respect and lifelong admiration for the man he knew only as Dr. Seminaro.

A quiet, well-respected physician, Dr. Seminaro specialized in combat neurosis. Decades ahead of his time, he possessed a keen intellectual understanding of combat-inflicted psychological trauma. He bristled at the humiliating "psycho" moniker and had no tolerance for the maltreatment of combat veterans. He was a strong advocate for suffering soldiers, and he wielded considerable and powerful influence on disposition boards. Dr. Seminaro immediately ordered that William be placed on rest and sent to Camp Chaffee Hospital for tests and surgery on his shoulder. William wrote to his worried wife.

> *My Darling Wife,*
>
> *Everything is okay. The Red Cross man came to see me today. I have been assigned to take care of the chapel . . . and a very kind doctor is helping me. Dr. Seminaro has helped me more than anyone ever has. Honey, maybe your prayers did some good.*
>
> *. . . I have been sick, but I am ok now. My arm is out of the sling but I still don't have much use. . . . I want to come home so bad, I don't know what to do. . . . You have been a perfect wife and have suffered so much . . . since you married me, you've had nothing but misery and loneliness as I have been away nearly the whole time. Honey, if I didn't have you and my babies to love me, I wouldn't care if I died or not.*
>
> *I love you, Your Bill*[12]

William's mood remained dark. As a result of the demeaning stigma attached to a diagnosis of combat fatigue, other soldiers shunned him. Psychiatric nomenclature was completely inadequate, resulting in a lack of understanding of combat neurosis—generically referred to as psychoneurosis. Unfortunately, psychoneurosis was confused with "psychosis" and the common term, "psycho" became the standard public perception of those diagnosed with combat neurosis.

Only after the Vietnam War, when PTSD finally received some legitimacy, was the stigma slightly diminished. As a result of the derogatory and lingering stigma, staggering numbers of World War II and Korean War combat veterans never sought treatment for PTSD, a disease that did not exist in name or understanding during their time. Among these aging veterans, the generational stigma associated with combat neurosis continues to persist decades later.

During a Christmas gathering, I was shocked to learn of my father-in-law's brother, who landed on Omaha Beach. Francis "Frank" Ganz landed with the hapless 29th Infantry Division on D-Day. A textbook case for the horrors of untreated combat neurosis, Frank physically survived the landing but was later gravely wounded in the fierce fighting to capture the city of Saint-Lo. After evacuation to the United States, he endured many months in a Veterans Administration hospital for treatment of his serious physical wounds—but like so many others prior to an understanding of PTSD, he remained largely untreated for his psychological trauma.

Living with his parents until the age of sixty-three, Frank was sometimes given a wide berth by family members, some of whom quietly described him as "crazy from the war." His nephew, a historian who knew well the intense combat Frank had endured, recalled that "He was a quiet old guy and a talented artist. I don't know if he had PTSD or if his war trauma was the reason he turned to alcohol or never married—but I never saw him act out in any way. He never talked about the war."[13]

A hero of D-Day, whose unimaginable sacrifice helped make possible our victory in World War II, Francis Ganz died alone in his room—thirty-three years after landing on bloody Omaha Beach.[14] Untreated for the painful and mysterious malady that possesses them, thousands of aging combat veterans like Frank currently live without empathy or understanding of the demons that hound their souls.

In studies of combat veterans who actually received some type of psychiatric treatment, 37 percent of World War II and an astounding 80 percent of Korean War veterans were diagnosed with current PTSD. Of the nearly 200,000 Korean War veterans who saw sustained combat, 24.2 percent became psychiatric casualties.[15] Military officials reported "very high rates of neuropsychiatric casualties" during the early months of the Korean War. Characterized by battlefields that were widely dispersed and shifting front lines, "forward psychiatry" remained a significant obstacle during the Korean War.[16]

Studies reveal that after experiencing combat decades earlier, these aging veterans continue to be plagued with life-altering symptoms of PTSD.[17] A National Vietnam Veterans Longitudinal Study revealed that nearly fifty years later, as many as 271,000 Vietnam veterans still suffer from PTSD and some form of major depressive disorder.[18]

After serving his country for eight years, two months, and two days, William received his honorable discharge coded for "Medical Disposition."[19] He was awarded 80 percent disability, and while his rank was restored, he never received his back pay. After being paid a reimbursement of $191.87 at the time of his discharge, William Steward walked away from the U.S. Army—but not the war that raged within him.

Before his death, I questioned my father about bringing David's body home and the weeks that followed. He often spoke of minute details but had difficulty articulating his feelings on more important issues. As he continued to talk, I listened without judgment. Finally, he began to divulge a profusion of incidents that likely had been sequestered in the corners of his mind for decades.

I had dear friends who endured some of the worst of war: a friend who was captured by the Japanese and endured the hell of the Bataan Death March, another who endured three years in a North Korean POW camp, and others who had seen vicious combat on Iwo Jima, at the Chosin Reservoir, and on Omaha Beach. Like my father, as these elderly heroes neared the end of their lives, there seemed to be a need to get things off their chests. They wanted desperately to tell their stories to someone they trusted, to someone who—without judgment—would simply listen. This effusion of unimaginable experiences and agonizing thoughts appeared to be medicine for their tortured souls. Sadly, many combat veterans of World War II, Korea, and Vietnam have been unable to confront the demons of war.

After combat in Europe, followed by the horrendous tragedy of his homecoming and the death of his eight-year-old brother—and finally upon the death of David in Korea—William was indeed a lost soul. As he aged, he was reluctant to discuss the events after David's funeral, but as I persisted, he finally whispered his innermost thoughts.

> Bug, it is a miracle that you are here. As I stood there on the edge of that Grand Canyon, looking into the most beautiful and terrifying thing I had ever seen, I was a millisecond from just giving in—I just wanted to fly off into it. I had watched and heard my friends die in the most horrible ways, ripped to shreds by machine gun and mortar fire, face down in a stinking rice paddy. I didn't want to die that way, but I knew it was coming. At one point I just resigned myself to get it over with. At least I would be near the people I loved—and you know, not in the mud or a stinking rice paddy but home on American soil.[20]

As William left Camp Chaffee Hospital for the last time, he saw a familiar face waiting for him. It was the compassionate army chaplain who had befriended and protected him through his darkest hours. As William embraced him, the chaplain placed a folded letter in his hands. "I was given this by the commander, son. It is something I know you wanted."

Leaving Wing C of the army hospital, William closed his eyes and held the letter to his pounding heart. On the outside of the envelope from Okinawa was the familiar handwriting of his brother David. Inside was David's letter, dated August 3, 1950, and a small piece of paper on which he penned his song "Blues in My Heart." It was the letter he requested months earlier from the officer's desk at the Camp Cooke guardhouse just before being led to his cell.

At the age of sixty-one, William finally received treatment from the VA for a diagnosis of chronic PTSD. But like the Korean War itself, my father's war did not end in victory. He would fight this war until the end of his days. Suffering several shoulder dislocations, William continued to fall from his bed during intense thunderstorms, the last time at the age of eighty—still ducking for cover from artillery fire.

21

FORGOTTEN CASUALTIES

I just get up and try to live another day. It might be the day they find Jack.

—DyAnna G., sister of 1st Cavalry MIA, Korea

INVISIBLE TO MOST OF US, casualties of America's wars are everywhere—in our homes, on school playgrounds, and in our hospitals. They live alone in nursing homes and on the streets of our cities. In a 2022 report to Congress, the National Coalition for Homeless Veterans found that 13 percent of all homeless adults are veterans.[1] The U.S. Interagency Council on Homelessness reported that more than 33,000 veterans were experiencing homelessness in 2022. Nearly half of these veterans are between the ages of thirty-one and fifty, and almost 50 percent have disabilities, including serious mental disorders.[2] Research has shown that veterans have a higher risk of homelessness than the general population, and combat veterans, especially those with posttraumatic stress disorder (PTSD), have an even higher risk of homelessness.[3] Even more shocking, the American Psychological Association reported that as many as two-thirds of homeless Iraq and Afghanistan veterans in one major sample had PTSD after returning home from the battlefront.[4]

While PTSD is belatedly well documented in scientific literature, relatively little is known about its effects on the spouses and children of combat veterans. The paucity of literature that exists, however, is chilling—some spouses and children of combat veterans with PTSD develop secondary traumatization. As a result, many have themselves been diagnosed with secondary traumatic stress disorder (STSD).[5]

The well-studied phenomenon of secondary traumatization is the transmission of stress from a traumatized individual to those close to them, such as counselors, spouses, or children. There is significant and compelling evidence of secondary traumatization among children of veterans with PTSD. Secondary traumatization as a result of war has most notably been identified among the children of Holocaust survivors, children of prisoners of war, and children of Vietnam veterans. Researchers have also found significant secondary traumatization among the children of World War II–Korea veterans diagnosed with PTSD.

It is important to note that not all veterans who experienced combat are diagnosed with PTSD, including those who have endured intense, sustained combat. Research indicates that some combat veterans may actually possess a greater predisposition to PTSD. But recent studies reveal that PTSD provides the significant link to secondary trauma in children, not simply the fact that their father endured combat.

Researchers found evidence supporting the argument that potential for secondary traumatization is increased among children of combat veterans diagnosed with PTSD—in addition to greater emotional impairment among the children of those combat veterans.[6]

Yale professor of psychiatry Robert Rosenheck described the effects of combat trauma and secondary traumatization upon the children of World War II combat veterans. "For these children," Rosenheck wrote, "life seems to have been a series of anticipation of, and reactions to, their father's moods, impulses, and obsessions."[7]

With recent advances in the biochemical and neurological mechanisms of PTSD, we are light years ahead of the old notion of combat fatigue—yet we are only beginning to understand the full effects of war upon the families of our warriors. Over half a billion dollars was allocated in 2017 for the treatment of PTSD in Iraq and Afghanistan veterans. But children and spouses of veterans with PTSD are afforded counseling only if deemed essential to the treatment of the veteran.[8] It is widely accepted that families, especially children of veterans with PTSD, are often deeply and adversely affected by secondary traumatization. Additionally, many studies have also shown that spouses of combat veterans with PTSD have higher rates of anxiety, marital distress, depression, and increased levels of stress compared to spouses of veterans without PTSD.[9]

Children of veterans suffering with PTSD are more likely to have social problems, difficulty coping with stress, and difficulty regulating emotions.[10] In a huge study of over 30,000 high school students in California, a University of Southern California professor found that one in four military children is likely to consider suicide—a much higher rate than nonmilitary children.[11]

The symptoms of children who develop secondary trauma are very similar to those seen in combat veterans with PTSD. Symptoms in these children may include emotional and behavior problems, dissociation, hypervigilance, and depressive problems.[12] Sadly, for many children who develop secondary trauma as the result of parental combat-related PTSD, the emotional and psychological problems continue to haunt them well into adulthood.

In one clinical study, researchers examined the effects of secondary trauma on the adult children of soldiers diagnosed with PTSD. Dinshtein, Dekel, and Polliak reported that adult children of combat soldiers with PTSD "exhibited greater psychiatric distress, higher levels of avoidance and intrusiveness, and lower capacity for intimacy" than those whose fathers served in combat but were not diagnosed with PTSD.[13] Some of those children continue to exhibit symptoms of secondary trauma for decades—or even lifetimes.

Nearly two million children have a parent or sibling who served in Iraq or Afghanistan since 9/11.[14] Many of these veterans remain untreated for PTSD. And as with World War II, Korea, and Vietnam veterans, the stigma of PTSD stubbornly persists, preventing many returning service members from disclosing combat neurosis or symptoms of PTSD. Many of these service members fear a diagnosis of PTSD will damage their future careers or military promotions. Remaining untreated, they are expected to make the immediate shift from a constant state of combat readiness and fear of death to domestic family life back at home. Unfortunately, their children and spouses often become collateral damage of the war that never ends for these veterans.

Even more disturbing, scientific research on PTSD has suggested that there may indeed be a genetic component. Still in its infancy as a relatively new and sometimes controversial field of study, epigenetic research has suggested that severe psychological trauma may actually result in the alteration of genetic information that is passed on to children. Epigenetics does not allow for alteration of our genetic code or DNA, but it is known to play a crucial role in gene expression.

In common language, epigenetic factors, such as environmental chemicals, nutrition, smoking, and severe stress often act like chemical light switches that are responsible for gene expression—turning some genes on and turning others off. It is well documented that humans and other animals produce powerful hormones in response to severe stress. These stress hormones have been shown to cause modifications in the DNA of animals, which in turn results in changes of gene expression—remarkably, these stress hormones may be the root of some epigenetic changes.[15]

The possible hereditary transmission of psychological trauma—and specifically PTSD—is not yet fully understood. But new and significant scientific research provides a compelling argument for further research into the transgenerational transmission of PTSD, especially in light of the vast numbers of combat veterans already diagnosed with PTSD.[16]

• • •

Sadly, the collateral damage of war is not limited to families of those with PTSD, but also includes the family members and especially the children of those who were killed, captured, or simply vanished as missing in action (MIA). Clinical psychologists often point to unique challenges facing families of the MIA. To give up on the return of a father or loved one creates guilt, but uncertainty often gives rise to intrusive thoughts, anxiety, and depression. Research has shown that significant unresolved grief is prevalent and long-lasting among the adult children of fathers who are MIA. One clinical researcher—herself the daughter of a missing-in-action airman, found that unresolved and life-altering grief was present in adult children of MIAs for as long as twenty-five years after notification of their father's MIA status.[17]

Many MIA family members spend their entire lives in a constant and ambiguous state of anguish. In some ways, they are the forgotten casualties of war, forever waiting for the return of their loved ones—with no confirmation of death, no resolution, and no closure. Their loss is ambiguous, their grief indefinite, and the tremendous emotional stress they must forever endure is unique and unfathomable.

"I call it the wound that never heals," said Rick Downes, the son of Lt. Hal Downes, who was shot down over North Korea in 1952. "After a while you get used to having it and it finds a place within you, and you go on, you live life."[18]

Twenty years of research into the death of my teenage Uncle David revealed voluminous detail, some of which will forever remain a heartbreaking burden on my soul. I learned the location of his death, the exact coordinates of his body, personal effects found on his body, and hundreds of other details. His Individual Deceased Personnel File revealed details for which I had long searched. And in some cases, details that may have been best left unknown.

There was much to learn about the tragic circumstances of David's death. And while many unanswered questions remain, after more than six decades there is at least a sense of closure. It is comforting to know that he was returned to his beloved piney wood home with his mother, father, and brothers. Unfortunately, for the family of men who are missing in action in World War II, Korea, and Vietnam, there is no closure.

"Our mom kept him alive for us," said the daughter of Lieutenant Downes. "I have his skates, his jersey, his wallet—every article you can imagine.... He was missing—he wasn't dead.... So we kept waiting for him to come home."[19]

> We had a wonderful upbringing, but every day of my life I wonder what happened to our father. We just know he was captured and marched off to a POW camp.
> —Evelyn B., daughter of MIA, Korea[20]

> My brother used to put me on the back of his Harley and take me to the five-and-dime for ice cream. I remember every single thing about him, he was a good brother. I don't have many years left now, but I pray every night that Jack will be brought home before I die.
> —DyAnna G., sister of MIA, Korea[21]

> It's been so long ago and you would think it would get easier... but it doesn't. In some ways, I think it gets worse. Every time I read an article or hear that one of our boys was identified in Korea, I get my hopes up. It just makes me think of him more, going through the same old questions we've asked for nearly seventy years. And even though I'm happy for the family of that young man, it just really makes it worse for me.
> —William B., brother of MIA, Korea[22]

Serving as group liaison for a return to Korea program, I had the honor of working with families of MIA Korean War heroes. Frozen in a perpetual state of ambiguity, their anguish and grief are heartrending. I traveled with them to Seoul, Korea, where 35,000 members of the Sae Eden Presbyterian Church paid homage to family members and those who gave their lives for freedom. The Korean people possess a grateful reverence for Americans who were killed, captured and died in prisoner of war camps, and especially for those who are still missing in action.

Since 2007, the Korean government and organizations such as Sae Eden Presbyterian Church have spent millions of dollars to fly family members of these American heroes to Seoul to be honored in weeklong memorial services and a once-in-a-lifetime journey. Family members are themselves treated as VIPs in what is often a first-time acknowledgement of the sacrifice their fathers and fallen family members made so long ago. And most importantly, there is finally acknowledgement of their own sacrifice as family of the fallen.

As liaison for MIA family members returning to Korea—just as I had done for my Uncle Davy—I spent many late hours studying the details of these soldiers and the locations where they were last seen. I studied their units, the battles where they made their last gallant stands, and the indelible faces which are forever ingrained in my mind and heart. I listened to children, sisters, brothers, nieces, and nephews as they recalled the smallest details of last seeing their fathers and family members. And as they conveyed their own unique stories, I witnessed a silent and immutable pain from each.

Although I never met them, I came to know these brave men just as I came to know and love my Uncle Davy. Meeting the people and visiting the land where these beloved men sacrificed their lives for freedom was both haunting and soul-lifting for families. For many, especially the aging children of Korean War heroes, these annual Korean events have provided a greater understanding of their fathers' sacrifice. The grateful South Korean people are free and prosperous as a result of the sacrifices made by their fathers and fallen family members.

Reduced to rubble during the war, Seoul is now a free and vibrant city, and once impoverished South Korea is now the tenth-largest economy in the world. Olympic stadiums and skyscrapers soar where battles once raged. Where South Korean people were once slaughtered as Communist forces poured across the border, children sing songs and play in schoolyards. Touching the soil where their fathers fought and died for the freedom of "a country they never knew and a people they never met," these American families—who have themselves sacrificed so much—are finally provided with a modicum of healing and closure.

The Defense POW/MIA Accounting Agency continues to oversee the recovery and identification of remains. With the return of fifty-five flag-draped containers from North Korea to the United States in 2018, there has been renewed interest in recovering remains. More family members are providing DNA samples in hopes of finding a lost loved one. But the son of one MIA explained the emotional upheaval that family members must endure in the effort. "You have to really watch your heart here because this all could just fizzle," said Rick Downes. "This could be nothing. It could be everything."[23] His sister, Donna, described the mixture of emotions that MIA families experience upon news of returning remains. "One family is going to get a set of dog tags. Dog tags can be right or wrong . . . but that's so much more than we used to have."[24]

Working with MIA families and learning the stories of those who made the supreme sacrifice is awe-inspiring. Utilizing the latest DNA technology, the remains of some of them were finally identified, including Sgt. Gilberto Sanchez. Nineteen-year-old Sanchez was a combat medic serving with the 32nd Infantry Regiment, Regimental Combat Team (RCT-31) as part of Task Force Faith. With temperatures plummeting to minus-thirty degrees Fahrenheit, Sanchez and the few remaining medics were forced to defrost morphine syrettes in their mouths.[25] The teenager dutifully administered medical attention to his soldiers until the end, when he went missing on December 2, 1950. In January 2015, Sanchez was finally returned to his family in Texas.[26]

Maj. Harvey H. Storms was a Texas Aggie—and one of America's greatest heroes. Serving with famed Gen. George S. Patton in North Africa, Sicily, and the Italian campaign, he saw fierce combat in World War II as one of "Patton's Aggies." While Storms served on the front lines of World War II, his wife, Helen, had a son—the spitting image of his father. Sam Storms was just a toddler when his father reenlisted in the army after World War II. Promoted to major, Harvey Storms was allowed to bring his family to Japan while he served as part of the occupational forces. The family grew with the arrival of younger brothers Ernie, Billy, and finally Robert, the baby of the Storms family.

As the situation in Korea became more desperate, in true Aggie fashion, Major Storms volunteered for duty with Headquarters Company, 3rd Battalion, 31st Infantry Regiment. Major Storms and the men of Task Force MacLean/Faith have been immortalized as part of the doomed move toward the Yalu River, east of Chosin Reservoir.

I first met Major Storms's son Sam as we prepared for a Korean journey to honor veterans and those who were killed or missing in action. The weeklong extravaganza was sponsored by the Sae Eden Presbyterian Church in Seoul. The eldest of Major Storms's four boys, Sam memorized passages from his father's letters back home. "We have the letters that Daddy wrote. His letters were very positive and he volunteered to go to Chosin."[27]

Referring to General MacArthur's promise that the boys would be home by Christmas, Sam recalled his father's words in a letter home. "They tell us it's going to be a cakewalk and we will be home by Christmas," Major Storms wrote. "I don't think we'll make it by then, but I should be home by May [1951]."[28]

Burned into his memory, Sam Storms recalled the events of more than six decades earlier.

> I was nine years old when my daddy left Japan for Chosin. It was early in the morning and no one else was there on the train platform. We were on another train because we were going back to the States—Daddy's train

was just down the platform. Mama told me to watch the suitcases while she and the younger boys walked down the platform to see him off. I was sitting on a suitcase guarding our bags and he was waving goodbye to all of us. The last time I saw him he was about 150 feet away from me and he turned around and looked at me. He didn't wave or say anything, just looked at me. That's the last time I saw my father.[29]

Sam and Robert later made the emotional journey to Korea. Along with brothers Ernie and Billy, they have spent much of their lives attempting to discover the details of their father's death and hoping for recovery of his remains. Although their mother died only ten years after their father went missing, both Sam and Robert believed they fared better than most children of MIAs due to her incredible strength and faith. "Mama was a very strong woman," Sam said, recalling his mother's painful lack of closure, "but 'til the day she died, she was looking for Daddy to show up as a POW [prisoner of war]."[30]

Living on their grandfather's cotton farm, the Storms boys were blessed with family and friends who helped raise them. The neighbor men and entire community took them under their wings. They were encouraged to play sports and become involved in their church. As he grew older, Sam came to realize that his father was not coming home. "It was a fact of life," Sam said. "Daddy was in the war and he's not coming back. I didn't want to let the past hold me back, but not a day goes by that I don't think, what would Daddy say?"[31]

Sam and Robert went to as many of the "Chosin Few" reunions as possible, hoping they would find someone who knew what had happened to their father at Chosin. Sam recalled learning the details of his father's last days.

> I finally found two fellows who were likely among the last Americans to see him alive on December 1, 1950. They told me my dad was scooting down the hillside on his rear. He was unable to stand and they said he was shot full of holes, must have been a dozen in his field jacket. There was no blood because it was too cold for him to bleed. The two soldiers asked my dad to come with them to try to make it back, but he just said, "No, I have fought the good fight. You kids go over the hill and knock out the road block. I'll go back down and get the rest of the men."[32]

With a profound and unforgettable look of sadness, my dear friend Sam, son of Maj. Harvey Storms, simply whispered, "I guess that's one of the last times anyone ever heard from my dad."

Robert, the youngest son of Major Storms, was born in February 1951, after his father was listed as missing in action. He recounted his own feelings as a child of an MIA.

> I accepted the fact that I didn't have a dad. I didn't see myself as a victim because we had such a blessed upbringing. I didn't blame anyone. We are blessed with the legacy and heritage we have. But I've had a lot of demons—part of it from not having a dad. We have three kids now, awesome kids. And I didn't want my kids to not have a dad.[33]

Sam, Robert, Ernie, and Billy continue to search for answers into the circumstances of their father's death. At a Chosin Few reunion they found a man who told them their father was loaded on a truck with the wounded men of Task Force Faith. When Chinese Communist forces overran the convoy, the wounded were burned with phosphorous grenades and killed in the trucks. Still searching for answers after almost seven decades, Robert wondered if his father's remains would ever be found. "We heard he was on a truck with the dead and wounded when they burned it," Robert said. "Maybe this is why no remains can be found."[34]

Sam expressed the feelings of many MIA children: "I often wonder, what if? My daddy and I were both track athletes. Maybe he could have given me some pointers, . . . Yes, it's been lifelong for me," seventy-seven-year-old Sam said. "And yes, I still shed a tear."[35]

In July 2019, Sam received a cell phone call that he almost ignored. He noticed the caller originated from Fort Knox and he quickly picked up the call.

"Are you Sam Storms, the son of Maj. Harvey Storms?" asked the caller.

"Yes, sir. I am."

"Well, I have wonderful news for you and your family," replied the gentleman. "The remains of your father have been positively identified. His remains were among those returned from North Korea in 2018."

Sam and his brothers later met with officials who described the "near-perfect match" of his father's DNA to that supplied by many family members, including Major Storms's then ninety-four-year-old sister.

To most Americans, the return of Korean War heroes after more than seventy years—and the life-changing solace it brings to families—is unimaginable. But the lives of the Storms brothers will never be the same. Remains of the proud Texas Aggie were given a hero's welcome upon landing at Dallas Fort Worth International Airport, touching Texas soil one last time on July 14, 2021.

To honor him were six Korean War combat veterans, including Lt. Gen. Richard Carey, who fought in the Battle of Chosin, where Major Storms died. Finally home on American soil, Major Storms was reunited with all four sons as he was interred at Arlington National Cemetery.

Jon Miller Kitts and I worked together for many years at the Ferris Mfg. Corp. medical device plant in Fort Worth—never knowing the common denominator that linked us. Pfc. Joseph Roth Miller, Jon's father, was a marine's marine, a true warrior. Like my Uncle Davy, Joseph was killed in action in Korea. By the age of twenty-eight, he was a seasoned combat veteran. Joseph fought with the 2nd Marine Division in some of the fiercest battles of the Pacific during World War II, including the hellish fighting on Tarawa.

As the war in Korea deepened, Joseph once again answered the call of his country and the United States Marine Corps. Just as he did in World War II, Joseph found himself in one of the worst battles of the war at Chosin Reservoir. In the early morning darkness of November 28, 1950, the 7th Marines of the 1st Marine Division found themselves overrun by thousands of Chinese in brutal subzero temperatures. In attempting to rally the men of his platoon, Joseph exposed himself to intense machine-gun, mortar, and small-arms fire in the epic Marine battle at Yudam-ni.

Leading his few remaining men, Joseph fearlessly moved in the open from foxhole to foxhole, directing fire until he fell mortally wounded. As a result of Miller's heroic actions, many marines of Company C were spared as they fought their way back to Hagaru-ri. Joseph was posthumously awarded the Silver Star "for conspicuous gallantry and intrepidity while serving as Squad Leader of Company C," west of Chosin at Yudam-ni.

A loving mother and stepfather raised Joseph's son, Jon Kitts. Maxine, a World War II navy nurse, remarried when Jon was three years old. Jon recounted memories of his childhood with loving parents, but he never stopped thinking about his father.

> My stepfather was a remarkable and wonderful man, and he treated me just like his own son. I always resisted the temptation to ask about my father out of respect for my stepfather—but yes, I wondered about him. When I was in grade school, about six or seven years old, my mother took me to the basement of my grandparents' house to show me my father's medals. They gave me his medals when I got married.[36]

Later in life, Jon began the quest to learn of his father's heroism. In a frontline letter from his father, Miller wrote to Maxine, "I wish I could have been there for Jon." As an adult, Jon traveled to Korea to look for his father's name on the Korean War Memorial Wall. After nearly seven decades, he decided to use the name of Jon Daniel Miller Kitts, in honor of his father.

"I wish I knew more about him," Jon said. "And I always wondered what it would be like to go back and meet my father. I'm so proud to be his son."[37]

Each family has its own unique and personal story, but so many commonly share the indefinite grief of never knowing. For most family members, there is a gaping hole in their lives—and closure is simply not possible. As with my Uncle David, I never knew these young men, but hearing eyewitness accounts of their courage and heroism has enriched my life beyond measure.

Like Major Storms and Private First Class Miller, there are thousands of fallen heroes, from the beaches of Normandy to the mountains of Afghanistan. David Steward and others were faithfully recovered, identified, and ultimately granted a final journey home. Untold others lay nameless, hastily buried in mass graves near Chosin and Unsan, in the jungles of Vietnam, and deep on the ocean floor of the Pacific.

Many of the "lucky ones" like William Steward, Francis Ganz who landed on bloody Omaha Beach, and thousands more were cast aside, wounded in mind and body. For now, they live on through their children, brothers, sisters, nieces, and nephews—themselves caught in the web of war, forgotten casualties in the struggle for freedom.

22

THE LITTLE CHRISTMAS MAN

Freedom is never more than one generation away from extinction.

—President Ronald Reagan

AS THE SECOND WORLD WAR mercifully came to an end, the misery and suffering began anew for innocent civilians who managed to survive. Still living in fear amid persistent postwar antisemitism and having no homes to return to, Jewish survivors of the Holocaust were placed in displaced persons camps. Most of these facilities housed large numbers of Holocaust survivors, many in the American and British zones. Tens of thousands of elderly Germans, women, and children—themselves victims of the Third Reich's carnage—were slaughtered as the Red Army advanced to Berlin. The winter of 1945–46 was not kind to German civilians, and the Red Army wanted revenge for Germany's invasion of the Soviet Union.

Maj. Gen. Edwin P. Parker Jr., commander of William Steward's 78th Lightning Division, was exceptionally proud of his troops. After enduring the horrors of Hürtgen Forest, battles for the Schwammenauel Dam, Remagen Bridge, and cleanout of the Ruhr Pocket, Parker wanted as many of them as possible to see Germany's famed capital city of Berlin.[1] Since rotations home were frozen for most soldiers, Parker's request for movement to areas surrounding Berlin was granted.

In late November 1945, the entire 309th and 310th Infantry Regiments moved out by convoy to Berlin and surrounding cities as part of the U.S. Army of Occupation in Germany. At 2:30 p.m. on November 22, 1945, the men of William's 309th Infantry Regiment arrived in the once-great city of Berlin.[2] Back home in America, the clinking of glasses toasted the end of war and a joyous Thanksgiving Day. President Harry Truman officially proclaimed the day as a day of national thanksgiving. For the men who survived, there was plenty to be thankful for as families anxiously awaited the return of their sons, husbands, and brothers.

William and his buddy Hob peeked out of huge canvas tarps on the back of their troop truck to witness the total devastation of war. Ingrained in their souls, the sight would remain in their memory for the duration of their lives. The ruined city had been bombed and shelled into oblivion. The entire countryside was littered with burned-out tanks, rubble from destroyed buildings, land mines, and complete structural devastation. More than 80 percent of Berlin's historic buildings lay in enormous heaps of rubble, at the bottom of which lay untold hundreds of corpses. From Ersen to Dresden, almost all of the surrounding cities and towns lay in ruins. Most water and sewage systems were completely destroyed. Deadly epidemics of diphtheria, typhoid, and dysentery added to the misery of ravaged citizens who miraculously survived the iron fist of the Third Reich.

Most hospitals, clinics, medical equipment, and medicines were completely lost during the war. Every resource was utilized for the German war machine—there was nothing left. Like the famed Berlin Palace, Germany's economy was also left in shambles. Overprinting as a result of inflation rendered the Reichsmark currency almost worthless and the once-vibrant economy was reduced to a bartering system for the remaining starving citizens.

Surviving German civilians were literally in shock, searching through rubble and mourning the loss of millions. The numbers were staggering, not only for those the Nazis oppressed but also for innocent German civilians. The war left more than 1.5 million Wehrmacht soldiers missing in action. Most historians now put the total German military casualties at nearly 11 million—5.5 million dead and more than 5 million wounded. Most women were widows and many had children to care for in a land with little infrastructure, food, or supplies.

Adding to the misery of innocents, mass atrocities were committed against German women and children—and not until decades later did the suffering of German women and children receive proper acknowledgement.[3] It is estimated that as many as two million women and girls as young as eight were raped, and many thousands were murdered in occupied Germany. Over 100,000 such attacks occurred in Berlin alone, most in the Soviet-occupied zones.[4] Word spread quickly among German civilians, and in one town flooded with over 15,000 German refugees, over a thousand German women and children committed suicide as the Red Army advanced on the town.[5]

William and his buddies personally witnessed their share of atrocities against innocent women and children, but few ever talked about their traumatic time as occupying soldiers. It is widely accepted that atrocities were committed on all sides of Germany's occupying forces, but atrocities against civilians were officially considered as war crimes and more severely punished by the Americans and British. Tensions between the Red Army and U.S. soldiers were running high. There was little policing in Soviet-occupied zones, and when brought to the attention of commanding Soviet officers, charges of rape-murders were often suppressed and considered a part of the spoils of war. One Soviet officer later recounted his time in occupied Germany.

> We were young, strong, and four years without women . . . we tried to catch German women. . . . There were not enough women; the entire population run [sic] from the Soviet Army. So we had to take young, twelve- or thirteen-year-old. . . . We thought it was fun. Now I cannot understand how I did it. A boy from a good family. . . . But that was me.[6]

William's only mention of the atrocities he witnessed during the occupation was finding a woman and her two daughters surrounded by Russian soldiers. William remembered the incident for the remainder of his life.

> They were being . . . well, I'll just say, tormented by a bunch of drunk Russians. It seemed like every one of them we ran into was drunk and raising hell. We told the bastards we would shoot every one of them, and all but one ran away from us. They knew we meant it . . . they knew we didn't like the [Red Army soldiers] . . . and we didn't . . . we hated 'em. The other guy was real drunk. He pulled his pistol and wouldn't let go of one of the little girls. Well, we took care of that piece of trash right then and there—and that was one coward that never hurt anybody again. The terrified mama and little girls just ran away, but for years I kept seeing them in my nightmares. I guess I'll never forget those poor little raggedy, blonde-haired girls and their big blue eyes full of tears.[7]

Before the war's end, as Allied air attacks on German infrastructure increased, hundreds of thousands of German children were evacuated from areas, such as the Rhine-Ruhr area. A tragic irony of the Second World War, thousands were sent to camps and "safe countries," where most met a grim fate. While there is still no accurate estimate of how many German children under the age of fifteen died in camps, tens of thousands are buried in graves throughout several countries. From Denmark to Hungary and what is now the Czech Republic, many of the grave markers are no longer visible. Scattered about Denmark alone are nearly 7,000 gray gravestones, some simply marked as "Unknown Child."[8]

In March 1945, the Danish Association of Doctors decided that children in camps would not be allowed medical care, and for reasons still unknown, the Danish Red Cross refused to take action against this decision. As a result, more than 80 percent of the small German children landing on the shores of Denmark lasted less than a few months. A Danish physician and historian recently reported that in Denmark alone more than 10,000 German children under the age of five died in the camps. [9]

There were thousands of orphans, living literally everywhere in Berlin and surrounding villages and towns. Many German orphans from East Prussia fled the Red Army to neighboring Lithuania, working on farms in exchange for food. Others roamed the countryside in order to survive. Due to malnutrition during both world wars, German and Italian children were nearly a half-inch shorter in height than those of prior generations.[10]

From Lithuania to Ersen and Berlin, they lived in shell holes, bombed-out buildings, boxes, and hollow trees. Searching for scraps of food and clothing to keep warm during the brutal winter, they roamed the surrounding forests, along the railroad tracks, and in the rubble of buildings. They were barefoot, covered with lice, and hungry. As a result of their pack-like behavior and wolf-like wandering, these children were collectively called Wolfskinder, the wolf children. Although the true Wolfskinder were orphans who fled East Prussia into Lithuania, American GIs often referred to all German orphans as wolf children. Their parents were killed in the war, their homes destroyed, they begged for food—and in 1945, they quickly learned that American occupation zones were the most fruitful.

William Steward was devastated not only by the plight of those persecuted by the Nazis but also by the misery of the German orphans and wolf children. He collected chocolate bars, blankets, socks, and food, sometimes with the permission of the U.S. Army—but mostly without. He vividly recalled his time with the orphans, whom he never forgot.

> I felt so sorry for those little kids . . . hungry, they didn't have any parents. Well, we got what we called a ration, it had cigarettes, candy, and stuff. It had chocolate bars—and I got some of this stuff for the kids. So I got me a nickname in this little town we were occupying. The town was called Ersen . . . Ersen, Germany. And the kids called me "*Der*

Kleine Weihnachtsmann." It means "the Little Christmas Man." Well, anyway, it took me a long time to find out what it meant, but I finally got somebody to tell me . . . and I was like the Pied Piper. I'd go up the street and I'd have half a dozen of 'em following me. I'm proud of that name. I don't mind it at all.[11]

William recalled that most of the children were quite young, but some were older siblings looking out for those only two or three years of age. Mostly he remembered that many had no parents, no coats, no shoes, and no food. It mattered not to William that they were German orphans—the children of his enemy—only that they were children and they were hungry and cold. And he knew exactly how that felt.

"They were like little birds, picking up the crumbs around the GIs," William remembered. "Almost all the guys were very good to them, scrounging up food for them, but the old cook didn't like 'em. He came out where we were eating and threw a pan of freezing water on those poor little hungry kids. It just flew all over me, so I coldcocked him. Believe me, I got into a lot a trouble over that, but I didn't care."[12]

In the waning days of his life, William recalled the horrors he witnessed in war and during his time of occupation. Like so many other Americans, he could not reconcile fighting and dying in a war to end persecution and suffering, only to witness more of it after the war was over.

By the end of his life, William began to speak again and again of the German orphans. Haunted by the sight of ragged children during the winter of 1945, he tearfully recalled the tiny voices calling out to him, "*Bitte Joe, Ich bin hungrig* [Please Joe, I am hungry]." After all the death and destruction William had witnessed—or perhaps because of it—the sight of German orphans would forever be a part of his soul, occupying his wounded heart and mind until the day he died.

• • •

Pop was plagued with many of the same anomalies common to members of his generation. Having received cigarettes in their K-rations from the time they entered war as teenagers, many veterans of World War II and Korea suffered the ill effects of tobacco and a host of diseases such as emphysema, COPD, and congestive heart failure. As Pop approached his eightieth birthday, his health began to falter. I moved my parents from their old home place to a new home near Baylor Hospital in the sprawling Dallas/Fort Worth metroplex. The home was strategically located ten minutes from my home and ten minutes from the hospital, where I spent many late nights in the emergency room. In typical fashion, Pop became the star of the show on his many visits to the Baylor Hospital emergency room.

"Here comes our war hero," the nurses invariably announced.

"Sing us your song, Pop," they called out as they stuck him with an IV drip. And no matter his condition, he could almost always muster a few words to the tune of "The Wabash Cannonball."

I heard that eighty-eight a comin' with a mighty screamin' start,
  By the time I got to my foxhole, I'd won the Purple Heart . . .

With an encyclopedic mind full of history, music, and literature, his fading blue eyes danced into the hearts of all who encountered him. Whether recounting the last days of war or the rough-and-tumble Depression days with his mischievous brothers, his storytelling was forever the center of attention.

With better health care, Pop's health began to moderately improve during my last few years as a high school teacher in Grapevine, Texas, near Dallas. It was during this time that I came to know and understand my father as never before. He was more tempered. I rarely saw the dark and mercurial father of my childhood, who struggled day to day to survive his demons.

He desperately sought forgiveness for the trauma and hardship he heaped upon his family in darker times. And as Pop neared the end of his life, he seemed to win over the darkness—life was finally tolerable. In a frenzy of seizing the moment, I took my elderly father and mother everywhere. We visited the National World War II Museum in New Orleans, traveled to 78th Infantry Division reunions, and witnessed the final congruence of Greatest Generation heroes at the dedication of the National World War II Memorial in Washington, D.C. While continually abiding his intermittent trips to the emergency room, I was determined to help Pop live the last few years of his tragic life to the fullest.

Like many World War II children, I juggled a full-time job while caring both for my own family and ailing elderly parents. To add to the tumult of my life, I had recently undergone a complete metamorphosis from thirty years as a career educator to the competitive world of sports medicine. Logging over 100,000 air miles a year, my new corporate position finally provided me with the financial means to care for my aging parents but required constant road trips.

Pop and I had a ritual as I left town on a work trip. He would follow me to my car, give me a big hug, followed by "I love you, Bug." And as I climbed into my seat, he would gently pat the hood of my car exactly twice—as if to say, "OK, you can now leave safely, Bug." But this time he appeared especially fragile, struggling to catch his breath on every step. The first day of December 2006 would foretell the coming of a cold and bitter Texas winter. As he struggled to make his way out to my car, I pleaded with him to go inside. Finally he whispered in defeat, "OK. I love you, Bug."

I was pushing my luck getting to the airport in time for the December 3 Baseball Winter Meetings in Orlando. Hurrying out of the driveway, I caught a final glimpse of the old soldier, weary and frail. Walking with his right shoulder slightly lower—as he had done since he stepped out of the Ruhr Pocket, he was wearing his signature black jeans and western shirt. As he shuffled back toward the house, I literally stomped the brakes, making a defiant effort to watch his every step.

"You just never know," I whispered aloud to myself.

It was the last time I saw my father, and "I love you, Bug," were the last words I heard him speak.

Gone forever was the familiar laughter as he told the frightening, albeit funny, story of the German sniper who shot off the heel of his boot, or of the pretty French girl who kissed him after Le Havre was liberated. Never again would I hear his cracking voice vividly recounting the sound of bullet-to-metal pings—or the sound of his Thompson machine gun as he made his way through the smell of smoke and fear during the crossing of "The Bridge."

The old soldier was silent now. But forever burned into my memory was the heartbreaking sound of an uncharacteristic stutter as he merely attempted to say the word, "Korea." I would never again hear the stories of his lifelong band of brothers—Cliff Fortune, who died next to him at the Sieg River; Bernard Shea, Whitey, and Doc Richardson—killed at the Rock Quarry; or of his teenage brother, David—and that which could not be spoken. I counted the most notable achievement of my own complicated life as having stuck by the old soldier's side through thick and thin, demon and torment.

When finally he was gone, it occurred to me that the last several years of my life were dedicated solely to helping him feel the goodness, rather than the pain of a life so fraught with sadness and tragedy. Now that Pop was gone I wondered what might possibly exist in life to fill such a void—or if ever again anything could.

Like so many of the Greatest Generation, William Steward's life was at once a tragedy and an enduring love story, reading like that of a Shakespearean play. He was like so many World War II and Korean War veterans who simply came home, got jobs, and set about raising their families amid the silent agony that endured until the end of their days.

William was a beloved husband to his wife of six decades. He was a survivor of the cruelty of the Great Depression and Dust Bowl—the only one of seven brothers to reach the age of thirty-six. Like so many others of his generation, he was a combat veteran quietly discarded by those who no longer remembered his sacrifice.

He was a gifted musician and songwriter, an astute historian, and a naturalist at a time when it was not yet fashionable. At the depths of his soul there resided a true adventurer, who despite his meager earnings taught himself and his children to explore the natural world, to scuba dive, and to always love and respect the beauty of nature.

Like so many who endured the Second World War and Korea, he taught his children to judge others not by their stature in life or the color of their skin but by their heart. He taught me to help the downtrodden, as he had helped the German orphans—and to stand for justice, even if it meant getting knocked down. He taught me to love freedom and to honor those who sacrificed all in its hallowed name. Most importantly, he and so many members of the Greatest Generation taught their children to get up, dust themselves off, and fight for right, as they had been forced to do so many times.

Some twenty years later, after the unremitting delays of life, I reached the end of a long and sometimes painful journey to complete this story—a story of two small-town Texas boys. Brothers and combat veterans, they were indeed the likeness of millions of others. This is a story not only of their individual sacrifice but of every American who sacrificed for the liberty of others. From the trenches of the Somme to the beaches of Normandy and the frozen ground of Chosin, to the jungles of Vietnam and the deserts of Afghanistan—our warriors and their families have paid an unreckonable price for freedom. Like so many of their time and generations to follow, our warriors have endured unimaginable hardships to become a part of something bigger than life itself, something most of us cannot fathom.

They answered the urgent calls to defend the freedom of people and nations they never knew. They asked nothing in return—and many, especially those who fought to free the South Korean people, received just that. With scant acknowledgement of and treatment for the horrifying psychological trauma that lingers still with many who remain, they demanded nothing, expected no privilege or entitlement. Returning with the scars of war—those who were lucky enough—sought only to raise their families and quietly live out the remainder of their storied lives.

Fighting our own battles in a desperate race against the clock, the families of these remarkable Americans endeavor to pass on the memories and legacies of fathers, brothers, sisters, uncles, and friends. Waging a war against time, we hope to teach our young people the worth and, ultimately, the price of freedom. We ask them to remember a time when the American people let down their guard. And we ask them to learn from our past, when the cost of American military unpreparedness was measured not in dollars but in the lives of brave Americans strewn about the Korean countryside.

We ask our children to forget the notion that war is inevitable, but to remember Thomas Jefferson's steadfast words: "The tree of liberty must be refreshed from time to time with the blood of patriots and tyrants." Most importantly, we ask the leaders of our nation to deepen their resolve to care not only for the warriors from whom we ask so much but for their families, the forgotten casualties.

In a few years, the last of their breed will vanish from this earth, taking with them the priceless and complicated lessons of defending liberty. Like so many sons and daughters of these heroes, I am at once grateful for having known them and deeply saddened in witnessing the fading shadows of their lives.

Like so many of our warriors, being an American soldier defined the brief life of sixteen-year-old David Daniel Steward—a hero I never knew but always loved. Being a soldier was the defining point in the life of William, the Little Christmas Man. And in so many ways, being a soldier's daughter and niece has defined my own life. I will always see the world through their eyes.

You are men who in your "lives fought for life . . . and left the vivid air signed with your honor."[13]

ACKNOWLEDGMENTS

MANY WONDERFUL INDIVIDUALS have informed this narrative. It is befitting that my son, David Steward Sessions, great-nephew of his "Uncle Davy," was of paramount importance in the development of this book. Engaging his brilliant journalistic skills over many months, Dave's help and encouragement were invaluable in bringing this true story to life.

I was honored to interview some of America's greatest heroes. None was more important to me than Lt. Gen. Richard E. Carey. His knowledge of the Battle of Chosin Reservoir is unequaled—he lived it. This extraordinary patriot took me under his wing and never gave up on me. Watson Crumbie, another member of the Chosin Few, provided me with his incredible memories of the Battle of Chosin. I was deeply honored to learn from these great men; both are my heroes.

Larry Kinard, a Korean War veteran and the past national president of the Korean War Veterans Association, taught me not only about the Korean War but about the urgency of honoring those who sacrificed there. Mr. Kinard reviewed the manuscript in its earliest form and helped shape its content. He, more than anyone, helped me see the virtue of our sacrifice in Korea.

I am deeply grateful for Col. John H. Ansohn, a twenty-six-year U.S. Army and emergency physician whose authentic knowledge of PTSD was exceptional. David Murphy, my high school track coach and Uncle David's best friend, shared his beautiful memories of my uncle and the Depression years. James Sharp, combat veteran of the 8th Cavalry Regiment, provided me with personal insight into the vicious fighting endured by those in the regiment, including my Uncle David. Capt. Richard Halferty, a Korean War veteran and Gold Star brother: thank you for your compassion and your family's sacrifice. I was encouraged and learned from the Korean War veterans of the Gen. Walton H. Walker Chapter 215. All are heroes who have enhanced my knowledge of the Korean War. John Martin, of Ferris Mfg. Corp., took time out of his busy schedule to review an early version of the manuscript.

My dearest Aunt Judith Steward-Wilson endowed me with my most precious gift—the handwritten letters of my Uncle David from army camps and the battlefront of Korea. The words of my teenage uncle provided me with steadfast resolve to forever honor the memory of our fallen heroes.

My mother, Callie, lost her vision as I neared the completion of this book. She encouraged me to finish the story, anxiously waiting for me to read it to her. Sadly, she passed away just as I completed the manuscript. She was the personification of the selfless sacrifice made by devoted spouses of our combat veterans. My dear aunts Helen, Donna, and Alma Ruth provided me with important facts, which were integral in unraveling this complicated story.

I am grateful to my friends at Sae Eden Presbyterian Church in Seoul. My dearest friends, R. Adm. (Ret.) Kim Chong Dae and senior pastor Rev. and Dr. So-Kang Suk, allowed me to peer through the darkness of the Korean War into the light of freedom. Admiral Kim arranged for me to speak to hundreds of high school students in Seoul, many the same age as my Uncle Davy. After more than sixty years, the beautiful faces of these young South Koreans taught me that our little David did not die in vain.

I am eternally grateful to Jon (Miller) Kitts and to Sam and Robert Storms, whose heartfelt interviews gave me new insight into the lives of those who grew up without fathers. Through them, I have come to know Pfc. Joseph Roth Miller and Maj. Harvey Storms, two heroes who gave their lives for the freedom of others. I am forever grateful to the Storms family, for giving me the privilege of allowing Major Storms to "touch Texas soil one last time." It was indeed one of the greatest honors of my life.

I am thankful for the many family members of MIA and KIA who shared stories of their loved ones and provided me with a new understanding of the devastating—and continuing—cost of the Korean War.

I had extraordinary teachers. The brilliant books of Lt. Col. Roy E. Appleman, Clay Blair, T. R. Fehrenbach, Hampton Sides, and David Halberstam unraveled the mind-boggling complexity of the Korean War. But I also had mentors from the very different world of primatology. Without them, I would never have developed a love of research and science, which undoubtedly enhanced this book. I am eternally grateful to Dr. Jane Goodall and Dr. Biruté Galdikas, whose pioneering scientific work led me to some of the most remote regions of the earth. They provided me with far more than scientific knowledge. From their work, I learned that compassion is in no manner unique to the human species.

Acknowledgments

I am honored to display the incredible talent of Mr. Steve Walkowiak of SWmaps. An extraordinary map designer and son of a Korean War hero, Steve's beautiful Chosin Reservoir map is truly a work of art. I am eternally grateful for the World War II and Korean War veterans who shared their stories with my Grapevine High School students and faculty during my thirty years as an educator. To an amazing teacher, Ruthann Parham, thank you for believing in me. I am deeply humbled and appreciative for Andy Bronckers and Frederik Vranken, two special young men I met at the seventieth anniversary of D-Day in France. Every year, without fail, they make the journey to Henri-Chapell American Cemetery in Belgium to lay a wreath on the grave of my father's beloved friend, Bernard Shea, who was killed in action in World War II. I am grateful for my brother, sister, and mother, who long ago traveled this sometimes difficult journey with me. Finally, I am grateful and honored to have shared the life and memories of two combat veterans. Like thousands of unnamed others, William and David Steward embodied the true price of freedom.

NOTES

Prologue

1. Korean War Veterans Memorial, Washington, DC, https://www.abmc.gov/about-us/history/korean-war-memorial

Chapter 1: The Blue House

1. Lamott, *Bird by Bird*, 24.
2. Author interviews with William Steward. 1999–2006, Vivian, Louisiana, and Trophy Club, Texas.
3. American Battle Monuments Commission, 2022, accessed August 15, 2023, https://www.abmc.gov/node/533519
4. Defense POW/MIA Accounting Agency, accessed August 15, 2023, https://dpaa-mil.sites.crmforce.mil/dpaaFamWebKorean
5. Defense POW/MIA Accounting Agency, "Progress on Korean War Personnel Accounting," updated September 14, 2023, https://dpaa-mil.sites.crmforce.mil/KoreanWar/PersonnelAccounting
6. Ibid.
7. WDAF-TV/TNS, Kansas City, Missouri, subsidiary of FOX News, "Local Veteran Who Died in Korean War Finally Identified, Comes Home to Leavenworth." April 25, 2019.
8. Defense POW/MIA Accounting Agency, "Johnnie Johnson List," accessed August 16, 2023, https://www.dpaa.mil/Our-Missing/Korean-War/Johnnie-Johnson-List/
9. Estabrook, "Lady Tigers," 24th Infantry Division Association, accessed September 20, 2023, https://24thida.com/stories/estabrook_lady_tigers.html

Chapter 2: The Picture

1. Steward, David D., Certificate of Vital Record, Cass County, Texas, Bureau of Vital Statistics, Texas State Department of Health, Standard Certificate of Birth and Family Census Record for public school entry, March 16, 1943; Steward,

David D., Texas State Department of Health, certificate of birth number 10857, filed February 5, 1934, Bureau of Vital Statistics, Atlanta, Cass County, Texas.
2. Ibid.
3. Procter, Ben H., "Great Depression," *Texas State Historical Association*.
4. Ganzel, "Walter Ballard," *Dust Bowl Descent*.
5. "Honorable Discharge from the Army of the United States" (original handwritten document), Form Number 525, A.G.O. August 26, 1919.
6. Cook, Seager, and Smerdon, "The Worst North American Drought Year."
7. Kristen Steagall, "Twelve Things You Might Not Know about the Dust Bowl," *Mental Floss*, July 8, 2008.
8. Armstrong, Conn, and Pinner, "Trends in Infectious Disease Mortality," 61–64.
9. Author interview with David Murphy, July 11, 2022, Atlanta, Texas.
10. Ibid.
11. Author interview with David Murphy, July 12, 2022, Atlanta, Texas.
12. William Henry Steward, *Federal Census of 1940, Cass County, Texas*.

Chapter 3: Replacements

1. Linder, "Hitler's Trial Speeches," *Famous Trials*.
2. Author interviews with the Steward wives, Helen Steward-Reeder, March 2012, Phoenix, Arizona.
3. "Honorable Discharge from the Army of the United States" (original handwritten document), Form Number 525, A.G.O. August 26, 1919, 1.
4. Ibid.; U.S. World War II Draft Registration Card, military records for William Henry Steward, Serial Number 1287, Texas, April 27, 1942.
5. Fishback, "Did Coal Miners 'Owe Their Souls to the Company Store'?"
6. John Jackson Steward, *Federal Census of 1900–1910*.
7. Ibid.
8. "Honorable Discharge from the Army of the United States" (original handwritten document), Form Number 525, A.G.O. August 26, 1919, Enlistment Record, 2.
9. Gallagher and Pigeon, *Infantry Regiments of the United States Army*, 179.
10. Owen, "Dulce et Decorum Est," in *Poems by Wilfred Owen*, 24.
11. Gallagher and Pigeon, *Infantry Regiments of the United States Army*, 176–77.
12. "Honorable Discharge from the Army of the United States" (original handwritten document), Form Number 525, A.G.O. August 26, 1919, Enlistment Record, 2.
13. Gallagher and Pigeon, *Infantry Regiments of the United States Army*, 177.
14. Joy, "Historical Aspects of Medical Defense against Chemical Warfare," 90.
15. Fitzgerald, "Chemical Warfare and Medical Response during World War I."
16. "Honorable Discharge from the Army of the United States" (original handwritten document), Form Number 525, A.G.O. August 26, 1919, Enlistment Record, 2.
17. D'Este, *Patton: A Genius for War*, 254.

18. "The Big Show: The Meuse-Argonne Offensive," Doughboy Center, accessed August 30, 2023, http://www.worldwar1.com/dbc/bigshow.htm
19. U.S. World War II Draft Registration Card, military records for William Henry Steward, Serial Number 1287, Texas, April 27, 1942.
20. Author interview with Judith Ann Steward (sister of William and David Daniel Steward), August 3–4, 2022, Yuma, Arizona.
21. "Honorable Discharge from the Army of the United States" (original handwritten document), Form Number 525, A.G.O. August 26, 1919, Enlistment Record, 2.
22. "Texas in World War II," Texas Historical Commission.
23. *William H. Steward Memoirs*, compiled by Sherri Steward, 1999–2006, and David Steward Sessions, original videography of *William H. Steward War Memoirs*, 1992, digitized 2012.
24. United States Holocaust Memorial Museum, "Allied Military Operations in North Africa."
25. Rantz, "Hemolytic Streptococcal Infections," 231.
26. Author interview with William Steward, *William H. Steward Memoirs*, 1999–2006, Vivian, Louisiana, and Trophy Club, Texas.
27. Klinek, "The Army's Orphans," 102, 162, 179, 205–6.
28. Ibid., 107.
29. Matloff, *Strategic Planning for Coalition Warfare, 1943–1944*, 367–75.
30. Ibid., 197–98.
31. Ibid., 127–28.
32. Vento, "The U.S. World War II Troop Replacement Policy."
33. Klinek, "The Army's Orphans," 227–28, 327.
34. Forty and Forty, *Infantry Warfare, 1939–1945*, 88.
35. Hastings, "The Wehrmacht Was the Better Army."
36. Balkoski, *Beyond the Beachhead*, 223.
37. Klinek, "The Army's Orphans," 137.

Chapter 4: Baptism

1. Tillman, *The D-Day Encyclopedia*.
2. Miller, *A Dark and Bloody Ground*.
3. Bell, "Costly Victory in Hürtgen Forest," 35.
4. Phil McCombs, "The Human Face of Armed Forces," *Washington Post*, January 24, 2003, https://www.washingtonpost.com/archive/lifestyle/2003/01/24/the-human-face-of-armed-forces/1b60a953-d29b-4771-a009-108accad8736/
5. Author interview with William Steward, *William H. Steward Memoirs*, 1999–2006, Vivian, Louisiana, and Trophy Club, Texas.
6. Hanks, "Architecture of France."
7. Dave Sessions, interview with William Steward, 1992, Vivian, Louisiana.
8. Ibid.

9. Ibid.
10. Ibid.
11. Ibid.
12. Ibid.
13. Ibid.
14. Author interview with William Steward, *William H. Steward Memoirs*, 1999–2006, Vivian, Louisiana, and Trophy Club, Texas.
15. Dave Sessions, interview with William Steward, 1992, Vivian, Louisiana.
16. Ibid.
17. Ibid.
18. Ibid.
19. Author interview with William Steward, *William H. Steward Memoirs*, 1999–2006, Vivian, Louisiana, and Trophy Club, Texas.

Chapter 5: Miracle at Remagen

1. Lockhart, *Diehard*, 12.
2. Miller, *A Dark and Bloody Ground*, 190.
3. Ibid., 191.
4. Lockhart, *Diehard*, 17.
5. Ibid., 14.
6. Ibid., 20.
7. Ibid., 23.
8. Author interview with William Steward, *William H. Steward Memoirs*, 1999–2006, Vivian, Louisiana, and Trophy Club, Texas.
9. Diamond, "Assault on Ludendorff Bridge: The First Allied Crossing of the Rhine."
10. Ibid.
11. Drozdiak, "Veterans Bridge Enmity at Remagen."
12. Diamond, "Assault on Ludendorff Bridge."
13. Holles, *Unconditional Surrender*, 336.
14. The Division Historical Association, *Lightning: The History of the 78th Infantry Division*, 179.
15. Felton, "Luftwaffe Jets vs. Remagen Bridge."
16. Hechler, *The Bridge at Remagen*, 163.
17. Semmens, "The Remagen Bridgehead."
18. Author interview with William Steward, *William H. Steward Memoirs*, 1999–2006, Vivian, Louisiana, and Trophy Club, Texas.
19. "V-2s on Remagen; Attacks on the Ludendorff Bridge," V2Rocket.com, accessed September 3, 2023, http://www.v2rocket.com/start/deployment/v2s-on-remagen.html
20. National WWII Museum Service on Celluloid, *Minisode to the Bridge at Remagen*, accessed November 17, 2023.

21. Hechler, "The Significance of Remagen Bridge," *The Bridge at Remagen*, 233.
22. Ibid., 232.
23. National WWII Museum Service on Celluloid, *Minisode to the Bridge at Remagen*, accessed November 17, 2023.
24. Eggenberger, *A Dictionary of Battles*.

Chapter 6: The Rock Quarry

1. Author interview with William Steward, *William H. Steward Memoirs*, 1999–2006, Vivian, Louisiana, and Trophy Club, Texas.
2. Hastings, "The Wehrmacht Was the Better Army."
3. Author interview with William Steward, *William H. Steward Memoirs*, 1999–2006, Vivian, Louisiana, and Trophy Club, Texas.
4. Ibid.
5. Ibid.
6. Ibid.
7. Lockhart, *Diehard*, 25–27.
8. Dave Sessions, interview with William Steward, 1992, Vivian, Louisiana.
9. Ibid.
10. Author interview with William Steward, *William H. Steward Memoirs*, 1999–2006, Vivian, Louisiana, and Trophy Club, Texas.
11. Lockhart, *Diehard*, 207–11.
12. Author interview with William Steward, *William H. Steward Memoirs*, 1999–2006, Vivian, Louisiana, and Trophy Club, Texas.
13. Citino, "Death in the West."
14. Johnson et al., "Impact of the Homecoming Reception."
15. Ibid.
16. PTSD Basics, National Center for PTSD, accessed September 3, 2023, https://www.ptsd.va.gov/understand/what/ptsd_basics.asp

Chapter 7: The Homecoming

1. Hendin and Haas, "Suicide and Guilt as Manifestations of PTSD."
2. Pyle, "Ernie Pyle's Last Column."
3. Author interviews with the Steward wives, Helen Steward-Reeder, March 2011, and June 9–12, 2012, Phoenix, Arizona.
4. Ibid.
5. Author interview with David Murphy, July 11, 2022, Atlanta, Texas.
6. Author interviews with the Steward wives, Donna Wilson, October 28–30, 2017, Hemet and El Centro, California (based upon recollections as told by her husband, Mickey Steward).
7. Author interviews with the Steward wives, Callie Steward, April 25, 2017, Trophy Club, Texas (based upon conversation with William and hearsay recollections).

8. Author interviews with the Steward wives, Helen Steward-Reeder, June 9–12, 2012, Phoenix, Arizona (present at time of accident).
9. Ibid.
10. Author interviews with the Steward wives, Donna Wilson, October 28–30, 2017, Hemet and El Centro, California (based upon recollections as told by her husband and sister-in-law).
11. Author interviews with the Steward wives, Helen Steward-Reeder, June 9–12, 2012, Phoenix, Arizona (present at time of accident).
12. Ibid.
13. Ibid.
14. Steward, Howard Neil, Texas State Department of Health, Certificate of Death #11512, filed March 20, 1946, Bureau of Vital Statistics, Atlanta, Cass County, Texas.
15. Enlisted Record of Report of Separation, Honorable Discharge, January 22, 1946.

Chapter 8: Demons

1. Author interviews with the Steward wives, Helen Steward-Reeder, June 9–12, 2012, Phoenix, Arizona.
2. Ibid.
3. Ibid.
4. Bentley, "A Short History of PTSD."
5. K. Cook, "Dying to Get Home."
6. Ibid.
7. Alcott, *Hospital Sketches*.
8. Samit et al., "Posttraumatic Stress Disorder."
9. Bentley, "A Short History of PTSD."
10. Bell, "Costly Victory in Hürtgen Forest."
11. Owen, "Mental Cases," in *Poems by Wilfred Owen*, 8.
12. Atkinson, *The Guns at Last Light*, 325.
13. Slawenski, *J. D. Salinger*, 366.
14. Atkinson, *An Army at Dawn*, 147.
15. Axelrod, *Patton*, 117.
16. Atkinson, *An Army at Dawn*, 147.
17. Axelrod, *Patton*, 118.
18. Blumenson, *The Patton Papers*, 329.
19. *The Perilous Fight*.
20. Ibid.
21. Schultz, "The Breaking Point."
22. Ibid.
23. U.S. Department of Veterans Affairs Post-Traumatic Stress Disorder Processing Claims Improvement Act of 2021, accessed September 14, 2023. https://www.congress.gov/bill/117th-congress/senate-bill/1664/all-info

24. Zarembo, "As Disability Awards Grow."
25. U.S. Department of Veterans Affairs Office of Inspector General, Office of Audits and Evaluations, Report 20-00608-29, December 9, 2020.
26. Handwerk, "Over a Quarter-Million Vietnam War Veterans."
27. Flory and Yehuda, "Comorbidity between Post-traumatic Stress Disorder."
28. Ibid.
29. Glantz, "Investigation."
30. U.S. Department of Veterans Affairs, "VA Releases Veteran Suicide Statistics by State," September 15, 2017, https://www.va.gov/opa/pressrel/pressrelease.cfm?id=2951
31. U.S. Department of Veterans Affairs, *2021 National Veteran Suicide Prevention Annual Report* (Washington, DC: U.S. Department of Veterans Affairs, 2021).
32. Bremner et al., "Neural Correlates of Exposure."
33. Bremner, "Traumatic Stress."
34. Gurvits et al., "Magnetic Resonance Imaging Study."
35. Bruce et al., "Altered Emotional Interference Processing."
36. Author interviews with the Steward wives, Helen Steward-Reeder, June 9–12, 2012, Phoenix, Arizona.
37. Ibid.
38. Author interview with Donna Wilson, October 29–30, 2017, Hemet and El Centro, California.

Chapter 9: The Promised Land

1. Author interview with William Steward, *William H. Steward Memoirs*, 1999–2006, Vivian, Louisiana, and Trophy Club, Texas.
2. Ibid.
3. Author interviews with the Steward wives, Helen Steward-Reeder, March 2012, Phoenix, Arizona.
4. Author interview with William Steward, *William H. Steward Memoirs*, 1999–2006, Vivian, Louisiana, and Trophy Club, Texas.
5. Steward, David, D., Texas State Department of Health, Bureau of Vital Statistics, February 5, 1934. On file, Cass County Seat, Linden, Texas.
6. Steward, David Daniel, State of Texas, County of Cass Family Census Blank, March 16, 1943. Cass County Seat, Linden, Texas.

Chapter 10: Boy Soldier

1. David D. Steward Letters, Fort Ord, CA. CO-L, 8th Infantry Regiment, February 10, 1950.
2. "Kids in the Civil War."

3. Brooks, "Child Soldiers in the Civil War."
4. Ibid.
5. "Don't Count Him Out Yet!" As told to Tony Welch, American Veterans Center, accessed September 4, 2023, https://www.americanveteranscenter.org/2012/02/veterans-of-underage-military-service/
6. Roberts, "Uncovering Resilient American Soldier Audie Murphy."
7. Fontaine, "Meet the Youngest Surviving WWII Veteran."
8. Ibid.
9. Pollarine, "Children at War."
10. Stachura, "Hitler Youth," 479.
11. "16-Year-Old EC Student Dies in Korea."
12. "Individual Deceased Personnel File for David D. Steward," U.S. Army Total Command, file 293, 1999.
13. Steward, Judith Ann (sister of William and David Daniel Steward), presentation of David Steward letters to author, December 24, 2004, Argyle, Texas.
14. Ibid.
15. Ibid.
16. Ibid.
17. David D. Steward Letters, Fort Ord, California, February 10, 1950.
18. David D. Steward Letters, Okinawa, Japan, 29th Infantry Regiment, Korea, 1st Cavalry Division, July/September 1950.
19. David D. Steward Letters, Fort Ord, California, CO-L, 8th Infantry Regiment, May 6, 1950.
20. David D. Steward Letters, Camp Stoneman, California, CO-F, Replacement BN, June 21, 1950.
21. David D. Steward Letters, Camp Stoneman, California, CO-F, Replacement BN, June 28, 1950.
22. Bland, "Rheumatic Fever."
23. Ibid.
24. David D. Steward Letters, Camp Stoneman, California, July 3, 1950.

Chapter 11: The Hermit Kingdom

1. David D. Steward Letters, Camp Stoneman, California, and San Francisco, June 29, 1950.
2. "The Treaty of Portsmouth." For the text, see https://portsmouthpeacetreaty.org/process/peace/TreatyText.pdf
3. Fehrenbach, *This Kind of War*, 16.
4. Yoshiaki, *Comfort Women*.
5. Gersen, "Seeking the True Story."
6. Min et al., "Posttraumatic Stress Disorder in Former 'Comfort Women.'"
7. Asian Boss Media, "Life as a Comfort Woman."

Notes to Pages 103–113

8. "Crimes of Sexual Violence," United Nations International Criminal Tribunal for the Former Yugoslavia, accessed September 4, 2023, https://www.icty.org/en/features/crimes-sexual-violence
9. Asian Boss Media, "Life as a Comfort Woman."
10. "The Cairo Declaration," released on December 1, 1943, the Wilson Center Digital Archive.
11. Blair, *The Forgotten War*, 37.
12. Beschloss, *Our Documents*, 194.
13. Sparrow, *History of Personnel Demobilization*, 382–85.
14. Ibid., 383.
15. Blair, *The Forgotten War*, 6.
16. Ibid., 8.
17. Harry S. Truman Presidential Library and Museum, "Letters to the Commandant of the Marine Corps League and to the Commandant of the Marine Corps," September 6, 1950.
18. Blair, *The Forgotten War*, 13.
19. Maw, *Freedom Is for Those Willing to Defend It*, 163.
20. Fehrenbach, *This Kind of War*, 60.
21. Blair, *The Forgotten War*, 88.
22. Ibid., 90–92.
23. Ibid., 92.
24. Ferrell, *Harry S. Truman*, 322.

Chapter 12: Land of the Morning Calm

1. David D. Steward Letters, Okinawa, Japan, CO-F, 29th Infantry Regiment, July 1950.
2. Lopez, "Rededicated Korean War Memorial Lists Names of Fallen."
3. Defense POW/MIA Accounting Agency (DPAA), accessed September 4, 2023, https://dpaa-mil.sites.crmforce.mil/dpaaFamWebKorean
4. Alan Marsh, "POWs in American History: A Synopsis," National Park Service, 1998, https://www.nps.gov/ande/learn/historyculture/pow_synopsis.htm
5. Department of Defense, CNN Library.
6. Fehrenbach, *This Kind of War*, 4.
7. "Radio and Television Report to the American People on the Situation in Korea," Harry S. Truman Library and Museum, recorded by National Broadcasting Company, September 1, 1950.
8. "The President's News Conference, June 29, 1950," Harry S. Truman Presidential Library and Museum, discussion of "police action" terminology, accessed September 8, 2023, https://www.trumanlibrary.gov/library/public-papers/179/presidents-news-conference-0
9. Appleman, *South to the Naktong*, 8–12.

10. Blair, *The Forgotten War*, 89.
11. Helm, *Prairie Boys at War*, 59.
12. Blair, *The Forgotten War*, 99.
13. Fehrenbach, *This Kind of War*, 73.
14. Millett, *The War for Korea*, 138.
15. Cleaver, *The Frozen Chosen*, 66.
16. David D. Steward Letters, Okinawa, Japan, CO-F, 29th Infantry Regiment, July 20, 1950.
17. Blair, *The Forgotten War*, 132.
18. Ibid., 127.
19. Ibid.
20. Halberstam, *The Coldest Winter*, 150.
21. Fehrenbach, *This Kind of War*, 95.
22. Ecker, *Battles of the Korean War*, 6.
23. Catchpole, *The Korean War*, 22.
24. Blair, *The Forgotten War*, 137.
25. David D. Steward Letters, Okinawa, Japan, CO-F, 29th Infantry Regiment, July 20, 1950.
26. Berg, "Few Know of the 'Tragic 29th' in Korea."
27. Ibid.
28. Blair, *The Forgotten War*, 165–66.
29. David D. Steward Letters, Okinawa, Japan, CO-F, 29th Infantry Regiment, August 3, 1950.
30. David D. Steward Letters, "Blues in My Heart," Okinawa, Japan, CO-F, 29th Infantry Regiment, August 3, 1950.
31. David D. Steward Letters, Okinawa, Japan, CO-F, 29th Infantry Regiment, August 4, 1950.
32. David D. Steward Letters, Okinawa, Japan, CO-F, 29th Infantry Regiment, August 9, 1950.
33. "Korean War 1950–1951," 1st Cavalry Division Association, http://www.first-team.us/tableaux/chapt_04/
34. Ecker, *Battles of the Korean War*, 32.

Chapter 13: Stand or Die

1. David D. Steward Letters, Okinawa, Japan, CO-F, 29th Infantry Regiment, August 1950.
2. Bell, "South Korea/U.S. Remember Korean War Sacrifices."
3. Alexander, *Korea: The First War We Lost*, 127.
4. David D. Steward Letters, Okinawa, Japan, August 16, 1950.
5. Bradbury. *Dandelion Wine*, 151.
6. Halberstam. *The Coldest Winter*, 150.

7. David D. Steward Letters, Korea, CO-L, 8th Cavalry Regiment, 1st Cavalry Division, September 1, 1950.
8. Fehrenbach, *This Kind of War*, 139.
9. Ibid., 141.
10. Appleman, *South to the Naktong*, 418.
11. Fehrenbach, *This Kind of War*, 157.
12. Appleman, *South to the Naktong*, 349.
13. Library of Congress, *Korean War Atrocities Report*.
14. Blair, *The Forgotten War*, 259.
15. Ibid., 258.
16. Anderson, "1st Cavalry Division."
17. Korean War Legacy Foundation, "Changing the Game at Incheon."
18. Author interview with General Richard E. Carey, June 2016, Seoul, Korea.
19. Ibid.
20. Sides, *On Desperate Ground*, 50–51.
21. Ibid., 51–52.
22. Weintraub, *MacArthur's War*, 157–58.
23. Fehrenbach, *This Kind of War*, 171.
24. Sobieski, "1127 Days of Death."
25. Blair, *The Forgotten War*, 308.
26. Chong Dae, *Battle Stories of the Korean War Heroes*, 90–91.
27. Ibid.

Chapter 14: A Million Miles from Home

1. Individual Deceased Personnel File for David D. Steward, Battle Casualty Report 14499, October 3, 1950; Letter # 276003, Major Edward F. Witsell, October 5, 1950.
2. Individual Deceased Personnel File for David D. Steward, Report # 284029, Major Edward F. Witsell, October 16, 1950.
3. Author interviews with the Steward wives, Helen Steward-Reeder, March 2012, Phoenix, Arizona.
4. Individual Deceased Personnel File for David D. Steward, photocopied letter, Delta Ray Steward to Colonel James R. Clearwater, 1951.
5. Individual Deceased Personnel File for David D. Steward, photocopied letter, Delta Ray Steward to Colonel James R. Clearwater, 1951.
6. Defense POW/MIA Accounting Agency, accessed September 4, 2023, https://dpaa-mil.sites.crmforce.mil/dpaaFamWebKorean

Chapter 15: Lost Battalion

1. "The Korean War Controversy: An Intelligence Success or Failure"? Central Intelligence Agency, June 25, 2015, https://www.cia.gov/stories/story/the-korean-war-controversy-an-intelligence-success-or-failure/#the-cia-in-1950

2. Ibid.
3. Halberstam, *The Coldest Winter*, 373.
4. Blair, *The Forgotten War*, 377.
5. Halberstam, *The Coldest Winter*, 366.
6. Ibid., 369.
7. Roe, *The Dragon Strikes*, 150.
8. Ibid., 156.
9. Halberstam, *The Coldest Winter*, 10–11.
10. Carlson, "This Week in History."
11. Halberstam, *The Coldest Winter*, 23.
12. Fehrenbach, *This Kind of War*, 190.
13. "Battle of Unsan," Defense POW/MIA Accounting Agency, accessed June 28, 2022, https://dpaa-mil.sites.crmforce.mil/dpaaFamWebInBattleOfUnsan
14. Halberstam, *The Coldest Winter*, 40–41.
15. Wenzl and Heying, *The Miracle of Father Kapaun*, 23.
16. Lange, "Medal of Honor Monday."
17. Wenzl and Heying, *The Miracle of Father Kapaun*, 68.
18. Ibid., 68–70.
19. Defense POW/MIA Accounting Agency, "Chaplain Accounted for from Korean War."
20. Ibid.

Chapter 16: Changjin

1. Harry S. Truman Presidential Library and Museum.
2. Cohen, "The Chinese Intervention in Korea, 1950."
3. Wolf, "The Chosin Reservoir."
4. Author interview with General Richard E. Carey, June 2016, Seoul, Korea.
5. Appleman, *Escaping the Trap*, 37.
6. Seelinger, "Nightmare at the Chosin Reservoir."
7. Sides, *On Desperate Ground*, 142.
8. Appleman, *Escaping the Trap*, 37.
9. Storms-Cook, *Helen and Harvey, Last Letters*, letter from Harvey Storms to Helen Storms, November 12, 1950.
10. Storms-Cook, *Helen and Harvey, Last Letters*, letter from Harvey Storms to Helen Storms, November 9, 1950.
11. Storms-Cook, *Helen and Harvey, Last Letters*, letter from Harvey Storms to Helen Storms, November 20, 1950.
12. Storms-Cook, *Helen and Harvey, Last Letters*, letter from Helen Storms to Harvey Storms, November 12, 1950.
13. Fehrenbach, *This Kind of War*, 242.
14. Halberstam, *The Coldest Winter*, 441.

15. Defense POW/MIA Accounting Agency, Personnel Profile, Col. Allan Duart MacLean, accessed September 4, 2023, https://dpaa-mil.sites.crmforce.mil/dpaaProfile?id=a0Jt00000001VHiEAM
16. Storms-Cook, *Helen and Harvey, Last Letters*, letter from Helen Storms to Harvey Storms, November 30, 1950.
17. Chong Dae, *Battle Stories of the Korean War Heroes*, 80.
18. Appleman, *East of Chosin*, 269.
19. Chong Dae, *Battle Stories of the Korean War Heroes*, 80.
20. Appleman, *East of Chosin*, 209.
21. Blair, *The Forgotten War*, 520.
22. Seelinger, "Nightmare at the Chosin Reservoir."
23. Appleman, *Escaping the Trap*, 158.
24. Author interview with Watson Crumbie, June 22, 2017, Robson Ranch, Texas.
25. Sides, *On Desperate Ground*, 172.
26. Ibid., 176.
27. Ibid., 250.
28. "The only way they could overwhelm us": Author interview with General Richard E. Carey, June 2016, Seoul, Korea.
29. Ibid.
30. Chong Dae, *Battle Stories of the Korean War Heroes*, 18.
31. "War: Retreat of the 20,000."
32. Author interview with Watson Crumbie, June 22, 2017, Robson Ranch, Texas.
33. Appleman, *Escaping the Trap*, 37, 158.
34. Storms-Cook, *Helen and Harvey, Last Letters*, letter from Helen Storms to Harvey Storms, December 7, 1950.

Chapter 17: Grave 182

1. Individual Deceased Personnel File for David D. Steward; letter from James B. Clearwater to Mrs. W. H. Steward, October 31, 1950.
2. Hughes, "Army Helicopters in Korea, 1950–1953."
3. Cook, "Graves Registration in the Korean Conflict."
4. Individual Deceased Personnel File for David D. Steward, Statement and Field Report of Sergeant Charles Wilson, February 5, 1951.
5. "U.S. Military Casualties—Korean War Casualty Summary," Defense Casualty Analysis System, https://dcas.dmdc.osd.mil/dcas/app/conflictCasualties/korea/koreaSum
6. Individual Deceased Personnel File for David D. Steward, James B. Clearwater letter, 1951.
7. Individual Deceased Personnel File for David D. Steward, R. J. Provost letter, 1951.
8. Individual Deceased Personnel File for David D. Steward, S. Zablocki, Commanding Officer, QMC, 1951.

9. Individual Deceased Personnel File for David D. Steward, letter from James B. Clearwater to Mrs. W. H. Steward, 1951.
10. Heather and Chain, "The Sequence of Sequencers."
11. Chial and Craig, "mtDNA and Mitochondrial Diseases."
12. Girish, Rahman, and Tippu, "Dental DNA Fingerprinting."
13. Vergun, "After 62 Years."
14. Higgins, "One Hero Home, 83,000 to Go."
15. Defense POW/MIA Accounting Agency, "Our Missing—Past Conflicts."
16. Cheek and Cassidy, "Robert Emmett Cassidy Collection."
17. Ibid.
18. *William H. Steward Memoirs*, letter from William Steward to Callie Steward, Korean battlefront, 1951.
19. Author interview with William Steward, *William H. Steward Memoirs*, Vivian, Louisiana, and Trophy Club, Texas.

Chapter 18: Finding Davy

1. Mauldin, *Up Front*, 39.
2. Sartin, "Infectious Diseases during the Civil War."
3. Halberstam. *The Coldest Winter*, 552.
4. Fehrenbach, *This Kind of War*, 266.
5. "Recapturing Seoul," *Korean War Legacy Foundation*, 2022, https://koreanwarlegacy.org/chapters/recapturing-seoul/
6. Author interview with William Steward, *William H. Steward Memoirs*, "Letters from the Front," William Steward to Callie Steward, May 2, 1951, from Korean battlefront.
7. "President Truman Address to the Nation."
8. Douglas MacArthur, "Old Soldiers Never Die."
9. "Giving Them More Hell"; Ponnuru, "Did Truman Really Call MacArthur That?"
10. Letter from William Steward to Callie Steward, June 10, 1951, from Korean battlefront.
11. "Daddy," poem included in a letter from William Steward to Callie Steward, June 10, 1951, from Korean battlefront.
12. Individual Deceased Personnel File for David D. Steward, letter from Mrs. W. H. Steward to Colonel James B. Clearwater, July 20, 1951.
13. Author interview with William Steward, *William H. Steward Memoirs*, letter from William Steward to Callie Steward, June 10, 1951, from Korean battlefront.
14. Individual Deceased Personnel File for David D. Steward, Case # 6219 Narrative.
15. Individual Deceased Personnel File for David D. Steward, notification from Colonel Broderick to Mrs. W. H. Steward, August 27, 1951.
16. Steward, "The Boy Soldier," 22.

Chapter 19: Piney Wood Home

1. Murrie and Petersen, "Last Train Home."
2. Steward, "The Boy Soldier," 22.
3. Ibid., 23.
4. Lessig, "Getting Them Home: Army Vet Served as Escort for the Fallen."
5. Steward, "The Boy Soldier," 24.
6. Ibid.
7. Ibid.
8. Ibid., 25.
9. Steward, "The Boy Soldier" (original version), *William H. Steward Memoirs*, 1999–2006, Vivian, Louisiana, and Trophy Club, Texas, 1999–2006. 17.
10. Ibid., 18.
11. Steward, "The Boy Soldier," *William H. Steward Memoirs*, 1999–2006, Vivian, Louisiana, and Trophy Club, Texas, 26.
12. Ibid.
13. Author interviews with the Steward wives, Helen Steward-Reeder, March 2012, Phoenix, Arizona.
14. Ibid.

Chapter 20: The Abyss

1. Author interview with William Steward, 2005, Trophy Club, Texas, *William H. Steward Memoirs*.
2. Jones and Palmer, "Army Psychiatry in the Korean War."
3. Author interviews with the Steward wives, Donna Wilson, July 14, 2015, Orlando, Florida.
4. Ghaemi, "Winston Churchill and His 'Black Dog' of Greatness."
5. Author interview with William Steward, 2005, Trophy Club, Texas, *William H. Steward Memoirs*.
6. Author interview with Callie Steward, June 6, 2015.
7. Letter from William Steward to Callie Steward January–February 1952.
8. Author interview with William Steward, 2005, Trophy Club, Texas, *William H. Steward Memoirs*.
9. Ibid.
10. Ibid.
11. Bernucci, *Forensic Military Psychiatry*, 477.
12. William Steward, Camp Chaffee Letters, U.S. Army Hospital, Chaffee, Arkansas, 1952.
13. Author interview with Carl Ganz Jr., August 15, 2022, Raritan, New Jersey.

14. Ibid.
15. Friedman, Schnurr, and McDonagh-Coyle, "Post-Traumatic Stress Disorder."
16. Pols and Oak, "War and Military Mental Health."
17. "Aging Veterans and Posttraumatic Stress Symptoms," U.S. Department of Veterans Affairs, National Center for PTSD, accessed September 4, 2023, https://www.ptsd.va.gov/understand/what/aging_veterans.asp
18. Marmar et al., "Course of Posttraumatic Stress Disorder."
19. Honorable Discharge for William H. Steward, Ft. Chaffee, Arkansas, Form Number 1569.
20. Author interview with William Steward, February 8, 2005, Trophy Club, Texas, *William H. Steward Memoirs*.

Chapter 21: Forgotten Casualties

1. "How Many Homeless Veterans Are There?" National Coalition for Homeless Veterans, accessed September 15, 2022, https://nchv.org/veteran-homelessness/
2. U.S. Interagency Council on Homelessness, November 3, 2022.
3. Thurston, "Why Veterans Remain at Greater Risk of Homelessness."
4. DeAngelis, "More PTSD among Homeless Vets," 22.
5. Dekel and Goldblatt, "Is There Intergenerational Transmission of Trauma?"
6. Dinshtein, Dekel, and Polliack, "Secondary Traumatization among Adult Children."
7. Rosenheck and Nathan, "Secondary Traumatization in Children."
8. *CBS News This Morning*, March 16, 2014.
9. Jordan et al., "Problems in Families."
10. Klaric et al., "Psychological Problems in Children."
11. *CBS News This Morning*, March 16, 2014; Rabb, "A Lesser-Known Group."
12. Cook et al., "Secondary PTSD in Children."
13. Dinshtein, Dekel, and Polliack, "Secondary Traumatization among Adult Children."
14. Morin, "Effects of Military Deployment on Children."
15. Wein, "Stress Hormone Causes Epigenetic Changes."
16. Hunter, Rijal, and Ressler, "A Review of Epigenetic Contributions."
17. Campbell and Demi, "Adult Children of Fathers Missing in Action."
18. Martin, "Son of Korean War Soldier."
19. Kornacki, "67 Years Later."
20. Author interviews with MIA family members, Korean War Appreciation Gala, June 2016 in Seoul, Korea, and June 2017 in Houston, Texas.
21. Ibid.
22. Ibid.
23. Martin, "Son of Korean War Soldier."
24. Ibid.

25. Author interviews with MIA family members, Korean War Appreciation Gala, June 2016 in Seoul, Korea, and June 2017 in Houston, Texas.
26. Defense POW/MIA Accounting Agency, "Soldier Missing from Korean War Accounted For (Gilberto Sanchez)," January 16, 2015, https://www.dpaa.mil/News-Stories/News-Releases/PressReleaseArticleView/Article/569578/soldier-missing-from-korean-war-accounted-for-sanchez/.
27. Author interview with Sam Storms, June 2016, Seoul, Korea, and June 2017, Houston, Texas.
28. Ibid.
29. Ibid.
30. Ibid.
31. Ibid.
32. Author interview with Sam Storms, June 2016, Seoul, Korea.
33. Author interview with Robert Storms, June 2018, Seoul, Korea.
34. Ibid.
35. Author interview with Sam Storms, June 2018, Northlake, Texas.
36. Author interview with Jon Kitts, November 2019, Ft. Worth, Texas.
37. Ibid.

Chapter 22: The Little Christmas Man

1. Lockhart, *Diehard*, 30.
2. Ibid., 30–31.
3. Heineman, "The hour of the Woman."
4. Tilman, "The Battle for Berlin in World War Two."
5. Hofmann, "End of WWII."
6. Aleksievich, *War's Unwomanly Face*, 33.
7. Author interview with William Steward, 2005, Trophy Club, Texas, *William H. Steward Memoirs*.
8. Ertel, "A Legacy of Dead German Children."
9. Lylloff, "Causes of Death of German Refugee Children."
10. Daniele and Ghezzi, "The Impact of World War II."
11. David Steward Sessions, interview with William Steward, original videography, 1992.
12. Author interview with William Steward, *William H. Steward Memoirs*, Vivian, Louisiana, and Trophy Club, Texas, 1999–2006.
13. President Ronald Reagan, "In the Words of Stephen Spender," Pointe du Hoc, France, 1984. Barrett Bowdrie, "Remembering D-Day," American Enterprise Institute, June 6, 2012, https://www.aei.org/foreign-and-defense-policy/remembering-d-day/.

BIBLIOGRAPHY

Articles and Media

American History TV. "The World War II Army Replacement Program." C-SPAN, February 19, 2016.

Anderson, Clarence L. "1st Cavalry Division Distinguished Service Cross Korean War Recipients." 1st Cavalry Division Association. https://1cda.org/history/distinguished-service-cross/dsc-korean-war/

Armstrong, Gregory L., Laura Conn, and Robert W. Pinner. "Trends in Infectious Disease Mortality in the United States during the 20th Century." *Journal of the American Medical Association* 281, no. 1 (1999): 61–66. https://jamanetwork.com/journals/jama/fullarticle/768249

Asian Boss Media. "Life as a Comfort Woman: Story of Kim Bok Dong." Interview, October 27, 2018. Updated September 8, 2023. https://www.youtube.com/watch?v=qsT97ax_Xb0

Bell, Kelly. "Costly Victory in Hürtgen Forest." *WWII History* 14, no. 3 (April 2015): 30–38.

Bell, Kevin. "South Korea/U.S. Remember Korean War Sacrifices during Nakdong River Battle Ceremonies." U.S. Army, October 15, 2021. https://www.army.mil/article/251198/south_koreau_s_remember_korean_war_sacrifices_during_nakdong_river_battle_ceremonies

Bentley, Steve. "A Short History of PTSD: From Thermopylae to Hue Soldiers Have Always Had a Disturbing Reaction to War." *The VVA Veteran* (March–April 2005). https://www.myptsd.com/threads/a-short-history-of-ptsd-from-thermopylae-to-hue.77663/

Berg, Tom. "Few Know of the 'Tragic 29th' in Korea." Interview of Jesus Rodriguez. *Orange County Register*, June 21, 2010. https://www.ocregister.com/2010/06/21/few-know-of-the-tragic-29th-in-korea/

Bernucci, Robert J. *Forensic Military Psychiatry*. Washington, DC: U.S. Army Medical Department, Office of Medical History, 1966.

Biography.com. Audie Murphy. April 2, 2014. https://www.biography.com/military-figures/audie-murphy

Bland, Edward F. "Rheumatic Fever: The Way It Was." *American Heart Association Journals* 76, no. 6 (December 1987): 1190–95.

Bowdrie, Barrett. "Remembering D-Day." American Enterprise Institute, June 6, 2012. https://www.aei.org/foreign-and-defense-policy/remembering-d-day/

Bremner, Douglas J. "Traumatic Stress: Effects on the Brain." *Clinical Neuroscience* 8, no. 4 (December 2006): 445–61.

Bremner, J. D., L. H. Staib, D. Kaloupek, S. M. Southwick, R. Soufer, and D. S. Charney. "Neural Correlates of Exposure to Traumatic Pictures and Sound in Vietnam Combat Veterans with and without Posttraumatic Stress Disorder: A Positron Emission Tomography Study." *Biological Psychiatry* 45, no. 7 (April 1999): 806–16.

Brooks, Rebecca Beatrice. "Child Soldiers in the Civil War." *Civil War Saga*, December 16, 2011. https://civilwarsaga.com/child-soldiers-in-the-civil-war/

Bruce, Steven E., Katherine R Buchholz, Wilson J. Brown, Laura Yan, Anthony Durbin, and Yvette Sheline. "Altered Emotional Interference Processing in the Amygdala and Insula in Women with Post-Traumatic Stress Disorder." *NeuroImage: Clinical* 2 (2013): 43–49.

Campbell, Cathy L., and Alice S. Demi. "Adult Children of Fathers Missing in Action (MIA): An Examination of Emotional Distress, Grief, and Family Hardiness." *Family Relations* 49 (2000): 267–76.

Carlson, Cody K. "This Week in History: China Enters the Korean War." *Deseret News*, November 26, 2014.

Cheek, Helen, and Robert Emmett Cassidy. "Robert Emmett Cassidy Collection (AFC/2001/001/31154)." Veterans History Project, American Folklife Center, Library of Congress, 1951.

Chial, Heidi, and Joanna Craig. "mtDNA and Mitochondrial Diseases." *Nature Education* 1, no. 1 (2008): 217.

Citino, Robert M. "Death in the West." *World War II*, June 20, 2016. HistoryNet Archives, accessed September 8, 2023. https://www.historynet.com/death-in-the-west/

Cohen, Eliot A. "The Chinese Intervention in Korea, 1950." CIA Historical Review Program, September 22, 1993. https://www.cia.gov/readingroom/docs/1988-11-01.pdf

Cook, Benjamin I., Richard Seager, and Jason E. Smerdon. "The Worst North American Drought Year of the Last Millennium: 1934." *Geophysical Research Letters* 41, no. 20 (2014): 7298–305.

Cook, Christine R., Andrea A. Slater-Williams, and Lynn R. Harrison. "Secondary PTSD in Children of Service Members: Strategies for Helping Professionals." Paper based on a program presented at the 2012 American Counseling Association Conference, San Francisco, March 23–25.

Cook, LTC John C. "Graves Registration in the Korean Conflict." *The Quartermaster Review*, March–April 1953. https://www.quartermasterfoundation.org/graves-registration-in-the-korean-conflict/

Cook, Kevin L. "Dying to Get Home: PTSD in the Civil War." *Civil War Quarterly* 7, no. 1 (Summer 2016).
Daniele, Vittorio, and Renato Ghezzi. "The Impact of World War II on Nutrition and Children's Health in Italy." *Investigaciones de Historia Económica* 15, no. 2 (June 2019): 119–31.
DeAngelis, Tori. "More PTSD among Homeless Vets." *American Psychological Association* 44, no. 3 (March 2013): 22.
Defense POW/MIA Accounting Agency. "Chaplain Accounted for from Korean War" (Kapaun, E.)." News release, May 14, 2021. https://www.dpaa.mil/News-Stories/News-Releases/PressReleaseArticleView/Article/2525763/chaplain-accounted-for-from-korean-war-kapaun-e/
Defense POW/MIA Accounting Agency. "Our Missing—Past Conflicts." Updated May 2023. https://www.dpaa.mil/Our-Missing/Past-Conflicts/
Dekel, Rachel, and Hadass Goldblatt. "Is There Intergenerational Transmission of Trauma? The Case of Combat Veterans' Children." *American Journal of Orthopsychiatry* 78, no. 3 (2008): 281–89.
Diamond, Jon. "Assault on Ludendorff Bridge: The First Allied Crossing of the Rhine." *WWII Quarterly* 6, no. 1 (Fall 2014): 80–86.
Dinshtein, Yula, Rachel Dekel, and Miki Polliack. "Secondary Traumatization among Adult Children of PTSD Veterans: The Role of Mother-Child Relationships." *Journal of Family Social Work* 14, no. 2 (March 2011): 109–24.
Drozdiak, William. "Veterans Bridge Enmity at Remagen." *Washington Post*, March 8, 1985.
Ertel, Manfred. "A Legacy of Dead German Children," *Spiegel International*, March 16, 2005. https://www.spiegel.de/international/denmark-s-myths-shattered-a-legacy-of-dead-german-children-a-355772.html
Felton, Mark. "Luftwaffe Jets vs. Remagen Bridge—Germany's Last Air Operation in the West 1945." Mark Felton Productions, April 2022. https://www.youtube.com/watch?v=dxMZyJz5Q6o
Fishback, Price V. "Did Coal Miners 'Owe Their Souls to the Company Store'? Theory and Evidence from the Early 1900s." *Journal of Economic History* 46, no. 4 (December 1986): 1011–25.
Fitzgerald, Gerard J. "Chemical Warfare and Medical Response during World War I." *American Journal of Public Health* 98, no. 4 (April 2008): 611–25.
Flory, Janine D., and Rachel Yehuda. "Comorbidity between Post-Traumatic Stress Disorder and Major Depressive Disorder: Alternative Explanations and Treatment Considerations." *Dialogues Clinical Neuroscience* 17, no. 2 (2015): 141–50.
Fontaine, Scott. "Meet the Youngest Surviving WWII Veteran." *Tacoma News Tribune*, November 18, 2008. Scripps Howard News Service, https://web.archive.org/web/20111113190843/http://www.scrippsnews.com/node/38026
Friedman, Matthew J., Paula P. Schnurr, and Annmarie McDonagh-Coyle. "Post Traumatic Stress Disorder in the Military Veteran." *Psychiatric Clinics of North America* 17, no. 2 (June 1994): 265–77.

Gersen, Jeannie Suk. "Seeking the True Story of the Comfort Women." *New Yorker*, February 25, 2021. https://www.newyorker.com/culture/annals-of-inquiry/seeking-the-true-story-of-the-comfort-women-j-mark-ramseyer

Ghaemi, Nassir. "Winston Churchill and His 'Black Dog' of Greatness." *The Conversation*, January 23, 2015. https://theconversation.com/winston-churchill-and-his-black-dog-of-greatness-36570

Girish, K. L., Farzan S. Rahman, and Shoaib R. Tippu. "Dental DNA Fingerprinting in Identification of Human Remains." *Journal of Forensic Dental Science* 2, no. 2 (July–December 2010): 63–68.

"Giving Them More Hell." *Time*, December 3, 1973. https://content.time.com/time/subscriber/article/0,33009,908217,00.html

Glantz, Aaron. "Investigation: Suicide Rates Soaring among World War II Vets." New America Media/Bay Citizen Online, November 11, 2010. https://news.yahoo.com/investigation-suicide-rates-soaring-among-wwii-vets.html

Gurvits, Tamara V., Martha E. Shenton, Hiroto Hokama, Hirokazu Ohta, Natasha B. Lasko, Mark W. Gilbertson, and Scott P. Orr. "Magnetic Resonance Imaging Study of Hippocampal Volume in Chronic, Combat-Related Posttraumatic Stress Disorder." *Biological Psychiatry* 40, no. 11 (December 1, 1996): 1091–99.

Handwerk, Brian. "Over a Quarter-Million Vietnam War Veterans Still Have PTSD." *Smithsonian*, July 22, 2015. https://www.smithsonianmag.com/science-nature/over-quarter-million-vietnam-war-veterans-still-have-ptsd-180955997/

Hanks, Jane. "Architecture of France: Le Havre, This Is No Concrete Jungle." *The Connexion*, August 28, 2019.

Hastings, Max. "The Wehrmacht Was the Better Army." *Strategic Studies* 8, no. 4 (Summer 1985): 92–98.

Heather, James M., and Benjamin Chain. The Sequence of Sequencers: The History of Sequencing DNA." *Genomics* 107, no. 1 (January 2016): 1–8.

Heineman, Elizabeth. "The Hour of the Woman: Memories of Germany's 'Crisis Years' and West German National Identity." *American Historical Review* 101, no. 2 (1996): 354–95.

Hendin, Herbert, and Ann Pollinger Haas. "Suicide and Guilt as Manifestations of PTSD in Vietnam Combat Veterans." *American Journal of Psychiatry* 148, no. 5 (May 1991): 586–91.

Higgins, Will. "One Hero Home, 83,000 to Go." *Indianapolis Star*, republished in *USA Today*, May 26, 2013. https://www.usatoday.com/story/news/nation/2013/05/26/one-hero-home-83000-to-go/2360881/

Hofmann, Sarah Judith. "End of WWII: Entire Families Committed Suicide." *Deutsche Welle*, May 5, 2015. https://www.dw.com/en/end-of-wwii-entire-families-committed-suicide/a-18404064

Hooper, Charles A. "Suicide among Veterans: Are Veterans at a Higher Risk for Suicide?" American Addiction Center. Updated July 20, 2023. https://americanaddictioncenters.org/veterans/suicide-among-veterans

Hughes, Kaylene. "Army Helicopters in Korea 1950–1953." United States Army, October 28, 2016. https://www.army.mil/article/177302/army_helicopters_in_korea_1950_to_53

Hunter, Howie, Chuda M. Rijal, and Kerry J. Ressler. "A Review of Epigenetic Contributions to Post-Traumatic Stress Disorder." *Dialogues in Clinical Neuroscience* 21, no. 4 (December 2019): 417–28.

Johnson, D. R., H. Lubin, R. Rosenheck, A. Fontana, S. Southwick, and D. Charney. "The Impact of the Homecoming Reception on the Development of Posttraumatic Stress Disorder: The West Haven Homecoming Stress Scale (WHHSS)." *Journal of Traumatic Stress* 10, no. 2 (April 1997): 259–77.

Jones, Edgar, and Ian P. Palmer. "Army Psychiatry in the Korean War: The Experience of 1 Commonwealth Division." *Military Medicine* 165, no. 4 (April 2000): 256–57.

Jordan, B. K., C. R. Marmar, J. A. Fairbank, W. E. Schlenger, R. A. Kulka, R. L. Hough, and D. S. Weiss. "Problems in Families of Male Vietnam Veterans with Posttraumatic Stress Disorder." *Journal of Consulting and Clinical Psychology* 60, no. 6 (December 1992): 916–26 (rev. 2016).

Joy, Robert J. T. "Historical Aspects of Medical Defense against Chemical Warfare." In *Medical Aspects of Chemical and Biological Warfare*, Department of Medical History, U.S. Army. Washington, DC: Borden Institute, Walter Reed Army Medical Center, 1997.

"Kids in the Civil War." *American Experience*. Supporting article to *The Civil War*, a film by Ken Burns. PBS. https://www.pbs.org/wgbh/americanexperience/features/grant-kids/

Klaric, Miro, Tanja Franciskovic, Branka Klaric, Ante Kvesic, Ana Kastelan, Mirjana Graovac, and Ines Diminic Lisica. "Psychological Problems in Children of War Veterans with Posttraumatic Stress Disorder in Bosnia and Herzegovina: Cross-Sectional Study." *Croatian Medical Journal* 49, no. 4 (August 2008): 491–98.

Klinek, Eric William. "The Army's Orphans: U.S. Army Replacement System in the European Campaign, 1944–1945." Dissertation, Temple University, 2014.

Klinek, Eric William. "World War II Army Replacement Program." *American History TV*, C-SPAN3, February 19, 2016.

Korean War Legacy Foundation. "Changing the Game at Incheon." Accessed September 10, 2023. https://koreanwarlegacy.org/chapters/changing-the-game-at-incheon/

Kornacki, Steve. "67 Years Later: Lt. Hal Downes, MIA in Korea, Gains Spot in Hall of Honor." University of Michigan Athletics, November 14, 2019.

Lange, Katie. "Medal of Honor Monday: Army Chaplain Emil J. Kapaun." Department of Defense, March 22, 2021, https://www.defense.gov/News/Feature-Stories/story/Article/2539877/medal-of-honor-monday-army-chaplain-emil-j-kapaun/

Lessig, Hugh. "Getting Them Home: Army Vet Served as Escort for the Fallen." *Daily Press* (Newport News, Virginia), November 26, 2016. https://www.dailypress.com/military/dp-nws-evg-fallen-soldier-escort-20161126-story.html

Linder, Douglas O. "Hitler's Trial Speeches: Hitler's Opening Statement (February 26, 1924) (excerpt)." *Famous Trials*. https://famous-trials.com/hitler/2525-hitler-s-closing-speech-at-trial

Lopez, C. Todd. "Rededicated Korean War Memorial Lists Names of Fallen." U.S. Department of Defense, July 27, 2022. https://www.defense.gov/News/News-Stories/Article/Article/3107882/rededicated-korean-war-memorial-lists-names-of-fallen/

Lylloff, Kirsten. "Causes of Death of German Refugee Children in 1945." English abstract retrieved from NIH National Library of Public Medicine, originally published in *Ugeskriftet Danish Medical Journal* 162, no. 9 (February 2000).

MacArthur, Douglas. "Old Soldiers Never Die." Address to Congress, April 19, 1951. Library of Congress. https://www.loc.gov/item/mcc.034/

Manfred, Ertel. "A Legacy of Dead German Children." *Spiegel International*, May 16, 2005. https://www.spiegel.de/international/denmark-s-myths-shattered-a-legacy-of-dead-german-children-a-355772.html

Marmar, Charles R., William Schlenger, Clare Henn-Haase, Meng Qian, Emily Purchia, Meng Li, and Nida Corry. "Course of Posttraumatic Stress Disorder 40 Years after the Vietnam War: Findings from the National Vietnam Veterans Longitudinal Study." *JAMA Psychiatry* 72, no. 9 (2015): 875–81.

Martin, David. "Son of Korean War Soldier Hopes to Finally Lay His Father to Rest." CBS News, July 26, 2018. https://www.cbsnews.com/news/son-of-fallen-korean-war-soldier-hopes-to-finally-lay-his-father-to-rest/

Maw, Helene. *Freedom Is for Those Willing to Defend It: Stories of Men in War*. Victoria, BC: Trafford, 2002.

Min, Sung Kil, Chang Ho Lee, Joo Young Kim, and Eun Ji Sim. "Posttraumatic Stress Disorder in Former 'Comfort Women.'" *Israel Journal of Psychiatry and Related Sciences* 48, no. 3 (2011): 161–69. https://cdn.doctorsonly.co.il/2011/12/2011_3_5.pdf

Morin, Amy. "Effects of Military Deployment on Children." *VeryWell Family*, September 20, 2020. https://www.verywellfamily.com/the-effects-of-military-deployment-on-children-4150518

Murrie, James I., and Naomi Jeffery Petersen. "Last Train Home." HistoryNet, November 29, 2017. https://www.historynet.com/last-train-home/

Pollarine, Joshua. "Children at War: Underage Americans Illegally Fighting the Second World War." Master's thesis, University of Montana, 2008.

Pols, Hans, and Stephanie Oak. "War and Military Mental Health." *American Journal of Public Health* 97, no. 12 (2007): 2132–42.

Ponnuru, Ramesh. "Did Truman Really Call MacArthur That?" *National Review*, June 18, 2020. https://www.nationalreview.com/corner/did-truman-really-call-macarthur-that/

"President Truman Address to the Nation." Critical Past, April 11, 1951. https://www.youtube.com/watch?v=jAhBDiu3mqY

Pyle, Ernie. "Ernie Pyle's Last Column: On Victory in Europe." *Green Bay Press Gazette*, April 18, 2015.

Rabb, Dan. "A Lesser-Known Group at Risk of Suicide: Children of Servicemembers." *The War Horse*, April 15, 2020. https://thewarhorse.org/a-lesser-known-group-at-risk-of-suicide-children-of-servicemembers

Roberts, Jeremy. "Uncovering Resilient American Soldier Audie Murphy." Medium, June 27, 2018. https://medium.com/@jeremylr/uncovering-resilient-american-soldier-audie-murphy-dd763ca0e5

Rosenheck, Robert, and Pramila Nathan. "Secondary Traumatization in Children of Vietnam Veterans." *Psychiatric Services* 36, no. 5 (1985): 538–39.

Samit, S. Roy, Randi E. Foraker, Richard A. Girton, and Alyssa J. Mansfield. "Posttraumatic Stress Disorder and Incident Heart Failure among a Community-Based Sample of US Veterans." *American Journal of Public Health* 105, no. 4 (April 2015): 757–63.

Sartin, J. S. "Infectious Diseases during the Civil War: The Triumph of the "Third Army." *Clinical Infectious Diseases* 16, no. 4 (April 1993): 580–84.

Schultz, Duane. "The Breaking Point: Combat Stress in WWII." *World War II History*, June 2013. https://duaneschultz.com/article/the-breaking-point-combat-fatigue/

Seelinger, Matthew J. "Nightmare at the Chosin Reservoir." *On Point: The Journal of Army History* 6, no. 4 (2000): 7–10.

Semmens, E. Paul, Col. "The Remagen Bridgehead: A Decisive Victory for AAA Soldiers." *The Hammer of Hell*, chapter 6, archived from original article August 13, 2014, updated September 8, 2023. https://web.archive.org/web/20141129025742/https://skylighters.org/hammer/chapter6.html

"16-Year-Old EC Student Dies in Korea." *Imperial Valley Press*, October 1950. El Centro, California.

Sobieski, Anthony. "1127 Days of Death—A Korean War Chronology—Part 1, 1950." Military History Online, July 20, 2019. https://www.militaryhistoryonline.com/Korea/KoreanWarPartI

Steward, William H. "The Boy Soldier." *The Flash*, vol. 2022, no. 1, 22–28, a publication of the 78th Infantry Division Veterans Association.

Thurston, Andrew. "Why Veterans Remain at Greater Risk of Homelessness." *The Brink*, Boston University, November 9, 2022. https://www.bu.edu/articles/2022/why-veterans-remain-at-greater-risk-of-homelessness/

Tilman, Remme. "The Battle for Berlin in World War Two." *BBC History Magazine*, last updated October 3, 2011. https://www.bbc.co.uk/history/worldwars/wwtwo/berlin_01.shtml

"The Treaty of Portsmouth." *New York Times*, October 17, 1905.

United States Holocaust Memorial Museum. "Allied Military Operations in North Africa." *Holocaust Encyclopedia* (online), North Africa Series, accessed

September 21, 2023. https://encyclopedia.ushmm.org/content/en/article/allied-military-operations-in-north-africa

Vento, Carol Schultz. "The U.S. World War II Troop Replacement Policy." *Defense Media Network*, April 21, 2012. https://www.defensemedianetwork.com/stories/the-u-s-world-war-ii-troop-replacement-policy/

Vergun, David. "After 62 Years, Korean War Medal of Honor Recipient Rests in American Soil." U.S. Army Public Affairs, July 10, 2018. https://www.army.mil/article/101279/after_62_years_korean_war_medal_of_honor_recipient_rests_in_american_soil

"War: Retreat of the 20,000." *Time*, December 18, 1950.

WDAF-TV/TNS, Kansas City, Missouri, subsidiary of FOX News, "Local Veteran Who Died in Korean War Finally Identified, Comes Home to Leavenworth." April 25, 2019.

Wein, Harrison. "Stress Hormone Causes Epigenetic Changes." *NIH Research Matters*, September 27, 2010, https://www.nih.gov/news-events/nih-research-matters/stress-hormone-causes-epigenetic-changes

Wolf, Stanley I. "The Chosin Reservoir: Medical Care in Subfreezing Weather." *Leatherneck*, June 2012. https://www.mca-marines.org/wp-content/uploads/2018/12/Leatherneck-June-2012.pdf

Zarembo, Alan. "As Disability Awards Grow, So Do Concerns with Veracity of PTSD Claims." *Los Angeles Times*, August 3, 2014. https://www.latimes.com/local/la-me-ptsd-disability-20140804-story.html

Books and Reports

Alcott, Louisa May. *Hospital Sketches*. Boston: James Redpath, 1863.

Aleksievich, Svetlana. *War's Unwomanly Face*. Moscow: Progress Publishers, 1988.

Alexander, Bevin. *Korea: The First War We Lost*. New York: Hippocrene Books, 2003.

Appleman, Roy E. *East of Chosin: Entrapment and Breakout in Korea, 1950*. College Station: Texas A&M University Press, 1987.

Appleman, Roy E. *Escaping the Trap: The US Army X Corps in Northeast Korea, 1950*. Williams-Ford Texas A&M University Military History Series, vol. 14. College Station: Texas A&M University Press, 1990.

Appleman, Roy E. *South to the Naktong, North to the Yalu*. Washington, DC: United States Army Center of Military History, 1961.

Atkinson, Rick. *An Army at Dawn: The War in North Africa (1942–1943)*. The Liberation Trilogy, vol. 1. New York: Simon and Schuster, 2003.

Atkinson, Rick. *The Day of Battle: The War in Sicily and Italy, 1943–1944*. The Liberation Trilogy, vol. 2. New York: Henry Holt, 2007.

Atkinson, Rick. *The Guns at Last Light: The War in Western Europe, 1944–1945*. The Liberation Trilogy, vol. 3. New York: Henry Holt, 2014.

Bibliography

Axelrod, Alan. *Patton: A Biography*. London: Palgrave Macmillan, 2006.

Balkoski, Joseph. *Beyond the Beachhead: The 29th Infantry Division in Normandy*. Mechanicsburg, PA: Stackpole Books, 1989.

Beschloss, Michael. *Our Documents: 100 Milestone Documents from the National Archives*. Oxford: Oxford University Press, 2003.

Blair, Clay. *The Forgotten War*. New York: Times Books, 1987.

Blumenson, Martin. *The Patton Papers: 1940–1945*. Boston: Houghton Mifflin, 1974.

Bradbury, Ray. *Dandelion Wine*. New York: Doubleday, 1957.

Catchpole, Brian. *The Korean War*. London: Constable and Robinson, 2001.

Chong Dae, Kim. *Battle Stories of the Korean War Heroes: My Last Mission for Freedom*. Seoul: Sae Eden Presbyterian Church, 2017.

Cleaver, Thomas McKelvey. *The Frozen Chosen: The 1st Marine Division and the Battle of the Chosin Reservoir*. Oxford: Osprey, 2016.

D'Este, Carlo. *Patton: A Genius for War*. New York: Harper Collins, 1995.

The Division Historical Association. *Lightning: The History of the 78th Infantry Division*. 2d ed. Durham, NC: Washington Infantry Journal Press, 1973.

Ecker, Richard E. *Battles of the Korean War: A Chronology, with Unit-by-Unit United States Casualty Figures and Medal of Honor Citations*. Jefferson, NC: McFarland, 2004.

Eggenberger, David. *A Dictionary of Battles*. New York: Thomas Y. Crowell, 1967.

Fehrenbach, T. R. *This Kind of War*. Washington, DC: Brassey's, 1994.

Ferrell, Robert H. *Harry S. Truman: A Life*. Columbia: University of Missouri Press, 1994.

Forty, Simon, and Jonathan Forty. *Infantry Warfare, 1939–1945*. Barnsley, UK: Pen and Sword Books, 2021.

Gallagher, Kenneth S., and Robert L. Pigeon, eds. *Infantry Regiments of the United States Army: A Complete Guide to the History, Decorations, Honors and Colors of Each Infantry Regiment in the Regular Army*. New York: Military Press, 1986.

Ganzel, Bill. *Dust Bowl Descent*. Lincoln: University of Nebraska Press, 1984.

Halberstam, David. *The Coldest Winter*. New York: Hachette Books, 2015.

Hechler, Ken. *The Bridge at Remagen*. New York: Ballantine Books, 1957.

Helm, M. M. *Prairie Boys at War: Korea: Volume I: June–October 1950*. Fargo, ND: Prairie Boy Books, 2014.

Hess, Gary R. *Presidential Decisions for War: Korea, Vietnam, the Persian Gulf, and Iraq*. Baltimore: Johns Hopkins University Press, 2009.

Holles, Everett. *Unconditional Surrender*. New York: Howell Soskin, 1945.

Lamott, Anne. *Bird by Bird*. New York: Pantheon Books, 1995.

Library of Congress. *Korean War Atrocities Report of the Committee on Government Operations Made through Its Permanent Subcommittee on Investigations by Its Subcommittee on Korean War Atrocities*. Report No. 848, United States Congress

Archives. January 11, 1954. https://tile.loc.gov/storage-services/service/ll/llmlp/KW-atrocities-Report/KW-atrocities-Report.pdf

Lockhart, Thomas P. *Diehard: History of the 309th Infantry Regiment*. Durham, NC: 78th Division Veterans Association, 1973.

MacDonald, Charles B. *A Rhine Bridge at Remagen, U.S. Army in WWII: The Last Offensive*. Washington, DC: Center for Military History, Government Printing Office, 1973.

Matloff, Maurice. *Strategic Planning for Coalition Warfare, 1943–1944*. Washington, DC: Department of the Army, 1959.

Mauldin, William H. *Up Front*. New York: Henry Holt, 1945.

McManus, John C. *The Deadly Brotherhood: The American Combat Soldier in World War II*. New York: Random House, 1998.

Miller, Edward G. *A Dark and Bloody Ground: The Hürtgen Forest and the Roer River Dams, 1944–1945*. College Station: Texas A&M University Press, 1995.

Millett, Allan R. *The War for Korea, 1950–1951: They Came from the North*. Lawrence: University Press of Kansas, 2010.

National Archives. *Our Documents: 100 Milestone Documents from the National Archives*. New York: Oxford University Press, 2006.

Owen, Wilfred. *Poems by Wilfred Owen*. Mockingbird Classics Publishing, 2015.

Rantz, L. A. "Hemolytic Streptococcal Infections." In *Preventive Medicine in World War II*. Vol. IV. Washington, DC: Office of the Surgeon General, Department of the Army, 1958.

Roe, Patrick C. *The Dragon Strikes*. Novato, CA: Presidio, 2000.

Rose, Kenneth D. *Myth and the Greatest Generation*. New York: Routledge, Taylor and Francis, 2008.

Sides, Hampton. *On Desperate Ground*. New York: Doubleday, 2018.

Slawenski, Kenneth. *J. D. Salinger: A Life*. New York: Random House, 2011.

Sparrow, John C. *History of Personnel Demobilization in the United States Army*. Washington, DC: Department of the Army, 1952.

Spender, Stephen. "The Truly Great." In *Collected Poems 1928–1953*. New York: Random House, 1955.

Stachura, Peter D. "Hitler Youth." In *Modern Germany: An Encyclopedia of History, People, and Culture 1871–1990*, edited by Dieter K. Buse and Juergen Doerr. New York: Garland, 1998.

Tillman, Barret. *The D-Day Encyclopedia*. Washington, DC: Regnery, 2014.

Weintraub, Stanley. *MacArthur's War: Korea and the Undoing of an American Hero*. New York: Simon and Schuster, 2000.

Wenzl, Roy, and Travis Heying. *The Miracle of Father Kapaun*. San Francisco: Ignatius Press, 2013.

Yoshiaki, Yoshimi. *Comfort Women: Sexual Slavery in the Japanese Military during World War II*. Translated by Suzanne O'Brien. New York: Columbia University Press, 2000.

Bibliography

Databases and Websites

American Battle Monuments Commission: https://www.abmc.gov/
American Veterans Center: https://www.americanveteranscenter.org/
Ancestry.com: https://www.ancestry.com/
Arlington National Cemetery: https://www.arlingtoncemetery.mil/
Army Historical Foundation: https://armyhistory.org/army-history-center/
Bureau of Vital Statistics, Texas Department of Health: https://www.dshs.texas.gov/vs/
Central Intelligence Agency: https://www.cia.gov
CNN Library. Korean War Fast Facts: https://www.cnn.com/2013/06/28/world/asia/korean-war-fast-facts/
Defense POW/MIA Accounting Agency: https://www.dpaa.mil/
1st Cavalry Division Association: https://1cda.org/history/
1st Cavalry Division Association: http://www.first-team.us/tableaux/chapt_04/
Harry S. Truman Library and Museum: https://www.trumanlibrary.gov/
Human Diseases Forum: http://www.humanillnesses.com/original/Pre-Sei/Rheumatic-Fever.html
Korean War Educator: http://www.koreanwar-educator.org/home.htm
Korean War Legacy Foundation: https://koreanwarlegacy.org
National Center for PTSD: https://www.ptsd.va.gov/
National Coalition for Homeless Veterans: https://www.nchv.org/
National Institute of Health, NIH Research Matters: https://www.nih.gov/news-events/nih-research-matters/
National Park Service: https://www.nps.gov
Poetry Foundation: Dulce et Decorum: https://www.poetryfoundation.org/poems/46560/dulce-et-decorum-est
Texas Historical Commission: https://www.thc.texas.gov/
Texas State Historical Association: https://www.tshaonline.org/home/
24th Infantry Division Association: http://24thida.com/
U.S. Department of Veterans Affairs, National Center for PTSD, Aging Veterans and Posttraumatic Stress Syndrome: https://www.ptsd.va.gov/understand/what/aging_veterans.asp
U.S. Library of Congress: https://www.loc.gov/
U.S. National Archives: https://www.archives.gov/research/census/online-resources

Documentaries

Burns, Ken. *The Civil War*. PBS, 1990. https://www.pbs.org/kenburns/the-civil-war/
Burns, Ken. *The Dust Bowl*. PBS, 2012. https://www.pbs.org/kenburns/the-dust-bowl/
Horan, Don. *Korea: The Forgotten War*. TV documentary. Don Horan, director, Mort Zimmerman, producer. Narrated by Robert Stack. Produced by Syndicated Services, 1987.

Ives, Stephen, Amanda Pollak, and Rob Rapley. *American Experience: The Great War.* PBS, 2018. https://www.pbs.org/wgbh/americanexperience/films/great-war/

Lee, In-soo. *Back to Korea Again: Their Last Return.* Produced by Sae Eden Presbyterian Church, Seoul, Korea, 2016.

MacLowry, Randall. *American Experience: The Battle of Chosin.* PBS, 2016. https://www.pbs.org/wgbh/americanexperience/films/chosin/

The Perilous Fight, America's World War II in Color. "The Mental Toll." produced by KCTS Television. Martin Smith, series producer. PBS, 2003. https://www.pbs.org/perilousfight/

Memoirs, Oral Histories, and Private Collections

Carey, General Richard E. (WWII, Korean War, Vietnam, Chosin Few). Author interview, June 2016 (Seoul, Korea) and March 2020, Plano, Texas; writings and speeches.

Cassidy, Robert Emmett. Robert Emmett Collection (AFC/2001/001/31154). Veterans History Project, 8204th Army Unit, American Folklife Center, Library of Congress.

Crumbie, Watson A. (WWII, Korean War, Chosin Few). Author interview, June 22, 2017, Robson Ranch, Texas–Denton County.

Ganz, Carl, Jr. Author interview, August 15, 2022, Raritan, New Jersey.

Kinard, Larry Carlisle (Korean War). Author interview, June 2016, Seoul, Korea; Korean War Legacy Foundation, https://koreanwarlegacy.org/interviews/larry-kinard/

Kitts, Jon (son of Private Joseph Roth Miller, USMC). Author interview, June 2017 (Houston, Texas), June 2018 (Seoul, Korea).

Milligan, Alma Ruth (wife of Earl Wayne Steward). Author interview, 2015, 2017, Bloomberg, Texas.

Murphy, David (friend of David Daniel Steward). Author interview, July 11, 2022, Atlanta, Texas.

Sessions, David Steward. Original videography of *William H. Steward War Memoirs.* 1992, digitized 2012.

Steward, David Daniel. Letters and War Memoirs Collection. Private collection of Sherri Steward, 2004.

Steward, Judith Ann (sister of William and David Daniel Steward). Author interview, August 3–4, 2022, Yuma, Arizona.

Steward, William Howe. *William H. Steward Memoirs*, compiled by Sherri Steward. 1999–2006. Videography by David Steward Sessions, 1992.

Steward-Reeder, Helen (sister of William and David Daniel Steward). Author interview, March 2011, and June 9–12, 2012, Phoenix, Arizona.

Storms, Robert (son of Major Harvey H. Storms). Author interview, June 16–18, 2017, Houston, Texas, and May/June 2018, via telephone interviews from Northlake, Texas.

Storms, Sam (son of Major Harvey H. Storms). Author interview, June 2016 (Seoul, Korea) and June 16–18, 2017 (Houston, Texas).

Storms-Cook, Helen and Harvey. *Helen and Harvey, Last Letters*. Self-Published, 2021. Letters from Harvey and Helen Storms, front line near Chosin Reservoir, North Korea, and LaFeria, Texas.

Wilson, Donna (wife of Aubrey Carroll Steward). Author interview, October 29–30, 2017, Hemet, California.

Selected Museums and Monuments

Airborne Museum, Sainte-Mère-Eglise, France
Chosin Few Battle Monument, Quantico, VA
Dwight D. Eisenhower Presidential Library, Museum, and Boyhood Home, Abilene, KS
Harry S. Truman Presidential Library and Museum, Independence, MO
Imperial Valley Veterans Memorial, Imperial, CA
Korean War Veterans Memorial, Washington, DC
Korean War Veterans Wall of Remembrance, Washington, DC
Memorial Museum of the Battle of Normandy, Bayeux, France
National WWII Museum, New Orleans, LA
Normandy American Cemetery and Memorial, Colleville-sur-Mer, France
Peace Museum Bridge at Remagen, Remagen, Germany
War Memorial of Korea, Seoul, Korea

INDEX

Note: Photographs and illustrations are denoted by *fig.* and image number.

Afghanistan War soldiers and families, 199–201
agriculture and farms, 19–20, 22, 27, 84
Air Force, U.S., 133–34
Alcott, Louisa May, 73
Almond, Edward ("Ned"), 109, 130–31, 149–51, 153
Ambrose, Stephen E., 32
amygdala, 80
antiaircraft weapons, 49–50
antitank weapons, 38, 110, 115
Apocalypse Now, 78
Appleman, Roy, 154
artillery fire: Korean War, 112, 113, 128, 133; PTSD effects of, 198; WW II, 34, 38–39, 40–41, 46, 48–50, 54–57
Assarian, Bart ("Blacky"), 40, 41, 55, 57
Atlanta, Texas: David Steward's birth in, 18, 88; David Steward's funeral and burial in, 10, 182, 184–86; Depression effects on, 21; Kenneth Steward's burial in, 20, *fig.* 5
atomic bombs, 60, 110
Auschwitz concentration camp, 30
autobahn, 56, 58

B., Evelyn, 203
B., William, 203
Bachman, Claude, 165
bacterial infections, 31, 96–97
Baldwin, Stanley, 25
Ballard, Walter, 18–19
Barber, William Earl, 156–58
Baxter, Earl R., 129
Beauchamp, Charles E., 117, 118
Berlin, Germany, 60, 210–14
"Bill" (Korean War soldier), 176–77
Blackie, 95
Blair, Clay, 106, 119
Blue House, The, 7–10, 13–14
"Blues in My Heart" (D. Steward), 120–21, 198
Blue Star banners, 177
bombers and bombing campaigns: Korean War, 110, 113, 155; WW II, 27, 29–30, 35, 47, 49–50, 60
Bradley, Omar, 33, 106
brain, PTSD effects on, 79–80
Broderick, Col., 179
Bronze Star, 55, 89, 92
Broyles, Barbara ("Bobbie"), 170
Bulge, Battle of the, 32, 34–35, 76

Cadet Corps, 88–89, 137
Caesar, Julius, 46
Cairo Declaration, 104
Carey, Richard E., 130–31, 151–52, 158–59, 208, *fig. 16*
Cassidy, Robert Emmett, 171
casualties: of Korean War, 11–12, 101–102, 111–12, 115–19, 122, 124–34, 142, 145–50, 153–59, 163–74, 178–79, 189–209, *fig. 14*; of WW I, 27–29, 75; of WW II, 1, 10–11, 30–37, 44, 52, 57–60, 66, 211–12. *See also* missing in action; prisoners of war; *specific individuals*
Catcher in the Rye, The (Salinger), 76
Central Intelligence Agency, 143
Changjin. *See* Chosin (Changjin) Reservoir, battle of
chemical warfare, 19, 28–29
Chiang Kai-shek, 103–104
"Chicks"/"Rock of Chickamauga" (19th Infantry Division), 117–19
children and youth: Depression-era effects on, 20; MIA status of parent affecting mental health of, 202–209; post-WW II German, 211–14; secondary traumatization of from PTSD, 15–16, 199–202; suicide and suicide ideation among, 200, 211; as underage soldiers, 90–97, 120–21, 137, 186. *See also specific children*
Chiles, John, 143
China, Korean involvement of, 103–104, 105, 142–47, 149–59, 173–75, 178–79, *figs. 17, 27*
Chipyong-ni, battle of, 174
Chosin (Changjin) Reservoir, battle of, 105, 150–60, 169–70, 205–208, *figs. 15, 27*
Chosin Reservoir Battle Monument, 158
Churchill, Winston, 15, 103–104, 189, 191

Cimino, Michael, 78
Civil War soldiers, 73–74, 90–91, 117, 120, 174
Clearwater, James R., 139, 163, 166, 168, 177
Cline, Roy, 16
Clines Corner, 16–17
coal mining industry, 27
Coldest Winter, The (Halberstam), 117–18, 144
Cold War, 104–105, 176
combat fatigue/exhaustion, 73–78, 85, 194–96. *See also* posttraumatic stress disorder; shell-shock disorder
Combat Infantryman Badge, 89, 137, 171, 185
comfort women, 103
Communism, 104–105, 112
complex PTSD, 190. *See also* posttraumatic stress disorder
Conrad, Joseph, 78
Cook, John, 91, 163, 164
Coon, Frederick Eugene, 11
Coppola, Francis Ford, 78
Coulter, John B., 149
Craiglockhart Military Hospital, 75
Crick, Francis, 169
Crumbie, Watson, 151, 156, 159
Custer, George Armstrong, 74

Dachau concentration camp, 76
Daddy (poem, by "Bill"), 176–77
Daigneault, Bill, 183
Danish Association of Doctors, 213
Danish Red Cross, 213
Davis, Raymond, 157–58
D-Day, 34, 174, 196
Dean, William F., 114, 118
Deer Hunter, The, 78
Defense POW/MIA Accounting Agency, 11, 147–48, 204

de Gaulle, Charles, 36
Democratic People's Republic of Korea, 105. *See also* North Korean People's Army
Depression, Great, 2, 4, 18–22, 25–26, 69, 89
depression and sadness: in children and families of veterans, 200, 202; in combat fatigue, 75–76; of David Steward, 20, 88, 94–95, 120–21; for Howard Steward's death, 70–71, 80–81, 84–85, 88; in posttraumatic stress disorder, 61, 79, 80, 190, 196; secondary traumatization and, 200; of Sherri Steward, 8–10, 13; of William Henry Steward, 29; of William Steward, 15–16, 18, 66, 70–73, 80–81, 84, 87, 137, 177–79, 191
"Diehard" Regiment. *See* 309th ("Diehard") Infantry Regiment
Distinguished Service Cross for Valor, 129
DNA: identification of remains through, 11, 148, 169, 170, 204–205, 207; stress hormones affecting, 201
Downes, Donna, 204
Downes, Hal, 202–203
Downes, Rick, 202, 204
Drabik, Alexander A., 48
droughts, 19, 125
Dust Bowl, 19–20
dysentery, 125, 174, 211
Dziecialowski, Cpl., 164

East Hill, battle for, 158–59
East of Chosin (Appleman), 154
Edouard, Ann Marie Beatrix, 12
8th Cavalry Regiment, 129, 132–34, 144–46
Eighth Army, 108–109, 122, 124–25, 134, 149, 174

82nd Field Artillery Battalion, 122
8204th American Graves Registration, 170–71, 179
Eisenhower, Dwight: award by for repatriation of Korean War soldiers' remains, 171; military budget cuts and, 107; PTSD stance of, 77; Texas roots of, 30; in WW II, 33, 44, 47, 51, 77, 150
Eppernich, Germany, 45
Erpeler Ley, 47

Faith, Don Carlos, Jr., 152–54, 169–70
farms and farming, 19–20, 22, 27, 84
Fehrenbach, T. R., 108, 111, 127
Felhoelter, Herman, 118
15th Replacement Battalion, 122, 127
5th Cavalry Regiment, 145–46
52nd Field Artillery Battalion, 115
57th Field Artillery Battalion, 149
"fight or flight" response, 80
1st Cavalry Division, 109, 114, 122, 127–29, 132–34, 144–45, 149, *figs. 13, 24, 26*
1st Rifle Platoon, 41
First Army, 59
First World War soldiers. *See* World War I soldiers
flak guns, 38
food: Depression-era, 18–21, 26; farming for, 19–20, 22, 27, 84; fishing for, 66, 68, 72; hunting for, 21, 68, 69; for Korean War POWs, 147; post-WW II lack of, 213–14; WW II soldier rations of, 37, 46, 57, 59
Ford, Henry, 18
Forgotten War, The (Blair), 106
Fortune, Clifton ("Cliff"), 39–40, 57, 58–59, 60, 61, 65, 67, 216
Fox Hill, battle for, 156–58

"Frozen Chosin," 105, 151, 159. *See also* Chosin (Changjin) Reservoir, Battle of
Funchilin Pass, 159

G., DyAnna, 199, 203
Ganz, Francis ("Frank"), 196, 209
gas attacks, 19, 28–29
Gay, Hap, 133, 145
Goebbels, Joseph, 50–51, 52
Gold Star banners, 177
Goodall, Jane, 9
Graham, Calvin, 91–92
Grand Canyon, 189, 191–92, 197
Graves Registration unit, 140, 164, 166, 168, 170–71, 179
Great Depression, 2, 4, 18–22, 25–26, 69, 89
Great Dust Bowl, 19–20
Greatest Generation, 1–2, 215, 216–17. *See also* Korean War soldiers; World War II soldiers
Guthrie, Woody, 20

Hagaru-ri, battle of, 151, 155–59, 208
Halberstam, David, 117–18, 144
Hastings, Max, 33
Hazelbaker, P. F., 182, 183
health issues: of David Steward, 95–97, 119–22, 125–26, 136 (*see also under* mental health issues); of Delta Ray Steward, 138; Depression-era, 20; of Earl Steward, 66; of Eisenhower, 107; gas attacks causing, 19, 28; infections and infectious diseases causing, 31, 96–97 (*see also* pneumonia); of Korean War POWs, 147; mental (*see* mental health issues); in post-WW II Germany, 211, 213; PTSD and, 73–74; water shortage and, 125, 174; of William Henry Steward, 19, 28–29; of William

Steward, 31, 59, 84–85, 96, 174, 178, 214–16 (*see also under* mental health issues). *See also specific illnesses*
heart disease, 73–74, 96–97, 125–26, 214
Heart of Darkness (Conrad), 78
helicopters, 164
"Hermit Kingdom," 102–103, 108
Herodotus, 73
Higgins, Marguerite, 101
Hill 303 massacre, 128
Hill 314, 128
Hill 401, 129
hippocampus, 80
Hitler, Adolf: bridge destruction orders of, 46, 47–48, 49, 50–52; concentration camp leadership under, 30; last stand by Germany under, 53; Le Havre importance to, 35; Reichsautobahn under, 56; trial for treason of, 25; Yugoslavia reprisals by, 26
Hitlerjugend (Hitler Youth), 59, 92
Hobson, Norman ("Hob"), 39–40, 42, 50, 56–57, 60, 211, *fig. 9*
Hoengseong massacre, 174
Hoge, William M., 48
Holocaust survivors, 200, 210
homecoming experiences, 60–61, 65–71, 184–85
homelessness, 199
homesickness, 73–74, 77
Hoovervilles, 18
Hope, Bob, 144
horses, 29
Höss, Rudolf, 30
Hürtgen Forest battle, 32, 34, 37, 43, 44, 75–76

I Company, 56, 58
Imperial Irrigation District/Imperial Valley, 22, 84
Inchon Landing, 129–31, 132, 142, *fig. 25*

Individual Deceased Personnel File (IDPF), of D. Steward, 13–14, 140, 164, 168, 202
influenza, 20, 31
Inmun Gun (North Korean People's Army), 109–19, 122, 126–30, 132–34, 136, 142, 144
insomnia, 9, 61, 67, 80, 85, 180
Iraq War soldiers and families, 199–201

Jefferson, Thomas, 218
Johnson, Louis A., 106, 108
Johnson [rifleman], 58
Joint Prisoners of War/Missing in Action Accounting Command (JPAC), 170

Kapaun, Emil, 142, 146–48
K Company, 38–39, 42, 45, 49, 54, 58
Kennedy, Vera, 82–84, 86–87, 89
Kim Bok-dong, 103
Kim Il-sung, 126
Kitts, Jon Miller, 208–209
Kitts, Maxine Miller, 208
Kline, 57, 58
Kohara, Yukinari, 179
Korean War: beginning of, 109–10, 111–12; conditions and circumstances for, 101–23; as "Forgotten War," 1; as "limited war," 175, 176; maps of, *figs. 22, 23, 24, 25, 26, 27*; as police action not war, 113, 138, 172, 190; as political battle, 174–75; setting for, 102; soldiers and veterans of (*see* Korean War soldiers); 38th parallel demarcation line for, 104–105, 111, 132
Korean War Memorial Wall, 209
Korean War soldiers: casualties among, 11–12, 101–102, 111–12, 115–19, 122, 124–34, 142, 145–50, 153–59, 163–74, 178–79, 189–209, *fig. 14* (*see also specific soldiers*); at Chipyong-ni, 174; at Chosin (Changjin) Reservoir, 105, 150–60, 169–70, 205–208, *figs. 15, 27*; demobilization and discharge creating shortage of, 105–108, 115; escorting remains of, 10, 139, 173, 179–86; as forgotten, 1; health issues affecting, 96–97, 125, 174 (*see also under* Steward, David Daniel; Steward, William); at Hoengseong, 174; identification of remains and effects of, 138–40, 163–72, 179, 204–205, 207; Inchon landing by, 129–31, 132, 142, *fig. 25*; legacy of, 2–4, 216–18; mental health issues among, 67, 189–98, 216–18 (*see also under* Steward, David Daniel; Steward, William); as missing in action, 11–12, 111, 118, 122, 135–36, 140–41, 146, 202–209, *fig. 4*; peacetime enlistment and, 87, 89, 92, 94, 107, 137; as prisoners of war, 11–12, 111, 116, 118, 128, 133, 136, 146–47, 153, 155; at Pusan Perimeter, 122, 124–28, 130, 132, 134, 142, *fig. 23*; at Pyongyang, 144–45; recovery and repatriation of remains of, 11–12, 138–41, 142, 147–48, 160, 163–72, 173, 177–86, 202, 204–209; refugee evacuation by, 159–60; secondary traumatization of children of, 200; in Seoul, 131–32, 142, 174, *fig. 18*; stand or die command for, 124–34, 157; Steward (David) as, 93–97, 101, 108, 111, 116–29, 132–41, 163–68, 171–73, 177–86, 202, 209, *figs. 2, 4, 19, 20, 24* (*see also* Steward, David Daniel); Steward (William) as, 1–2, 8, 136–39, 142, 165, 171–98, 209, 216–18, *figs. 3, 10*; suicide by, 67; at Taegu, 126–29, 132–33; at Taejon,

Korean War soldiers (*continued*) 117–18, 119, 122, *fig. 24*; training, equipment, and preparedness inadequacy for, 107–10, 114–19, 122–23; underage, 91, 92–97, 120–21, 137, 186; unknown or unidentified, 11, 147–48, 163, 165–72, 186; at Unsan, 144–46, 149; Yalu River offensive by, 132, 143–45, 149–60
Koryzis, Alexandros, 27

"Land of the Morning Calm," 102, 111–12, 134, 142
Lange, Dorothea, 15, 18
Lee Hak-ku, 133
Le Havre, France, 35–36
Leonidas (King), 73, 149
"Lightning" Division. *See* 78th "Lightning" Infantry Division
Lincoln, Abraham, 135
Lipscomb, Andy, 44
Little Bighorn, Battle of, 74
"Little Christmas Man," 213–14
Ludendorff, Erich, 47
Ludendorff Bridge, 46–52, *fig. 8*
Luftwaffe, 27, 30, 47, 49

MacArthur, Douglas: Korean War tactics of, 109, 112, 114–15, 130–32, 142–44, 149–50; occupation of Japan under, 108; relief of command from, 175–76; Texas roots of, 30; on war crimes, 128
machine guns: Korean War, 110, 113, 115–16, 131, 133, 208; WW II, 40, 41, 45, 48–49, 54–55, 57
MacLean, Allan D., 152–53
Mao Zedong, 144
maps, Korean War, *figs. 22, 23, 24, 25, 26, 27*
Marine Corps, 106–107, 129–32, 149–52, 155–59, 208, *figs. 15, 25*

Marshall, George C., 32, 132
Mary Clare (Mother), 12
Mauldin, Bill, 35, 173
McCrea, John, 40, 55, 57
Medal of Honor, 90–91, 148, 154, 170
Meloy, Guy, Jr. ("Stan"), 117
"Mental Cases" (Owen), 75
mental health issues: of children and families of veterans, 15–16, 199–209; controversy on legitimacy of, 76–78; "cowards" disciplined for, 74–75, 76–77, 193; of David Steward, 94–95, 97, 120–21; depression as (*see* depression and sadness); of Earl Steward, 66–67; escorting deceased family members creating, 182–83; homecoming experiences and, 61, 65–71; Howard Steward's death triggering, 70–71, 72; replacements struggling with, 33; rest or breaks as relief from, 77–78; secondary traumatization and, 15–16, 199–202; of Sherri Steward, 8–10, 13; suicide, suicide ideation, and, 67, 79, 189, 191–92, 194, 200, 211; survivor's guilt and, 67; warfare-induced, 73–81, 85, 91, 189–98, 216–18 (*see also* combat fatigue/exhaustion; posttraumatic stress disorder; shell-shock disorder); of William Henry Steward, 27, 29; of William Steward, 2–3, 8, 10, 15–16, 18, 65–73, 80–82, 84–88, 137, 177–80, 189–98, 215–17
Meritorious Unit Citation, 171
Meuse-Argonne campaign, 19, 28–29
migration: Dust Bowl and Depression leading to, 18–20, 22; by William Steward and family, 8, 15–17, 80, 83–87, 89, 192
Miller, Edward, 34
Miller, Herbert ("Pappy"), 146–47, 148

Miller, Joseph Roth, 208–209, *fig. 12*
Miller Kitts, Jon, 208–209
Miller Kitts, Maxine, 208
Milligan, Alma Ruth, 3
"Miracle at Remagen," 51. *See also* Remagen, Germany
missing in action (MIA): children and families' mental health issues due to status of, 202–209; Korean War soldiers as, 11–12, 111, 118, 122, 135–36, 140–41, 146, 202–209, *fig. 4*; recognition of sacrifice of, 203–204; Vietnam War soldiers as, 202, 209; WW II soldiers as, 202, 209, 211
Mitchell, John W., 48
Model, Walter, 46
Moon Jae-in, 159–60
Mudgett, Charles ("Fritz"), 114
Mulheim Bridge, 47
Munoz, Frank, 126
Murphy, Audie, 30, 72, 91
Murphy, David, 21–22, 70
Murphy, Kenneth, 70
music: David Sessions and, 186; David Steward and, 82, 87–88, 90, 93, 94, 95, 120–21, 186; Depression-era, 20; Sherri Steward and, 10; William Steward and, 82, 83, 86–87, 137, 215; WW II soldiers listening to, 39, 58
Mussolini, Benito, 25

Naktong Bulge/Naktong Offensive, 126–28, 133, *fig. 23*
Nance, Elmer, 38, 40, 41, 57
napalm, 155
Napoleon, 46, 51
National Memorial Cemetery of the Pacific (Punchbowl), 11
National Museum of the Marine Corps, Chosin Reservoir Battle Monument, 158
National World War II Memorial, 215

National World War II Museum, 215
neurasthenia. *See* shell-shock disorder
Nichols, Joe D., 18, 71, 88
Nimitz, Chester, 30
955th Field Artillery Battalion, 172
19th Infantry Division ("Rock of Chickamauga"/"Chicks"), 117–19
9th Armored Division, 45, 48
9th Infantry Division, 126
Ninth Army, 59
North Korean People's Army (NKPA) (Inmun Gun), 109–19, 122, 126–30, 132–34, 136, 142, 144
nostalgia, 73–74
Nuzzo, John, 179

oil industry, 21, 29, 30
"Old Soldiers Never Die" speech (MacArthur), 175
Ondrick, John G. ("Uncle John"), 37–38
101st Airborne, 32
Operation Big Switch (1953), 118
Operation Bluehearts (1950), 109, 129
Operation Chromite (1950), 130–31
Operation Glory (1954), 11, 148
Operation Overlord (1944), 34
outposts, 58
Owen, Wilfred, 25, 75, 90

Paik Sun-yup, 124, 145
Palmer, Raymond, 133
Parham, Ruth, 13
Parker, Edwin P., Jr., 44, 210
Patton, Dale, 40
Patton, George S., 30, 76–77, 108, 205
Pearl Harbor bombing, 29–30
Petrified National Monument/Petrified Forest, 16
pets, 8, 16, 38
Plath, Sylvia, 7
pneumonia, 20, 31, 96, 147
Portsmouth, Treaty of, 102

posttraumatic stress disorder (PTSD): complex, 190; controversy on legitimacy of, 76–78; "cowards" disciplined for, 74–75, 76–77, 193; cultural references to, 78; disability claims for, 78–79, 196; epigenetic factors affecting, 201; heart disease and, 73–74; homecoming experiences affecting, 61; homelessness and, 199; medical discharge for, 194, 196–97; Murphy's experiences of, 91; neurological and brain alterations with, 79–80; recognition and awareness of, 78, 190, 195–96; research and study of, 15, 73–81, 199–202; secondary traumatization of children and spouses from, 15–16, 199–202; Steward's experiences of, 80–81, 194–98 (*see also under* mental health issues); stigma of, 195–96, 201; symptoms of, 61, 74, 190; treatment for, 76, 78, 190, 195–96, 198, 200. *See also* combat fatigue/exhaustion; shell-shock disorder
prisoners of war (POWs): complex PTSD among, 190; German WW II soldiers as, 45, 59–60, 92; Korean War soldiers as, 11–12, 111, 116, 118, 128, 133, 136, 146–47, 153, 155; secondary traumatization of children of, 200
Provost, R. J., 167
psychological trauma. *See* combat fatigue/exhaustion; mental health issues; posttraumatic stress disorder; shell-shock disorder
PTSD. *See* posttraumatic stress disorder
Punchbowl (National Memorial Cemetery of the Pacific), 11
Purple Heart, 39, 59, 66, 89, 92, 156, 185
Pusan Perimeter, battle for, 122, 124–28, 130, 132, 134, 142, *fig. 23*

Pyle, Ernie, 43, 53, 65, 67, 82
Pyongyang, battle for, 144–45

Reagan, Ronald, 1, 210
refugees: German, 211–13; Korean, 113, 132, 159–60
Regimental Combat Team 31 (RCT-31), *fig. 27*, 152–55, 205. *See also* Task Force Faith
Reichsautobahn, 56, 58
religion: Delta Steward's ministry in, 85, 138; Kapaun's practice of, 146–48; Kennedys' participation in, 82–84, 89; William Steward's views of, 80–81, 83–84, 172
Remagen, Germany, 46–52, *fig. 8*
Reno, Marcus, 74
Republic of Korea/ROK forces, 105, 112–14, 128–29, 132, 144–45, 159–60, 174
Rhee, Syngman, 105, 132
rheumatic fever, 31, 96–97, 119–21, 122, 125–26, 136
Richardson, Doc, 58, 61, 216
Ridgerunners, 157
Ridgeway, Matthew, 108, 174
"Rock of Chickamauga"/"Chicks" (19th Infantry Division), 117–19
Rock Quarry, 56–58, 67
Rodriguez, Jesus, 119
Rommel, Erwin ("Desert Fox"), 30
Roosevelt, Franklin D., 18, 29, 103–104
Roosevelt, Theodore, 102
Rosenheck, Robert, 200
Route 66, 16–17, 192
Rowland, Bill, 154
Ruhr Pocket, 58–60, 84–85

Sae Eden Presbyterian Church, 203, 205
Salinger, J. D., 75–76
Sanchez, Gilberto, 205

sawmill and timber industry, 21, 22, 26, 69
scarlet fever, 31, 96
Schwammenauel Dam, 43–45
Schwarzkopf, Norman, 34
Schwentker, Francis F., 96
2nd Infantry Division, 126–27, 174
2nd Rifle Platoon, 39–42, 49, 55–60, 84–85
secondary traumatization, 15–16, 199–202
Second World War. *See* World War II
Seminaro, Dr., 195
Seoul, battles for, 131–32, 142, 174, *fig. 18*
Sessions, David Steward, 3–4, 7–8, 10, 12, 186
7th Infantry Division, 109, 130, 149–53, 155
17th Infantry Regiment, 153
7th Cavalry Regiment, 133
70th Tank Battalion, 133
78th "Lightning" Infantry Division, 2, 37, 43–46, 48–49, 53, 58–60, 210, 215. *See also* 309th Infantry Regiment
sexual violence, 103, 211–12
Shakespeare, William, 53
Shea, Bernard, 61, 67, 216
shell-shock disorder, 29, 74–75. *See also* combat fatigue/exhaustion; post-traumatic stress disorder
Shelton, SFC, 164–65
Sieg River, 58
Silver Star, 153, 156, 208
Smith, Charles B., 114–15
Smith, Oliver P., 130, 132, 150, 152, 158–59
soldiers. *See specific wars and soldiers by name*
spouses, secondary traumatization of, 199–202
Stalin, Joseph, 104

Steward, Aubrey Carol ("Mickey"), 26, 66, 69–71, 81, 82–83, 191, *fig. 5*
Steward, Callie: children born to, 89, 137–38, 181–82 (*see also by name*); historical documents preservation by, 3; letters to, 171, 175, 176, 178–79, 192, 195; photograph of, *fig. 7*; William Steward courting and marrying, 69, 82–89, 137; William Steward's leave with, 191–92
Steward, David Daniel ("Davy," "Tex"): birth of, 18, 88–89; as boy soldier, 90, 92–97, 120–21, 137, 186; in Cadet Corps, 88–89, 137; David Sessions as namesake of, 3, 10, 12, 186; death of, 9–10, 12–14, 134, 136–37, 202, *figs. 20, 24*; Depression-era childhood of, 18–22, 69, 89; funeral and burial of, 10, 182–86; health issues of, 95–97, 119–22, 125–26, 136 (*see also under* mental health issues); identification of remains and effects of, 138–40, 163–68, 179; Individual Deceased Personnel File of, 13–14, 140, 164, 168, 202; as Korean War soldier, 93–97, 101, 108, 111, 116–29, 132–41, 163–68, 171–73, 177–86, 202, 209, *figs. 2, 4, 19, 20, 24*; letters of, 3, 90, 93–97, 101, 111, 116, 119–22, 124–25, 127, 136, 181, 198, *figs. 19*; letters on service and sacrifice of, 9, 135, 136; mental health issues of, 94–95, 97, 120–21; as missing in action, 135–36, *fig. 4*; as musician, 82, 87–88, 90, 93, 94, 95, 120–21, 186; photographs of, 9, 10, 17–18, *figs. 2, 5, 21*; recovery and repatriation of remains of, 138–41, 142, 163–68, 171–72, 173, 177–86, 202, 209; Sherri Steward's research and remembrance of, 9–10, 12–14, 15, 17–18, 93–94, 140, 186, 202, 218;

Steward, David Daniel ("Davy," "Tex") (*continued*)
William Steward's relationship with, 10, 17–18, 26, 27, 66, 72–73, 86, 88, 137, 171–72, 216

Steward, Delta Ray: childhood and background of, 138; children born to, 18, 25, 69, 138 (*see also by name*); David Steward's MIA and death notices to, 135–37, 138; David Steward's remains identification and repatriation efforts of, 138–40, 142, 163, 165–66, 168, 173, 177–80; health issues of, 138; homecoming experiences with, 67, 68, 71; photograph of, *fig. 5*; religious ministry of, 85, 138; William Steward's return from Korea efforts of, 139, 173, 177–80; William Steward's shared grief with, 182

Steward, Earl Wayne ("Bo"): David Steward's funeral role of, 184, 185; as Korean War soldier, 139; mental health issues of, 66–67; photograph of, *fig. 5*; siblings and behavior of, 26, 82–83; as WW II soldier, 66–67, 69, 139

Steward, Howard Neil: childhood of, 69; death of by rifle accident, 68–71, 72, 80–81, 82, 84–85, 88, 136, 186; photographs of, *figs. 5, 6*

Steward, John Jackson, 27

Steward, Kenneth Carl, 20, 26, 85, 88, 136, 186, *fig. 5*

Steward, Linda, 15–16, 138, 182

Steward, Michael, 15–16, 89, 137–38, 176–77, 179, 181–82

Steward, Robert, 25, 85

Steward, Sherri ("Sherri-Bug"/"Bug"): Blue House of, 7–10, 13–14; David Steward remembered and researched by, 9–10, 12–14, 15, 17–18, 93–94, 140, 186, 202, 218 (*see also* Steward, David Daniel); family celebrations with, 7–8; father's relationship with, 2–3, 8, 15–17, 197, 214–18 (*see also* Steward, William); historical research methods of, 3–4; mental health issues of, 8–10, 13; MIA status effects research by, 202–209; moving and school changes by, 8, 15–17; self-imposed perfectionist drive of, 8; siblings of, 15–16 (*see also by name*); war stories told to, 3, 197

Steward, William ("Billy"/"Dodie"/"Pop"): alcohol consumption by, 82–83, 86, 87; baptism of fire of war by, 33, 35–42, 173; birth of, 25; bullying and retaliation of, 25–26; Callie Steward courted and married to, 69, 82–89, 137 (*see also* Steward, Callie Kennedy); children's relationship with, 2–3, 8, 15–17, 138, 197, 214–18 (*see also by name*); David Steward's MIA and death notices to, 136–37; David Steward's relationship with, 10, 17–18, 26, 27, 66, 72–73, 86, 88, 137, 171–72, 216; David Steward's remains escorted by, 10, 139, 173, 179–86; death of, 216; Depression-era childhood of, 2, 4, 25–26; family celebrations with, 7; on first battle experience, 40–41; grandfather's relationship with, 86; health issues of, 31, 59, 84–85, 96, 174, 178, 214–16 (*see also under* mental health issues); homecoming experiences of, 60–61, 65–71, 184–85; Korean War military service of, 1–2, 8, 136–39, 142, 165, 171–98, 209, 216–18, *figs. 3, 10*; legacy of, 216–18; letters of, 3, 171, 175, 176–79, 192, 193, 195, 198;

medical discharge for, 196–97; mental health issues of, 2–3, 8, 10, 15–16, 18, 65–73, 80–82, 84–88, 137, 177–80, 189–98, 215–17; moving and fleeing of, 8, 15–17, 80, 83–87, 89, 192; as musician, 82, 83, 86–87, 137, 215; peacetime enlistment of, 87, 89, 137; photographs of, 9, *figs. 1, 3, 5, 7, 9, 10*; post-WW II occupation experiences of, 60, 210–14; at Remagen/Ludendorff Bridge, 46–52; at Rock Quarry, 56–58, 67; at Ruhr Pocket, 58–60, 84–85; as runner, 54–55; at Schwammenauel Dam, 43–45; siblings of, 4, 25–26, 66–71 (*see also by name*); suicide ideation by, 189, 191, 194, 197; unauthorized absence and punishment of, 192–94; in village-hopping campaign, 53–55; WW II military service of, 1–2, 20, 26–27, 29–33, 35–61, 210–18, *figs. 1, 9*

Steward, William Henry: birth and childhood of, 27; children born to, 18, 25 (*see also by name*); David Steward's MIA and death notices to, 135–37; Depression-era conditions for, 18, 19, 22; health of, 19, 28–29; Howard's death and, 71, *fig. 5*; military service of, 19, 20, 25, 27–29, 139; photograph of, *fig. 5*; post-WW II migration for work by, 83–86; William Steward's shared grief with, 182

Steward-Reeder, Helen ("Sis"): Callie Steward and, 69, 82–83; David Steward's relationship with, 95, 185–86; homecoming experiences with, 68–70; personal history shared by, 3; photograph of, *fig. 5*; siblings and behavior of, 26; on William Steward's mental health, 68, 72, 80–81, 137

Steward-Wilson, Judith Ann, 3, 93–94, 95
Stockwell, Elisha, 91, 120
Storms, Harvey H., 152–55, 160, 205–208, *fig. 11*
Storms, Helen, 152–54, 160, 205–206
Storms, Sam, Ernie, Billy, and Robert, 205–208
streptococcal infections, 31, 96–97
Stuka dive-bombers, 49–50
suicide and suicide ideation, 67, 79, 189, 191–92, 194, 197, 200, 211
survivor's guilt, 67

Taegu, battle for, *fig. 24*, 126–29, 132–33
Taejon, battle for, 117–18, 119, 122
tanks: Korean War, 112, 113, 115, 117, 119, 127, 133–34, 153; WW II, 41, 57. *See also specific armored divisions*
Task Force Faith, *fig. 27*, 152–55, 159, 205, 207. *See also* Regimental Combat Team 31 (RCT-31)
Task Force Smith, 114–17, 133
X Corps, 130–31, 143, 149, 151, 153, 155
3rd Armored Division, 46
3rd Cavalry Regiment, 133
31st Infantry Regiment, 152–54
34th Regiment, 109–10, 114–15, 117, 118
309th ("Diehard") Infantry Regiment, 37–38, 40, 43–46, 48–49, 52, 53–60, 210
310th Infantry Regiment, 57, 60, 210
311th Infantry Regiment, 44, 45
Tiger Death March, 11–12
Timmermann, Karl, 48
Toktong Pass, 156–58
torture, 103, 128, 132, 136, 147, 173
Truman, Harry S.: Korean War service recognition by, 9; Korean War stance of, 112–14, 132, 137–38, 143–44, 174–76; military discord

Truman, Harry S. (*continued*)
and reduction under, 106–108, 175–76; thanksgiving for WW II end by, 210–11; Truman Doctrine and Cold War under, 105, 176
Truman Doctrine, 105
21st Regiment, 114–15
24th Infantry Division, 108–10, 114, 118–19, 122, 133–34
25th Infantry Division, 109, 127
29th Infantry Regiment, 29th Regimental Combat Team, 97, 101, 108, 118–19, 122, 133, 196
Typhoon Helene, 122

underage soldiers, 90–97, 120–21, 137, 186
United Nations: Korean War forces of, 112–13, 114, 117, 122, 126, 128, 132, 142, 144, 149–52, 159, 173–75, *figs. 17, 18, 22*; military cemeteries of, 164, 166, 167, 171; Republic of Korea elections supervision by, 105; on war crimes, 103
Unknown Soldier X-5000, 166–68, 179. *See also* Steward, David Daniel
Unsan, battle for, 144–46, 149

V-2 ballistic missiles, 50
veterans. *See specific wars and soldiers by name*
Veterans Administration/Veterans Affairs: PTSD claims to and response by, 78–79, 196; suicide statistics by, 79; underage soldiers' benefits from, 92
Vietnam War soldiers: homecoming experiences of, 61; mental health issues for, 67, 78, 79, 190, 195–96; as missing in action, 202, 209; secondary traumatization of children of, 200; suicide by, 67

Vlatten, Germany, 45
Volkssturm, 45, 53, 58, 59–60

Walker, Walton H. "Johnnie," 108–109, 124–25, 128, 145, 174
Wallesheim, Germany, 45
war crimes, 103, 128, 132, 136, 211–12
Watson, James, 169
Wehrmacht, 47, 49–50, 53, 211
Weissmuller, Johnny, 25
Wellington, 58
Whitey, 57, 61, 216
Wilkerson, "Wilky," 39
Willoughby, Charles, 143
Wilson, Charles E., 164–65
Wilson, Donna, 3, 81, 191
Witsell, Edward F., 135, 136
Wolfskinder, 213
Wood, James Theodore, 67, 86, 89, 192
Wood, Ollie, 67
work and employment: Depression-era, 18, 19, 21, 22, 26; Stewards' post-WW II, 83–84, 86–87, 137
World War I soldiers: casualties among, 27–29, 75; chemical warfare and gassing of, 19, 28–29; mental health issues among, 29, 74–75; Steward (W.H.) as, 19, 20, 25, 27–29, 139
World War II: beginning of, 26–27; end of, 60, 210–11; Korean War affected by policies following, 103–10, 115; occupation following, 60, 210–14; soldiers and veterans of (*see* World War II soldiers)
World War II soldiers: at Battle of the Bulge, 32, 34–35, 76; casualties among, 1, 10–11, 30–37, 44, 52, 57–60, 66, 211–12; demobilization and discharge of, 105–108, 115; enlistment of, 29–30; as "Greatest Generation," 1–2, 215, 216–17;

health issues affecting, 31, 96 (*see also* mental health issues *subentry*); homecoming experiences of, 60–61, 65–71; in Hürtgen Forest battle, 32, 34, 37, 43, 44, 75–76; legacy of, 2–4, 216–18; in Le Havre, 35–36; mental health issues for, 67, 73, 75–78, 79, 91, 190, 195–96, 216–17 (*see also under* Steward, William); as missing in action, 202, 209, 211; post-war occupation experiences of, 60, 210–14; recovery and repatriation of remains of, 181; at Remagen/Ludendorff Bridge, 46–52, *fig. 8*; replacement system for combat division of, 32–33, 35; at Rock Quarry, 56–58, 67; at Ruhr Pocket, 58–60, 84–85; at Schwammenauel Dam, 43–45; secondary traumatization of children of, 200; Steward (William) as, 1–2, 20, 26–27, 29–33, 35–61, 210–18, *figs. 1, 9*; suicide by, 67, 79; underage, 91–92; in village-hopping campaign, 53–55

Wuppertal, Germany, 60

Yalu River, offensive to, 132, 143–45, 149–60
Yellow Knife, 74
Yudam-ni, battle of, 151–52, 156–58, 208

Zablocki, S., 167
Zamora, Anselmo, 12
Zangen, Gustav von, 46

ABOUT THE AUTHOR

Sherri Steward served as liaison for families of MIA and KIA soldiers in Korea, and as the only nonveteran member of the 2018 National Korean War–Korean Defense Mission and Vision Committee. As a member of the National and Chapter 215 Korean War Veterans Association, she served as funding chair of the Korean War and Korean Defense Veterans Memorial in Arlington, Texas. Sherri and her son, David Steward Sessions, were honored to be chosen to carry the banner for veteran families in the Seventieth Anniversary of D-Day Parade in Sainte-Mère-Église, France.

Sherri has dedicated much of her life to teaching young people about the sacrifices made for democracy and freedom. As a result of her work with students, she was the recipient of Disney's Outstanding American High School Teacher and the Texas Veterans Commission, Outstanding Texas Teacher Award. She has appeared in radio and television broadcasts and in the Korean documentary *Back to Korea, Their Last Return*. Sherri has made public appearances on behalf of veterans throughout Texas and Korea.

As an avid adventurer, Sherri summited Mount Kilimanjaro in Africa, completed the Inca Trail, and has been scuba diving around the globe. She has competed in six National Track & Field Championships and five marathons. An ardent supporter of the sciences, Sherri served as *Scientific American Frontier's* Teacher Ambassador, working with actor Alan Alda and world-renowned biologists in the Galapagos Islands. She has worked with Dr. Biruté Galdikas in Borneo and Dr. Jane Goodall in Africa, and she has completed many humanitarian projects for schoolchildren around the globe.

Praise for *Bringing Davy Home*

"*Bringing Davy Home* unveils a deeply personal story of [the author's] PTSD-afflicted father, an infantryman in WWII and Korea, and her teenage uncle, a fallen hero of the Korean War. This well-researched book informs us all of the toll of war—not only upon our warriors, but also upon their families, the 'forgotten casualties.'"

—Lt. Gen. Richard E. Carey, US Marine Corps (Ret), Chosin Few, Korean and Vietnam Wars

"With WWII and Korean War savagery as a backdrop, the author presents a gripping view of the psychological trauma heaped upon warriors and their families. This important book reveals the true price of freedom."

—Col. John H. Ansohn (1949–2023), US Army (Ret), command surgeon in support of Operations Desert Shield and Desert Storm

"Scholarly and poignant—this is a tale of American sacrifice. Only those who have lost freedom know the true value of that sacrifice."

—Capt. Richard Halferty, US Navy (Ret), Korean War, Gold Star brother

"The author accurately portrays the bitter fighting endured by the 1st Cavalry during the breakout of the Pusan Perimeter. Her account of the 8th Cavalry Regiment's demise at the Battle of Unsan is painfully accurate. I was one of the lucky ones."

—Sgt. James Sharp, US Army (Ret), 1st Cavalry Division/ 8th Cavalry Regiment, survivor of the Battle of Unsan